Proud owners - Bill Tucker and Jerry Walker

# MOVING HOME PLATE

## THE MIRACLE ON I-5

### A TRUE BASEBALL STORY

BY

## BILL TUCKER   AND   JERRY WALKER

**Volcano Press**
**1999**

Library of Congress Catalog Card Number : 99--97554

Tucker, Bill
Walker, Jerry

Moving Home Plate
   (The Miracle on I-5)

390 Pages  includes 142 photos or illustrations

Includes index
ISBN Number : ISBN 0-9663169-1-6


Subject: Relocation of a minor league baseball franchise and
         construction of a new ballpark

Published by Volcano Press
         P.O.Box 20936
         Keizer, Oregon 97307

Manufactured in the United States of America

Other book by these authors: DP—Or Billy and Jerry In
The Promised Land

Published: 1998

Subject: Two friends from opposite
sides of the continent buy a minor league
baseball franchise and operate it

THANKS

# THANKS

A book of this nature does not come to fruition simply by someone sitting at the word processor and typing in the events as they remember them. It requires the assistance and time of many people. Others have more personal recollections of certain events and allow the writer to portray the intended picture more accurately. Those people gave freely of their time and effort both in researching the questions and in telling their part of the story. After that is all done, they again contribute their time and energy in proofing the manuscript and providing any and all corrections needed. We owe a debt of gratitude to them. There are simply too many who helped in that fashion to be able to safely name them here. However, we would like to thank those people for the record.

Dotty Tryk and Dennis Koho added considerably to the accuracy of the transcript. Both of them were the most outstanding public supporters of the stadium proposal from the start. Without their help and determination, at some personal cost, there would be no story here, no stadium and no need for a book. We cannot thank them enough for everything they did for us, which was virtually everything.

Then there was the contribution of Al Miller. The near-genius suggestion he made to amend the Urban Renewal Map to add in the area for the stadium was the technical trigger that enabled the bond financing possibility without which the entire idea might have been stopped in its tracks. The amendment consisted of a thin sliver running between one huge bulge which outlined the City boundary and another smaller bulge where the stadium property was located. The final lines resembled a boy holding a balloon. The new area had to be connected to the original Urban Renewal area to be valid. This proposal took care of that necessity. Including the stadium parcel in the Urban Renewal District made the City eligible to issue Urban Renewal Bonds to fund the City's part in the enterprise. We are indebted to Al Miller for that and all his help and steadfast loyalty throughout the entire process.

We are eternally grateful to the slim majority of one that sustained the effort at the critical City Council vote. Messrs. Miller, Newton and Beach, along with Mayor Dennis Koho, provided the approving majority that ended the long debate on our side of the ledger to allow the project to proceed. The rest is history. The entire process, from idea to fruition stands as an outstanding example of democracy at work and of its success. It also represents a tribute to those political people who were willing to sacrifice their reputations and political futures to see something that ought to be and make it happen. They recognized the value of professional baseball and what it represents and how it does so many things beyond the limits of the diamond. It improves the quality of life where ever it goes. Those people were willing to risk a lot to benefit their constituencies. The quality of courage is a noble trait to be admired wherever it is found.

Both the Statesman Journal and the Keizer Times played significant roles in the development of and adherence to those democratic processes. We are indebted to both of them for their participation while the issue was being decided. Their accounts were complete and accurate and allowed the public to have their input after an informed consideration. The Statesman Journal stories were the source of many of the details in this book. The KeizerTimes offered to make many of their photos available to us, and we appreciate their kindness in doing so.

We also thank Tracey Davis who acted as secretary to the City Council and provided us with transcripted details of those critical meetings . That allowed us as writers to be considerably more specific than we ordinarily could have been. The result is a more accurate product and better public record of that brief but important period of Keizer history. Jeanne Schroeder helped out with the technical typing.

The contractors, Cory Redding and the architects, Arbuckle, Costic and many others too numerous to name here played pivotal roles in defining the limits within which we could work. They kept the project on an even keel to completion within a difficult deadline. It was a near impossible task. It was and is truly a miracle.

But of all of those involved, the recurring names of Koho, Tryk, Miller, Newton, Beach, Redding and Costic stand out along with the fans of Salem and Keizer and team sponsors that have taken this team to their hearts and have done it all. To them, all of them, we owe an eternal debt of gratitude that we can never repay, but will constantly try to do. We are happy and proud to call all these people our friends.

From idea to dream, from dream to reality, the entire enterprise covered many, many people in glory. A select group of them will for decades to come be celebrated as those who were willing to sacrifice and labor to bring something to a community that could not otherwise have been accomplished. Their satisfaction and recognition has to come from the gratitude of generations of families and their children who will continually enjoy the activities the stadium has made available to them. We owe much to those individuals, alone and collectively, who helped us to bring the ballpark to where it is and who welcomed us into their cities and accepted us so readily.

Then there is the Walker family. From the day we purchased the franchise in Bellingham, they have been important people in our baseball lives, often going unnoticed among the crowds at the game performing jobs that we never had to think about once they were assigned to them. We knew those jobs would be done well. Ivan Walker, who died near the end of 1997, had been the original voice of the team on radio and in the ballpark announcing the players. Janet Walker is a daily contributor on many levels. An important personage in her own right, she is the author of several cookbooks, she pitches in every night to keep the show running. Her daughter Jennifer Knudson, along with her two sons, Philip and Gary, and her husband Gary, are all part of the daily ritual. EVERYONE in the Walker clan works, including Jerry and Lisa, as well as Nate and Lois Holeman, John and Joyce Fowler, Jim Walker and Betsy, and Jerry's girls Tracey and Brittany. Even Mickey is already a fixture at the ballpark. The earlier book characterized the Walker family as our Most Valuable Players. That was an understatement. We owe them a big debt of gratitude.

Our staff deserves a great word of thanks too. Rick Nelson gave his talents to this book by completing the dust jacket . From the previous book we know what a difficult chore that was and it came out splendidly. He joined us in the winter of 1996 and his presence allowed Jerry to participate more fully in other aspects of the entire process. Katrinka Rau runs the onfield chores daily and does a very good job. She pours her heart and soul into the operation and does many, many behind-the-scenes tasks far too numerous to mention here. We have been blessed with many other loyal and very competent people who came to work with us over the three years and who hopefully will stay, or return, or at least revisit, as the case may be. People like Tony Brown, Kim Spicer, Christy Shannon and many others make or made the game experience a little bit better every game.

Then there is Pat Lafferty, the consummate professional. He is the ultimate in preparedness. He works many hours before the games preparing statistics and acquainting himself with the players, both home team and others.

He searches for those many interesting facts he works into his broadcasts. He puts in many hours after the games making certain the after game broadcast and all details are carefully worked out for historical purposes. It is mostly to satisfy his own inner demands for perfection. Pat is "class" personified and he has brought the Volcanoes a great deal of that class and infused the spirit and love of baseball into our staff. He pitches in to do just about everything, finding no task to be above his stature. He is well known in the Oregon area and knows almost everybody too. His knowledge of sports matters in the Northwest is virtually limitless and he is a great source of information and advice. Jerry and Bill, the entire staff and the fans are better for knowing him. He has brought a great deal of professionalism to the team and we consider ourselves very fortunate to have him associated with us.

But most of all, it has been the fans and sponsors and people of Keizer and Salem who make it all such a grand success. They are the true heroes of this story. It was their background voice and support for the stadium idea that the elected representatives were able to hear and feel and turned the tide in our favor. Without them and their steadfast loyalty, things may have come out differently. We cannot thank them enough. We are happy in Salem-Keizer, hope to be there a long, long time, and will strive to be contributing members of the community. To all those who helped, we ask them to accept our thanks for everything.

Bill Tucker   and   Jerry Walker

# DEDICATION

## by Bill Tucker

Few of us have the opportunity to write one, let alone two books in our lifetime. Therefore, even the dedication of this, my second book, requires a great deal of consideration. After all, I have been blessed with a great family. My wife Dolores, to whom I dedicated the first book, is a fine person who I love for many reasons, one of which is the great effect she has had on my life. My children, Andy, Tom and Mary Alice are three of the nicest and finest persons I have met. I am very proud of what they have achieved and of their pleasing personalities and outstanding kindness and consideration for others. Those traits mark you as a great human being.

I am fortunate that my children are each married to wonderful people. Andy married Marlene Lapere and together they gave us Matthew William and adopted a little lady from Xiang Xia, China who they named Caroline Li, both of whom are magnificent. Tom married Susan Roberts and they have given us two grandsons, Jeremy and Justin, who have already made us proud and who will make us even prouder. Mary Alice married Gary Barter and moved around the corner from our home where she is raising her wonderful twins, William James and Kathleen Grace. Any one of them alone, would warrant the dedication of this book.

However, life takes many twists and turns and from time to time your priorities change , mostly due to events beyond your control. Dolores and I have a traditional family party we host on July Fourth each year. It is a whole day's exercise, beginning early in the day, through lunch and dinner and for some time after. We usually get over 60 people, including lots of children who tend to spend most of the time in our heated swimming pool. In between chow calls and swimming, we manage to get in a traditional whiffle ball game in which just about everyone plays, including some of the neighborhood kids who tend to float in. All are welcome.

It was at that traditional party in 1992 that my nephew John O'Hara , who was also my Godson and unquestionably one of my favorite persons of all time , asked some of us about a little mole-like growth that he had noticed recently on the right side of his head above his ear. It was small, actually tiny, and an outsider would not have noticed it unless your attention was called to it. Nobody thought it was anything important.

Shortly thereafter, his firm, Bear, Stearns, made available to all employees one of those mass medical screenings for just such growths. John was not inclined to participate but his wife, Paula, insisted that he have them take a look at it anyway. It couldn't hurt. Those medical people told him he should have some concern with that tiny spot and to have it looked at by a specialist. That began John's battle for his life.

The doctors called it melanoma. It was a death sentence for all but the extremely lucky few. There was no known cure and no truly effective slowdown medications. John's prescribed course of treatment was to have the growth surgically removed. The operation turned out to be more difficult than expected but we all thought it had been successful. Most of us anyway. To stretch his skin over the wound, the doctors inserted a tiny expansion device that had a tag hanging out of

2

it. John loved to joke that the doctors took a break for tea in the middle of the operation and  mistakenly left one of the bags inside.

John had to submit to radiation to "make sure" the site was clean.  He stuck to his program faithfully.  Some of us in his family actually thought all was well with him.  He was a happy and jovial person all the time, just as he was before. Nothing in what he said or did would lead you to believe that he was harboring even the tiniest germ of that fatal disease. But he knew it.

With his immediate family around his home, everything went on as usual.  The children continued in their little league, soccer, scouting and school programs.  John went to their games and participated in their homework exercises and did all the fatherly things  he always did. He played games with them and worked on their computer skills. Nothing seemed wrong.  He took his son Danny with me on a trip to see the Baltimore Orioles play in CamdenYards.  John even drove. We had a great time coming, going and while we were there.

Behind that happy exterior, John was fighting a painful but quiet battle to prolong his life and maybe even beat the disease. On the eve of his 38th birthday in November 1997, a second growth appeared in the same general area as before. The doctors again suggested surgery followed by more radiation. After that operation,  you could notice that his gait was not quite the same and that his shoulder sort of slumped a little. He was almost in constant pain but he managed at that time to hide  it well. John also enrolled in an experimental vaccine program that had him receiving shots which were expected to build up an immunity to future melanoma episodes. The program was hoped to be good for him but would certainly benefit others some day.

He bore the pain privately. He went back to work for short days. His parents, who were like saints throughout the entire experience, helped out by driving him back and forth from New Jersey to work in Brooklyn. Through that second radiation program and the injections, he still kept life at home with his wife Paula and the children in a special cocoon where bad messages were not allowed. He had decided he would be living with his cancer rather than be dying from it.

The melanoma was relentless though. In the Summer of 1998, he began to experience persistent pains in his back again. At first, nobody wanted to ascribe those symptoms to cancer, but they were just that. The cancer had spread to his back and was now very aggressive. It was inoperable at that stage so he was scheduled for some chemo therapy, a process which uses highly toxic chemicals to eliminate all your white blood cells, good and bad. He found it difficult to bounce back completely and he began to get blood transfusions to help rally him.

Through it all, he kept up his façade of having life at home go on as usual. The children knew Daddy was sick, but they did not know how sick he was. Paula was great through it all. He then took a quick trip with Paula to Lourdes in Southern France to ask the Blessed Mother for a miracle, if he could get one. At the end of the trip he had a private audience with the Pope which had been arranged by his father. He came home to his family, his entire family, who were praying for him all the while.

4

At Christmas time 1998, he began to experience problems with keeping food down. Each day he grew weaker as his body hungered for the nourishment it needed. Finally, he was admitted to the hospital and fed intravenously to restore his strength. Those of us who saw him then thought he would not be coming home alive. However, his will to live was very strong and he began to rebound and was able to come home.

John seemed to feel a lot better with the chemo and the blood transfusions working for him. Now he and Paula told the children that Daddy was very sick and might not live a long time. They would have to be strong and bear up with God's will. They did just great.

John courageously held sessions with the children separately and together. He told them they always had to work hard, in school and at whatever they chose to do in life. He stressed the importance of being kind and compassionate to others and helping those less fortunate than themselves. John told them their success in life would not be measured in dollars and cents but in what others thought of them and how they conducted themselves at all times. They did not have to be the smartest kids in the class but if they combined their talents and abilities with those other worthy character traits, they would succeed and lead happy, and good lives. He would watch and know about it somehow.

The Summer came and he was enjoying the first signs of the season when it struck again. This time, in the hospital, he did not seem to rebound and each day he seemed to lose a little bit more ground. Eventually, the disease reached some most vital parts and the end was in sight. He was able to have time for some parting thoughts with his wife and children and other close family members and friends. On June 24,1999, this wonderful and gifted human being died. He was only 39, or as John loved to say, just barely in his thirties. All the world suffered a great loss, even those whose lives he did not directly touch.

I have such magnificent memories of John. I lived with my sister and brother-in-law, Shirley and John O'Hara in their Brooklyn house when John was born. I was proud to be his Godfather and watch him grow up. I can remember him as I would turn the corner onto his street while coming home. He would run at top speed into your arms. His greeting was just like you were a king, and he made you feel that way. I got the same greeting from him even after I got married, left the house and would return on visits.

That exuberance as a child continued with him throughout his lifetime. He was always smiling and happy. He found the good side of everything. He had a personality that made everyone like him. One summer he worked as a messenger in my law office. His hours ended at four each day but at five o'clock you could still see John saying goodbye to the people he would be seeing again the very next day. He was that kind of person. He cared for everyone and was kind to them. I was happy to see him marry Paula and for the children to be born. They had a wonderful family life. He was a terrific father, the kind everyone would like to be or have. He was my hero.

While he was on his sickbed, he would be up through many pain-filled nights. He read some of the proofs of this very book which I gave him for enjoyment. He made some excellent suggestions which are incorporated into this book. I was amazed that despite his constantly painful condition and the fate that was staring him square in the face, he would not only read for his enjoyment but would also try to help me out.

Throughout this entire saga, which lasted in varying degrees of severity, for seven years, his family circled the wagons around him. While what he was going through was a purely personal thing, his family was strong and supportive through it all. Everyone, his brothers, Michael, Peter and Jimmy and sisters, Patricia and Mary Anne, especially, but most of all his wife Paula and his parents, John and Shirley O'Hara, were constantly at his side. He knew and appreciated the love and affection he was receiving. One of his lifelong friends, Bobby Higgins, visited him in the hospital almost every day. There is no question his ability and desire to cloak the pain he endured made the process somewhat more bearable for all of us and John wanted it that way. That was why he did it.

He was working for Bear Stearns up to his death. That firm was magnificent to John at all times throughout this ordeal and the firm deserves all the plaudits and credits we can give. The people at the job stuck with him personally and many of them visited him regularly in the hospital. Others who didn't see him during his times in the hospital or confined to bed at home by the pain he had to endure, found it difficult to believe he was so gravely ill since he looked so good until almost the very end.

John's attributes in life need not be embellished . If you were one of those that loved John O'Hara, and there were many of us, you knew he was something special. He glowed with a sweetness of character and his charm and enthusiasm were contagious. His family life was exemplary even before he had to undergo the ordeal he was to experience and that was to claim him. John was outstanding in everything he did . Everyone I ever met enjoyed just being with him. His wake and funeral were attended by literally hundreds of people, all of whom loved him.

From the moment he was diagnosed, John knew he was in a fight for his life. He knew the odds were stacked against him. He guarded that secret carefully and some of us, myself included, thought to the end he was going to win the war even if he lost some of the battles. With all of us around him, he was still alone as he marched to battle with that dreaded enemy.

If you could have seen the dignified way in which he conducted himself through it all, the way he managed his home life and the upbeat way in which he  mustered the resolve to be friendly, smiling and enjoyable at times when the pain must have been unbearable, you could not  help but admire this young man and hold him in your highest esteem. John faced a bleak future with high hopes but with a realistic view of the final outcome, and never complained. His determination, faith and courage should be beacons for all of us for the future.

As the years pass, nature tends to blur our  memories of details of persons, places, events and things. I have written this type of dedication so that his children, Sean, Lauren, Danny and Juliann, in future years as they grow up will know how truly great their father was, and how many of us so loved him.

I am very proud just to have known him. I am prouder to be related to him and to be his Godfather. I miss him every day. I am honored to dedicate this book to such a fine person. He had the courage of a whole pride of lions.

To John Francis O'Hara, Jr.
November 16, 1959 to June 24,1999

with love, forever.

Uncle Billy

1999

# DEDICATION

## By Jerry Walker

My part in this book is dedicated to the memory of my father, Ivan Walker. Dad was an integral part of the success of the franchise from the time of its purchase in 1989 until his death on December 18, 1997.

Dad did it all for the team. Immediately after we bought the team, Dad came to Bellingham and created a marketing program for the Bellingham Mariners. He would commute daily one hour each way from his home in Everett.

In the early days we operated out of a 9' x12' concrete office at the Stadium. The room more closely resembled solitary confinement than an office. It had no windows, no heat, no carpet and no rest room facilities. These nonexistent facilities did not stop Dad, he never complained, it just made him more determined.

Later Dad became the first ever radio play-by-play voice of the Bellingham franchise. He also did color commentary when our games were televised. Later he became "the voice" of the stadium as he graced the ballpark each game with his public address announcing. His energy was contagious and it excited the fans and motivated the team.

He will be long remembered for bringing a state of the art computer graphics scoreboard to Joe Martin Stadium in Bellingham. At the time, it was by far the nicest and best scoreboard in the League, possibly in any A-league short season stadium. He accomplished what seemed impossible as he sold sponsorships to cover the entire cost of the scoreboard and its installation. The scoreboard, which still stands today, was and is the best part of the Stadium. In fact, its grandeur looks somewhat out of place in an otherwise very modest ballpark.

I am thankful that our great fans in Salem-Keizer got to meet my father. I've never met anyone who didn't like him. I am also very happy that Dad saw the building of Volcanoes Stadium and was able to experience the excitement of Volcanoes baseball during our inaugural season. In many ways he was responsible for a great deal of the excitement during the Volcanoes' inaugural season as he did the public address announcing during the Volcanoes' games at the Stadium.

He was always very supportive of bringing baseball to Salem-Keizer and did anything he could to make it a reality. Dad even rallied support for the building of the Stadium by creating a petition for potential fans to sign. Dad spent hours in front of local supermarkets obtaining signatures, talking with the people and explaining how the Stadium would benefit the citizens. In all, he got over 500 people to sign his petition which asked the City officials to approve the Stadium project. The petitions were presented to the City Council at the beginning of an important meeting and the impact was overwhelming. It is appropriate that a permanent bronze plaque, in his memory, now adorns the Stadium concourse. It features his likeness. He seemingly is looking over the Stadium with a sense of satisfaction, happiness and tranquility. The

Stadium press box was also named in his honor the "Ivan M. Walker Memorial Press Box."

Not only was Dad an integral part of the baseball team, he was truly a terrific father. He defined the word father. He was always there for me and was supportive of everything I did. Dad got me started in baseball. Somehow getting me on his Fobes Tigers little league team at the age of 6. Everyone else on the team was much older and you had to be 8 to even sign up to play. But I was big for my age and Dad got me on the field. He also taught me how to win. The Fobes Tigers had back-to-back undefeated seasons going 31-0 each year. Dad ended his managing career as an undefeated coach, when his life ended he was undefeated in anything he wanted to do. He taught me those qualities and if I can achieve half of what he did in his life, I will be truly happy.

I have been blessed with a terrific family, a wonderful wife, Lisa, and with beautiful children,Tracey, Brittany and Mickey. But the foundation for my success must be credited to my Dad and my Mother, Janet, as they raised me they instilled in me how to succeed. I am still fortunate as Mom is with us daily during the baseball season and we see her frequently in the off season. We all miss Dad--more than words can express. He was a true legend and his memory will never fade.

Jerry Walker

1999

# CHAPTER ONE : IN THE BEGINNING

It's all history now. It was and is a terrific story about Jerry Walker and Bill Tucker and how they came to be in baseball together. It began rather casually. Both Jerry and Bill received birthday gift tickets to the Mickey Mantle-Whitey Ford Fantasy Camp in Fort Lauderdale Florida in 1986. It was a coincidence, or was it, that they had lockers right next to each other and became friends. They did not play on the same team that year but hung around together and ate lunch in their neighboring locker spaces between games of the daily doubleheader . It also was a coincidence, or was it, that they were two of the only three guys who had their ladies with them. As a result, they tended to go to dinners together and got to know each other a lot better than would ordinarily have been the case.

They hung around with Mickey and Whitey of course and also became friends with the other former Yankee players in camp, such as Jake Gibbs, Hank Bauer, Moose Skowron, Johnny Blanchard and Mike Ferraro. Those guys were classy and the motivation that drove those two guys to that camp was fully realized by those friendships.

But the greatest friendship that grew out of that camp was unquestionably the one between Jerry and Bill. Having stayed in touch with many of the campers over the years, they are always impressed by the recognition they have attained among the group and their interest in what Jerry and Bill have achieved together. That is a story that simply had to be told. So it came to pass that Jerry and Bill together wrote a book entitled "DP-Or Billy and Jerry in the Promised Land." It is a unique story. It chronicles the entire history of their meeting, becoming friends and deciding to get into baseball as an avocation, having been denied the opportunity by a lack of skills from getting into the game as players.

Sometimes referred to as the Bellingham adventure, the story was just not that simple. The pair eased their way into the Winter Baseball Meetings, using their credentials as representatives of the Everett Giants to break into that closed fraternity. That event was in Atlanta and there they were able to meet many of the Northwest League bigwigs, a factor that became increasingly important as the situation developed. Their first approach for information on a team to purchase was to Rook Von Halm who was the representative of the Bellingham franchise at that meeting. He unequivocally told them Bellingham was not for sale so they were at a loss as to what to do next.

They badly wanted to be in the Northwest League since Jerry was going to run the team on a daily basis. That general locale, with teams in Everett, Bellingham, Spokane, Medford, Salem (which then moved to Yakima),Eugene, Bend and Boise, would be less disruptive to Jerry's life. They wanted the Everett franchise because that was precisely where Jerry lived and where he was well known. However, that was not for sale. Their next choice was Bellingham, only 60 miles north of Everett, but they understood from Rook that franchise was not on the market. They wandered the lobby of the Hyatt Hotel aimlessly, as they tried to jell their plans as to their next step.

Almost at the point of giving up, they chanced into a hotel lobby restaurant for a hamburger. There at the next table was a gentleman named George DeLange and his wife,Lois, who were associated with the San Bernardino team. He overheard the discussion between Jerry and Bill and, fortunately, butted in.

He knew how they should proceed, he said, they should contact an agent. It so happened he knew one and would recommend him . In fact, he would have the agent call Jerry when they got home and discuss the matter with him. How about that? Is there any doubt that Jerry and Bill were correct when they believed their destiny was to be in baseball and some super mystical force was looking out for them to help! That is why the first book is partly entitled "DP" for Divine Providence. But that plot thickens.

Shortly after Jerry returned to Everett, he had a call from an agent named Roy Engelbrecht . He discussed with Jerry that he had a franchise for sale in the Northwest League and he believed it could be worked out in our price range. He finally told Jerry the franchise he had in mind was the Medford team, an affiliate of the Oakland A's and located in southern Oregon. This would be at least eight to ten hours driving from Everett so it meant the commute would have to be restricted at the very least. Nevertheless, Jerry called Bill and outlined the proposition. Both agreed to go forward and Jerry flew to Medford.

There he met Fred Herrmann and his partner Ed Zander. They discussed the sale, said they would stay in as part owners if we wanted. They indicated they would take back some financing if we wanted (meaning they would hold a mortgage or other lien on the franchise until we paid them in full, a customary ingredient in minor league franchise sales.) It would be an expensive proposition for us but we could swing it, although in our hearts we really wanted Everett first and then Bellingham.

Jerry went out to see the facility and was somewhat disappointed. It was not modern in any sense of the word . It showed the results of some expensive modernization the owners had accomplished with their own funds, but it still needed major improvements. It was in a sense giving a haircut to an ugly kid. He looks better, but is still just an ugly kid.

Negotiations dragged on for a number of reasons and opening day was rapidly approaching. The spring meeting of the league was scheduled to be held soon by conference call. Fred

Herrmann suggested we take advantage of the opportunity to get league approval so that condition would be eliminated when and if we signed a contract to buy the franchise. That conference call would be the best example of DP being present and in our corner.

At the league meeting (conference call) they conferenced in Jerry and Bill. We were to be interviewed as to our interest in the team, how we would pay for it and our ability to do so as well as how we would operate it. Several league owners, including Rook, spoke up in our behalf since we had met them at the winter meetings. Approval was swift although not easy since they asked all the right questions and got the answers they wanted. They were obviously experienced in this sort of thing. The league approved us. Jack Cain the president instructed us to get the deal closed fast . We were then excused from the meeting although we were invited to stay on the line if we wanted, and we did. Enter DP!

The next item of business was discussion of the sale of the Bellingham Franchise. We were dumbstruck. We had been told unequivocally the Bellingham franchise was not for sale, but here it was on the agenda-AFTER our item. We listened and the tide turned against the purchase and sale and the league did not approve it. Now we were in a quandary.

We had no formal contract with Medford and really didn't want it if Bellingham was available. Immediately following the end of the league meeting, Jerry called Bill and together they resolved any doubts or issues they may have had and decided to go all out for Bellingham. Jerry was probably on the road north from Everett within minutes and arrived in Bellingham late that afternoon. He was quickly able to discover the names of the important people in the sale and contacted them. By noon the next day the deal was signed and sealed and almost entirely delivered.

We had to inform Fred Herrmann of the events and why. We had to stand for league approval again and did. We had to settle with the unapproved Bellingham proposed purchaser to ensure the league there would be no lawsuits and pay Fred's legal expenses, which were minimal. Bellingham was ours. Tell us now that there is no DP, if you can!

We closed on the sale on opening day, which was really a night game. We had a press conference that afternoon at which one of the local sportswriters announced the bombshell that the team's general manager had resigned. Now the team was truly in the hands of the inexperienced. In fact, we didn't even know where the switch was to turn on the lights for the game. Fortunately it didn't get dark up there until late allowing us the time for a frantic and frustrating search for the switch. It was an opportunity for our new landlord, the Parks Department to come to our rescue,and they did.

The game was outstanding. We trailed Everett by two runs going into the bottom of the ninth when Corey Paul, an outfielder, pulled a pitch over the right field wall for a three-run homer and the game. Exciting. We even had live television coverage for that game due to a school project undertaken by the Western Washington University located in Bellingham. As a result, we have a full tape of our opening day ceremonies for the year and for our baseball careers and the full game. We were instant heroes. DP or what?

However, we now had to roll up our sleeves and get to work. The program planned for the year by our predecessors lacked just about everything and it had to be supplemented. Jerry became the owner in residence and worked what has come to be a magical change to elevate the program to a better position. As Bill flew back and forth between Brooklyn and Bellingham, Jerry worked with a barebones staff to acquaint himself with the neighborhood and to acquaint them with him. He did gangbusters.

The program was reworked and the general manager who had left so precipitously, returned. He signed on for the rest of the season and his experience was helpful. He was the only one who really had hands-on game experience and we needed it, at least in the very beginning. As the season wore on, Jerry became more and more expert and took over the running of the show on his own. Forgotten (until our book) were the foulups we went through such as not having a game ball available to throw out the ceremonial first ball on opening day (by the Mayor's designee) and problems with the sprinkler system coming on unexpectedly during games and many others. These are detailed in the first book which deserves your reading.

We did a lot of things right though. We greeted all fans as they came through the turnstile (we had only one) and thanked them for coming on the way out. We became personalities there and appeared on talk shows and in newspaper columns. We had the support of the local paper somewhat (there still is no local TV) and generated sufficient ink to stimulate attendance. Jerry became the man about town and was popular with the Lions Club, Kiwanis and other organizations.

We were an affiliate of the Seattle Mariners, in fact their first affiliate and the only one then still with them from their beginning. When we got to Bellingham, there was considerable doubt about how long that relationship would continue. Seattle was dissatisfied with the conditions of the field and the facilities and disliked the virtually empty stands night after night. They wanted their future stars to be playing in front of many fans to give them that special enthusiasm that only crowds can give. There is no question we were in grave danger of losing our Player Development Contract (PDC) with them.

A Player Development Contract, known as a PDC for short, is an affiliation agreement between a major league baseball team and a minor league franchise. Under that agreement, the major league team binds itself to send players, managers and coaches to the minor league team. These players are at a certain level of development according to the league in which the minor league franchise plays. The big league team selects the players and managerial staff, pays them, outfits them in uniforms selected by the minor league team, and provides the players with an opportunity to develop. The major league team has the entire say about those players. They can move them at will to another affiliate, cut them, trade them or teach and play them.

The managerial staff files reports with the development division of the major league team following every game. Their comments and opinions are carefully considered to determine the fate of these young men, to progress or not through the system. It is an expensive process and major investment for the big league club and has to be managed carefully so as not to waste resources and to avoid missing out on a player's talents.

The local franchise owners have no say whatsoever in what happens to the players either before or after they are assigned to a minor league team. Our job is to promote the team and its players so that fans come to see them play and fill the house to the extent possible. Playing before crowds is a big part of the professional baseball experience and learning to do that is just one more step in their developmental process.

We do arrange for their travel and for staying at the various stops in the league as they play out the schedule. We advance money to them for meal allowances as directed by the big league team and generally serve as a buffer and conduit for interaction between the players and the public and between the managerial and coaching staff and the development office. Because it pays a major part of what would be the franchise overhead, it is a very valuable thing to each minor league operator. We wanted to sustain our PDC at all costs.

That was Job Number One. To play without a PDC would mean we would have to locate, hire and pay our players which would be difficult if not impossible to do profitably out of the pitiful attendance they were getting.

We didn't win the pennant that year, but developed a relationship with the team and the City that was really good. We had a honeymoon period with Seattle which took a cautious position preferring to wait and see what we could do. We have no doubt that had we not come in that would have been the last year of Bellingham's association with Seattle. We discussed it frequently because one of the teams in our league, Boise, was playing without a PDC and the owner was known to be a friend of the owner of the Seattle franchise. It was a genuine concern.

Even worse, the team was not truly competitive on the field. We lacked hitting and power and had only spotty pitching. We were no match for the affiliates of the older major league franchises. Seattle had never won and rarely if ever had a competitive team up to then. As a result , they had difficulty in signing their draft choices, forcing them to be realistic about their signing opportunities and deliberately drafting from lower in the pack to give them success in signings. That would change later, but the lack of wins had a serious impact on attendance.

Then there was the City culture. The fans were used to what were called "free nights." These were games, which were sold to sponsors for a flat fee . The sponsors would then distribute many, many tickets as widely as they could and  the fans came because it was free. The theory was good to a degree.  One would expect that someone who got in to the game free would spend more on the concessions but that was not the case. Statistics that have been scientifically obtained and validated and revalidated prove beyond doubt the reality is otherwise. They spend less.

There was no way that culture could be changed in the first year. In fact, despite everything we did, we were never able to overcome that expectation. Until the end, people would drive to the park, inquire whether it was free and, if not, go home. Painful, but it happened repeatedly.

The free nights did have some value. They added to the attendance figures since you counted everyone who came to the park, paying or not. They also provide certain cash for the treasury and added to the revenues, which might not otherwise have been too high on certain nights. This was especially true when we took over with such ordinarily low attendance. We reasoned that even if one in four attendees on a free night bought a hot dog or pizza we were ahead on concessions. And the increased attendance did not go unnoticed in Seattle where the relationship improved and flourished.

But worst of all was the ballpark itself. The playing field was immaculate and the Parks Department laid it on heavily. They manicured and nurtured the surface as if it was their own table or bed. We were rated one of the best infields in the league. But not everything about it was good. It had an incline around the outfield edge running from the beginning of the warning track to the fence, about ten feet wide. Outfielders had to run uphill for that last ten feet, causing some to lose their balance and the flight of the ball. It even gave some of the balls odd bounces when they caromed off that before or after hitting the wall. It made for some odd plays.

Joe Martin Stadium as it was called was named after one of the late legendary baseball men of Bellingham. After his playing days were over, he ran THE sporting goods store in town. He was so deeply involved in organizing baseball on all levels in Bellingham, and successful at it that they named the stadium after him in his honor. He had long since gone to his reward by the time we got there. But many still remember him and revere that memory. Bill once asked Mel Stottlemyre if he knew him and he proceeded to give a  somewhat long discourse on him and about playing at the stadium.

But the memory now exceeded the reality of the stadium's shortfalls.   It no longer did justice to Joe Martin or his memory.  The concourse was a concrete walkway that may at one time have had no cracks but now it was uneven, tilted and full of cracks.   We were constantly worried about people falling , especially at night since the lights did not shine too brightly there.

The bathrooms were atrocious.  They were near impossible to keep clean and were ugly and disgusting.  The urinals consisted of really only one big trough, which was used communally by three or more at one time, maybe four if you had children participating.  The ladies' room was even worse.  There were only two dirty stalls that needed constant attention to keep them working.  The lines of ladies waiting to"go" during games often if not always exceeded the lines at the concessions or beer booth.  Lighting in the concourse was hardly existent  but yet those conditions had been tolerated for a long time by the time we got there.   We wanted to improve those conditions.

The concession stands were hardly adequate.  They functioned with the help of antiquated equipment, some of which was borrowed from other organizations. They faced the back of the grandstand so that anyone on line was unable to see or hear the game while waiting.  The serving counters were narrow so that service was slow which was already slow enough because of the inexperienced young people we used there on a game day basis.  Pizza, french fries, ice cream and other items which are traditional in ballparks just were not offered there because of lack of equipment. Jerry cured that to a large degree. Many of the items had been  outpriced or outsized for the community.

We switched to reasonable quantities and prices and added the equipment by either buying it or renting it and served the other items.  Jerry added a barbecue pit and seating area that became very popular. He opened a souvenir stand to sell team oriented products and other items. He upgraded the team's baseball cards and made sure they were delivered long before the season's end so kids could get them autographed if they wanted. The old cards would arrive near the season's end so the kids would have to rush to buy them and hustle to get them autographed. Those cards contained almost nothing about the players individually and Jerry changed that too.

One of the worst things about the stadium was the concept itself. The ballpark had no changing areas and no shower or dressing facilities. The players had to walk about three hundred yards across the parking lot to the football stadium, down a ramp and there was the dressing room and shower facilities. That dressing room was shared with any other teams or track and field enthusiasts who used the football stadium or its track. There was no locked facility to protect the personal items of the players or the manager and coaches making it impossible to leave home team items in their lockers safely. The manager and coaches had no separate facilities and hung out in that same room with the players and trainer and the entire room opened up onto the community shower making the room hot and steamy after games. Players came out of the dressing room hotter than they went in, and sweatier too.

Even worse was the parking lot. It looked like the surface of the moon, scarred and deeply pitted. It had been surfaced originally when the football stadium was built and as an afterthought was pressed into service for Joe Martin Stadium too. It had not been surfaced, striped or repaired since and looked to be in awful disrepair.

Unlike ballparks in other towns, there was no possibility of charging for the parking to generate additional revenue. The public was used to parking free despite the condition of the lot. It was a Catch-22 situation. You couldn't raise money to repair the lot because it was in such poor condition nobody would pay to park there. It was made more hazardous at night because there was no lighting either. People navigated the treacherous way by the light that peeked over the grandstand from the ballpark and placed themselves in grave danger. The absence of striping and lack of interested supervision meant that everyone parked every which way and made it difficult to leave the lot safely.

The players had to navigate that hazard too, on foot. They usually walked close to a fence that protected the grass area within the football stadium from the public and used the fence as a guide and protector. It was not satisfactory to say the least.

When we came there in 1989, we thought the stadium and its environs was darn near heaven and the surrounding and shared facilities just great. It shows you what rookies don't know. Ignorance is really bliss. As we became more experienced and thought of the legal exposure we had for injuries and the legal nuisance it was, we became less and less happy. Our satisfaction turned to dissatisfaction as we saw the facilities of other teams and compared their good points against ours.

Shortly after we took over, the major leagues insisted on an audit of minor league facilities to judge them on their attributes and point out their shortcomings. It was an appropriate exercise and had to be done since there were many that didn't measure up. The major leagues, however, recognized that there were many older ballparks that the operators could do nothing about. They were antiquated and were owned by the cities which had little money in their coffers to spare and very little inclination to spend it on a ballpark. Therefore, although they audited them all, they grandfathered many despite their inadequacies and strongly suggested that something be done to correct the problems.

Joe Martin Stadium was among the latter group. Tom Leip came to do the audit and viewed the facility against the standards he had been given. Our playing surface was judged to be better than just adequate, except for the incline in the outfield warning track. The lighting passed, but just barely. It was really inadequate and there were huge dark spots in the outfield when full darkness finally arrived. It was difficult to follow and catch line drives and even more difficult to spot the ball on those really high flies.

There was no standard against which he could compare the rest. The concourse, broken and raised in spots was a hazard and the toilet facilities woeful. We got the lowest grades on that that were available but they should have created even lower categories just for us. The parking and team facilities were also in a league of their own and could not be adequately judged in a survey meant to cover more than one facility. It didn't fit well into any category. There was no other quite like it.

We knew we would fail but had no idea what to do about it. As we groped for solutions, Jerry as always came up with some ideas to make it more attractive. He redesigned the toilet facilities to make them cleaner and more user friendly. However , he couldn't get the City to pitch in to do the work without the application of considerable political pressure centered on the idea that the cost was minimal and that we had borne a part of the cost by paying for the redesign.

He pushed for some more attractive seating that could be sold to regular patrons as special or box seats. The City eventually bought 72, count them, seats, but they were the cheapest and thinnest plastic available and were easily broken by fans of the teams who misused the park when our team was not using it. Within the year, the seats were broken beyond hope of repair and many could not be raised or lowered. On many, the backs and seat surfaces themselves had been badly broken and cracked by vandals who were in there to play games. If you sat on them you were in mortal danger of getting a badly pinched heiny.

Jerry himself, with a few volunteers, designed and constructed four skyboxes above the grandstand , plus room for the press and radio. Those skyboxes were tough to take. Whenever you walked up there the entire roof would shake and you felt uneasy. There were no toilet facilities up there so patrons had to descend stairs the full height of the grandstand to"go" and then reascend those same stairs. No mean feat. The concession personnel who served up there, had to be in pretty good shape for the thirty or forty trips they had to make up and back each night.

Nevertheless, they were  innovative, and attractive too.  But they were not popular.  We were the only team in the league with skyboxes but we couldn't really sell them.  We were locked in an area that had a low per capita income and a culture that meant many only came to the park when admission was free.  We had provided a luxury in  a surrounding where luxuries were not appreciated and people spoke more of necessities. They did serve one significant functional purpose.  They provided us with skybox management experience we couldn't have gotten otherwise which stood us in good stead when we eventually moved to a modern facility.

The major league audit was not confidential.  It was given to the press everywhere and the Bellingham Herald wrote it up accurately.  It started people talking and thinking, especially us.  We began to take a hard look at the missing elements in Joe Martin Stadium and to put an approximate price tag on the cost of the improvements.  It was a shocking number, one we knew was conservative and would provide only the minimum of improvements to meet the major league criteria. It was a number that staggered the imagination and was far in excess of any possible expected profits from the franchise in twenty or more years, especially when we were not making money to begin with.

Something had to be done or the situation would continue to worsen beyond anyone's tolerance level. We could not expect the major leagues to be so understanding about a facility that only worsened over the years with little or nothing done beyond cosmetics to improve the conditions. What was accepted now would not always be accepted.

Teams were moving all around like checkers and getting new facilities. In our league alone, the Salem team had moved to Yakima into a new stadium. Boise had built its own state of the art facility. Medford invested some meaningful money into park improvements. Everett was angling for statewide help to upgrade its facility which was already better than ours.

Elsewhere, new stadia popped up everywhere. Lake Elsinore, Rancho Cucamonga, Norwich, Sparta, Trenton, Fishkill. They appeared out of nowhere and were spacious and nice. New York State was budgeting ninety million for new stadiums in Rochester, Batavia, Albany, Syracuse, Buffalo, Utica, Binghamton and other places. We would very soon be the only blackeyes on the minor league horizon and the pressure was on to get something done. We would stand alone as the lonely little petunia in the onion patch. Yet, we never thought of moving. Yet.

## CHAPTER TWO : SEASONS IN THE SUN

Had the major league auditor not have brought attention to the gross inadequacies of Joe Martin Stadium, it may never have come to a head. We were aware of the shortcomings of the ballpark but it was a blissful unawareness. We would probably have gone on year after year patching and trying to make minor improvements.

After the audit,we wanted to improve not only to comply but to better the facility for the fans and perhaps for ourselves. It was possible improved conditions might bring more people to the park. The need for tolerance would then be less. Then the less than fanatical baseball fan might , just might, come to the park occasionally to see for themselves what went on in that little hotbed of activity just off Lakeway Drive on Orleans Street. Compliance was the most remote of reasons to do something since being inexperienced we thought ourselves to be eternally safe with the noncompliance waiver in our pockets.

Our euphoria even reached to greater heights when we won the league championship in 1992. It was a delightful but hardfought season, full of ups and downs. Our team really didn't measure up fully against the rest of the league. This was especially so with the Bend Rockies. They were stacked with high draft choices which resulted from the major league Colorado team having been created through expansion with a fistful of high draft choices to start them off.

We had streak hitters who seemed to pick up the team by turns. Our pitching was pretty good though, and we were seemingly always in every game and won most of them.

Several of our guys made it to the majors eventually-not household names -but good ones. Guys like Lowe, Pozo, Widger, Bonnici, Estes, Wolcott, Hampton and a few others made it up to the show. But the entire team was something to be proud of, and we still are, including those who went no further than A-ball.

So, as we swung into 1993, we knew we had something good. But the string had just about stretched as far as it could go. The good karma we had gotten from the skyboxes (even though they went largely unused)and improved bathroom facilities and the barbecue space had just about waned. We always thought we could do much better in that town if we could give an improved product for the fans to watch in more comfort.

The mindset in Seattle had definitely changed and our years of being poor losers, almost perennially, were gone. The big team had actively sought to sign , and signed, its high draft choices and dreams of an eventual winner in Seattle were more of a reality. This bode well for improved attendance too.

Our lease on the stadium had one more season to run,1993. We knew we would have no difficulty in renewing it because it was a low cost item for the City and was being better attended than in years past. In fact, it was a civic attraction because the Chamber  of Commerce used it as one of the entertainment highlights in its propaganda to bring business and people to Bellingham

Let it be understood that Bellingham WAS a really nice place to live. The topgraphy around the City made it one of fantastic beauty, with panoramic scenes from snow-capped mountains, to steaming hills under which volcanoes lay dormant, to spectacular waterfalls, and Puget Sound and the vast Pacific.

The City was college oriented with a major segment of Washington's college commitment vested in Western Washington University which gave the City a cultural aura few cities could attain. The people were really very nice.

The downtown area had been truly redone in a burst of urban renewal . What once must have been a collection of shabby, antiquated buildings was transformed , almost miraculously , into several well-planned City blocks of shopping and cafes, all of which were eye-appealing and relatively prosperous. The proof of the pudding was in the fact that parking was scarce making one believe the area was already bursting with prosperity. The City seemed to have outgrown its planned parking in a short time.

It was in this atmosphere that in 1993 we entered upon an extension of the lease for the ballpark with the City. The negotiations were tough to say the least and Jerry was locked in a discussion of facts and opinions with the Parks Department chief, Byron Elmendorf. He was the one who husbanded the budgeted funds for the City and operated a very nice cluster of parks throughout the City that were well used and appreciated.

He drew the line on the ballpark, though, because he believed the facility was not as widely used by the populace as the other facilities and the stadium in part earned income for private parties. As a matter of deep personal principle, he felt the City should not pay to earn money for private enterprise. That type of thinking ran counter to the universal modern tenet of cities everywhere. Other cities were building specialty ballparks for professional teams and remodeling their environs, granting tax relief and financial encouragement to lure and then retain private entrepeneurs. The rationale for such civic action is very clear-it pays off in jobs, removal of urban blight and increases tax as well as private revenues which in turn are also taxed. Everyone gains.

But that did not tell the entire story. It was difficult to understand how anyone connected with the City would think we were not paying our fair share. Our team played only 38 of the 195 games played at Joe Martin Stadium every season. That works out to only 19% of the total games played there each year. Yet, it was a proven fact which could not be truthfully contested that our team nevertheless paid 85% of the total City revenue derived annually from the operation of that ballpark.

The Parks Department did not skimp on the playing surface. Its team of laborers worked long and hard manicuring the grass and infield skin. The bases were always freshly whitewashed and the foul lines and batters boxes were put in for every game with loving care and accuracy. These fellows liked the team and Jerry so they were like a bridge between the franchise and the Parks Department. So long as the field was well taken care of, Jerry did not really have to interface with anyone in officialdom, until lease negotiations.

Naturally, as one of the City's hired minions in an executive type position, Byron came before the City Council membership en masse or singly on many issues. He had their attention and support. In point of fact he ran a very good ship for the City and even for the ballpark-except that he felt we were not earning our keep or paying our share of the way.

In a City that was always close on its revenues, monetary issues held the spotlight whenever they were raised. Therefore, when Elmendorf conceived of a plan to increase revenues without additional taxpayer dollars to pay for the Parks Department efforts at Joe Martin and elsewhere, he received Council support and public praise. And so it came to pass that the idea was advanced that fees for ballpark rental should be increased for the professional team only. Part of the plan was the team should take over some of the chores at the park that were at the time being performed by Department personnel. So those items became the touchstones of the plan for the extended lease.

On the other hand, revenues for the team were not good. When we acquired the franchise, it was the third worst professional baseball franchise in North America, not just the United States. One should note that geographic area includes places like Canada, Mexico, Nicaragua, Guatemala and Panama. The franchise had been "drawing flies" as they say-about 450 people per night, many of whom got in free.

Jerry was eking out an existence barely above minimal levels at some risk,and even at times below that. If money was scarce in the City budget for ballpark improvements, it was even more scarce and more difficult to come by out of franchise revenues. To attract fans Jerry brought in professional acts at every opportunity, some of which were privately sponsored. The fans saw high class acts like the Blues Brothers, Myron Noodleman, Captain Dynamite, the Famous Chicken and even the Colorado Silver Bullets.

The latter was a team of female baseball players sponsored by the Coors Brewing Company. They played against a male team picked locally from among a group whose skills or former skills had to meet strict rules laid down by the Bullets. They obviously didn't want them to be too good and hopefully not too bad. The restrictions made for a polyglot collection of opponents who really couldn't pitch, run, throw or hit anymore, if they ever could. The Bullets were managed by (then) future Hall of Famer, Phil Niekro.

We dressed the "home" team in old Bellingham Bells uniforms and advertised the event well. That always proved to be the best fully paid attendance night we had as the women got behind the Bullets and came out in droves. All these acts were expensive and we could only hope for a good turnout, not expect it. But the Bullets almost always made out well for us. Without those events, we probably could not have made it.

Those events were new to Bellingham. We were therefore bringing to the City a form and media of entertainment that enlarged the available menu of fare the City was used to. They were appreciated by the people who came to the ballpark. The events never hit home with the City officials with the impact they should have had. The Chicken and the Silver Bullets were really class acts and were provided to the City populace with no extra charge beyond the regular price of admission, not even for The Famous Chicken whose act was especially expensive. Our predecessors had booked the Chicken in their last year there and made a slight increase in adult ticket prices. We were proud that we did not.

Despite that, when issues arose to the City Council level, the members naturally recognized the side they were most familiar with, especially when that side had a position adverse to the spending of public moneys. They knew Byron Elmendorf well, recognized his achievements which were truly commendable and understood he was not extravagant with tax revenues.

So when there came forth a plan which had as its centerpiece the saving of public moneys through having the team take on more of the work activities at the ballpark, and raising the game charges in the new lease, it was well supported. Only those Council members who came to the games, irregularly at best, recognized the value the franchise had to the City. They also realized the hardship such increased costs would have on the franchise and were reluctant to go along with that program.

Instead, they opted for leaving the entire situation as it was. After all, the City had shown it could afford it and the team was happy. Those Council members knew of the pitfalls of placing the City in jeopardy of losing the franchise by having it relocate elsewhere. They knew professional franchises were beginning to hear and heed the siren call of cities looking to add such jewels to their crown. They were aware that would leave a huge void in the entertainment available to the people and would create a stigma on the City. It would impair their efforts to attract residents and businesses. But they were in the distinct minority. The majority, well-intentioned as they were-sought always to publicly opt for the financial results most beneficial to the City whether only in the short term or otherwise.

Jerry also innovated meaningful giveaway nights. Gloves, bats, balls, photos, posters, baseball cards, t-shirts and other things were regularly given away. We had terrific fireworks shows, and a stirring program for July Fourth which featured a local cavalry exposition complete with lights and torches. All those things helped raise the level of attendance to about 1800 per night by the time we departed.

When you realize that 14 of the 38 home games (we are a short season team playing a 76 game schedule , half of which were at home) had either a giveaway or special event, you can appreciate the job that was done and the planning effort that went into it. Added to that number was about 6 or 7 "free nights" and the season was almost fully covered. You could come to the stadium and see a major league act or performance by a nationally known performer, get something or get in free, almost every night. And great baseball besides.

Into that supercharged atmosphere rode Jerry Walker, new resident of Bellingham and an entrepeneurial one at that, seeking to retain the same level of City support for private profit. With the deck somewhat stacked against him from the beginning, his pleas of small if any profits and increasing costs fell on deaf ears. They were just not interested and couldn't see why the team couldn't simply accept the new proposal and the new chores and charges. After all, the City's costs were said to be rising too.

Naturally, the public had its ear to the press as its only source of information. The press with its need to retain good relations with the City fathers printed the story as they received it but most of what they received, and thus printed, came from their regular sources in City Hall, not us.

Our side of the story would have to be gleaned from small bites of quotations and explanations printed in the body of the story, mixed with a large splattering of the opinions of City officials and the Council members. Since only a small percentage of the populace was attending the games, the issues of the park were mainly meaningless to many of the citizens and they got only a headline familiarity with what they felt was someone else's issue.

It also was not an issue that would be likely to arouse a public clamor even if the arguments for the team were entirely meritorious and the official side was entirely wrong. So the debate wore on with both sides being intransigent throughout the 1993 season. It so happened that the Bellingham Mariners were a pretty good team that year and the race for the pennant was close and interesting. We won the Northern Division pennant but lost the playoffs in a two game sweep by Boise. Nevertheless the team's success did translate into substantial public interest which resulted in some softening of the official position. This thing that operated for an intended profit (without actually getting one) over in Joe Martin Stadium was not so bad after all and should be retained, if not nurtured.

Therefore, it was deemed appropriate and wise for both sides to soften their positions and compromise the differences. A two year extension was drafted and approved. It called for the team to pick up the chore of cleaning the ballpark after its home games and to increase the field rental charges somewhat. There had been some dispute about practice time on the field for the team during the season with the City trying to impose a separate charge for each practice in addition to game charges. That was not acceptable, nor could we accept any limitation on the preemptive right of the team to practice whenever they wanted to, and without charge.

Nobody had won that war and the seeds that were sown during the period of hostility would bear bitter fruit in the future.

Cleaning the ballpark was quite a chore for us. We had to hire special staff to do it and only through sharp haggling were we permitted to use the City's existing equipment, but then had to maintain it. We found the people to do it alright but the quality of the job they did varied from day to day and consumed lots of time. Sometimes they were working right up to an hour before the gates opened.

For the next two seasons, through 1994 and 1995 , it seemed as if peace reigned. The issue faded from the papers and the ballpark functioned seemingly well. That was all on the surface though. Byron Elmendorf began to show up more frequently than before on game nights, or at least it appeared that way. We were never sure he understood the economics of franchise management, especially the "free" night culture. He may have misunderstood and done the simple arithmetic of multiplying the attendance figures by the average ticket price and added that figure to what he surmised to be the income from advertising and concessions to conclude prosperity was at hand.

We tried to give the impression all was well, and we really thought it was. Silence was golden. The new state of the art, electric scoreboard was a big hit and Ivan Walker's operation of it got the fans into the game in a big way.

We had made a deal with the City to replace the weathered, splintered and missing cedar slats that were woven through the chain link fence that surrounded the park. The deal was the Parks Department would buy new plastic blue slats to replace them IF we would furnish the labor to remove the old ones and slide in the new. It was an enormous project but Jerry got volunteers to do it and it was accomplished. The cast of volunteers also included Bellingham's retired mayor, and our late good friend, Reg Williams. Dolores Tucker even pitched in to do it when she was in town.

That did improve the look of the park tremendously when viewed from the grandstand. But it was really the same story as the ugly kid and the haircut. Nothing could hide the cracked and uneven concourse or the woeful concession stands or the cracked "new box seats." It worked no magic on the potholed parking lot or the inconvenience of the location of the clubhouse and showers.

We were not entirely innocent either. We had been tooling along and transporting the players between cities for games in the old bus we inherited with the franchise. It was decrepit and had no air conditioning to speak of, no toilet facilities so necessary on trips that were hours long, and its engine had such poor compression it was difficult to negotiate the high hills of the Cascades. It consumed oil relentlessly and left a wake of acrid exhaust that polluted the atmosphere terribly. We were genuinely concerned about the oil spray from its exhaust blinding following drivers on the freeway. Its breakdown in 1992 and forced replacement was really a benign event and was a vast improvement.

Perhaps the two worse aspects of the old bus were its frequent breakdowns and the absence of toilet facilities. Spyder Webb, the veteran Bellingham (Mariners) trainer, had sort of woven a legend about that bus. He created the lore of the breakdowns and turned what could have been disastrous events into an almost club-like adventure which everyone wanted to participate in. Many who never pushed the bus or suffered through long breakdowns along the highway would later claim veteran status in such events. It was sort of like being at the Polo Grounds for Bobby Thomson's home run in 1951. (You don't meet many people who were alive for that who weren't there!)

The lack of bathroom facilities on the bus was another issue. Many of our players were from South or Central America or from the Dominican Republic. They were just what the doctor ordered to be "let in" on the dangers of the bus. The trips throughout the league were over lonely highways with only sparse development. They took the team through mountain passes and huge forests.

Often the bus would stop for nature calls in remote, unlighted places. Some of those players were so intimidated by the stories of wild bears or animals attacking players while they relieved themselves along the road they were fearful of getting out of the bus. This made the stops longer than usual as they insisted on urinating from the last step in the bus doorway rather than getting out on the road alongside the bus. As a result, they went one at a time from the doorway.

That breakdown brought us to a point of decision. We came up with various ideas on how to use the old bus to offset at least part of the cost of the "new" one. One of the ideas was to hold a "break up the bus" party. Admission would be charged and everyone would bring their own sledgehammer. Then they would take smashes at the bus with their own sledgehammers until it was demolished. We thought however that the cost of cleanup and removal might outdistance the income we got from tickets. We even discussed the possibility that only part of the bus would be demolished and the remainder left standing, making removal even more difficult. We finally traded it in, in one piece.

Near the end of the 1995 season, the tranquility was broken again. The lease extension was coming to an end and the drumbeat started. The Parks Department was now more convinced than ever that we were raking in the dough hand over fist. Jerry's constant retorts that the franchise was far from a bonanza and that the major leagues were pushing for compliance with their standard requirements fell on almost deaf ears. Jerry was right on both counts. We had by now switched to the Giants from the Mariners affiliation (more about that in the next chapter) and the Giants, while happy with the affiliation, were pushing for upgrades all across the line. We wanted to secure the relationship too.

The Giants wanted better lighting in the bullpens, a more compliant bullpen mound as to material composition and other things. They wanted the manager to have a separate office where he could meet with the coaches, scouts and players privately. There was no question that office had to be in the clubhouse, accessible to the dressing room and showers. One problem was the clubhouse was already jammed with lockers, showers and trainer space , and was over several hundred yards away. That plus the fact the Parks Department hesitated to spend one nickel for any improvement to benefit the professional team made it a tough situation.

The economic issue was being pushed harder this time, determined to succeed, in getting more revenues from the team. The City declared it as an absolute that the game charges would have to be increased and demanded a share of ticket or concession revenues. Of course, the mere outlining of that program made Elmendorf a hero with the City Council since it appeared that he was an alchemist, creating budget income out of thin air. To assure himself that the share the City was expecting to get was correctly computed, he wanted open access to team financial records and all our confidential material.

That was anathema. These were private records of a private corporation. The City had no business asking or expecting access to them. However, in the press it sounded good for the City and made it seem as if we were trying to hide the true facts simply to avoid paying "our fair share." It seemed as if almost nobody at City Hall was listening to our side of the discussion. Only a few members of the Council were on our side. Nothing that was ever advanced as an argument either way ever changed anyone's position on the issue anyway.

It was not a stalemate but only because both sides seemed fearful of the results of a vote. Franchises were moving all the time and it seemed as if the process had accelerated in then recent months. Jerry hinted at our considering a move but it was only for bargaining purposes. We had not seriously considered it. However, it was enough of a ghost that the Council feared it and didn't want to be recorded for posterity that they were the ones whose intransigence lost professional baseball for Bellingham. Despite the rich tradition of the City for baseball and Joe Martin Stadium in particular, they were shrewd enough to realize they couldn't get a replacement team without spending enormous sums on stadium improvements.

The argument was a public matter now and people coming to the ballpark discussed it openly. Even the Seattle TV station sent someone up to get the varying points of view. We were interviewed on TV by a reporter who aired the sequence almost without editing. We tried to defuse the misconception that we were being selfish about it and not paying our share while reaping in a bonanza from public facilities. Even our old and good friend Bruce Weed thought we were holding back and were making a good profit there.

The true facts should have carried the day for us. We were being asked to pay the entire cost of the stadium upgrades and all the maintenance and whatever other expenses there were. There were 195 events that took place at the stadium each year, baseball, softball and other things. Of those 195 events, we played only 38 games! There were 157 other games there each year. That works out to our team's use being only 19% of the stadium's total use yet we paid 85% of the stadium's annual costs. Anyone should have been able to see the logic of our argument. The press never even repeated that fact. The Council refused to recognize the facts.

We laid it on the line. The franchise was no bonanza. The improvements we talked about were required for major league compliance and would benefit all the fans. WE were not the Bellingham Giants. Everyone who enjoyed the games and came to the park, mothers, children and fathers, were the Bellingham Giants. Our attendance eventually reached over 70,000 fans in a season--a number almost one and one half times the entire population of Bellingham. That was the point and we urged everyone to see.

We were encouraged by the results but we were still losing the war of rhetoric in the press. There the stories were distilled and the reporters naturally balanced the outcome in favor of their regular sources. After all, we only became an issue every two years, it seemed, as opposed to City Hall sources which were there every day for them. It also appeared that we were asking them to accept our word on finances, not showing the actual figures for one and all to evaluate. We looked to be obstinate in refusing to allow the issue to be resolved  by not cooperating by  providing financial details.

The truth was otherwise. We saw no benefit in making our financial records public since we were a private corporation. Our transactions were between us. We were the ones who had the entire risk of loss to the franchise. The City, no matter what we showed them, would never consider guaranteeing us a profit. If we lost money, as we usually did, it was our loss and we bore it entirely.

We also felt that no matter what we made public, it would redound to our disadvantage. The figures would be almost automatically denounced as fabrication by people in control who didn't want to think otherwise and could not be convinced. We were eventually proven correct on that point, unfortunately. In the end, Jerry and Lisa did reveal important records to the City Council and, as expected, they meant nothing to them.

There was no question this negotiation was going to be harder and rougher than the previous one. Byron Elmendorf was mobilizing his strength for an all-out fight at City Council , determined to get his way. He definitely wanted a vast increase in revenues from the team and now. He wanted the City to be an upside-only partner in the venture, but wanted no part of the losses, if any. He envisioned an expanded public parks program and facilities based solely on the team's income, which he saw as a public oil well. There was no turning back.

Jerry began to mobilize to meet the force. Reg Williams, former Mayor of Bellingham and an outstanding friend and fan, with all his political clout and savvy joined our side. Several other important people helped out as did many of the loyal fans who were regulars at games. Jerry enlisted several of the Councilmen who were known to be supportive and girded for an all out battle.

And a battle it was. Several meetings at City Hall were held. Many supporters from our side showed up to lend support and very vocally. Jerry and Lisa laid out for the Council our position and their arguments seemed convincing. Lisa was quoted as telling them our losses were not bogus. However, it was impossible to convince those Council members who came to the meeting with their minds already made up. Everything said by our side at the meetings fell on deaf ears.

Those statements were picked apart, edited and printed in the newspaper accounts of the meetings. We could not come out ahead. It was a frustrating time for Jerry, there in Bellingham almost alone, carrying the fight to the hostile side. Bill was three thousand miles away in Brooklyn, rooting hard, but without any influence at all. Lisa was with Jerry all the way and spoke up at the meetings to support our points of view. She was good and Jerry was better. But the issue was coming down to the predetermined end. We would have to sign and somehow compromise the issue of financial information sharing. And so it was done.

## CHAPTER THREE:  WE HAVE TO MOVE

The new lease was signed, sealed, and delivered.  It insured that there would be baseball at Joe Martin Stadium in Bellingham through the 1996 season.  In that respect it was a success for the City and for the team.  The team had to have a home and Joe Martin was it.  For the City Council it was a success because it had resolved a thorny issue, at least temporarily, and had thus preserved the status quo, or some part of it.  However, it left many issues unresolved and had planted seeds of discontent that were certain to rear up again and soon.

The lease was essentially only an extension for one year.  Jerry had been savvy enough and sufficiently fortunate to have negotiated in an option for another one year extension for the team on almost the same terms. If you looked at it one way you could say the team was protected through the 1997 season if it so elected.  Notice would have to be given by the team to the City by October 31 of 1996 if the team  was going to elect to remain at Joe Martin Stadium for the 1997 season.  Time was of the essence as to that date.

Nobody on either side really believed that if the notice was not timely or properly given that the City would evict the team. On the other hand, failure to give the notice timely or properly could create the predicament of having to commence full negotiations again and you just couldn't tell or trust how wide negotiations under those circumstances would be.  It might just be that the entire laundry list of wished-for items that the City sprung on us from time to time would form the basis of any new negotiations if there was no option protecting us.   That could prove disastrous.

The City negotiators had pushed to have a four year lease to defer as far into the future as reasonably possible the opportunity for us to move the franchise. We suspected they wanted to have wide open negotiations with everything on the table to gain the advantage and win some lucrative, long term, financial rights. The problem was they were working from what they felt were the correct economics of the team. Their reasoning was flawed and their calculations were way off the mark. They really thought they were correct in simply multiplying the ticket prices by the numerical attendance, adding a factor for concession profits and advertising and come out with the team's bottom line. Dead wrong!

The trouble was that once they rationalized themselves into that position no amount of logic or facts could persuade them to revisit the subject. Despite the virtual continual stream of financial facts that Jerry began to provide, they remained adamantly convinced their calculations were correct and ours were slanted to achieve our private purposes. They just could not believe that the franchise which had literally risen from the ashes through Jerry's fabulous efforts was not coining currency. And it wasn't!

The issue therefore had resolved principally into a debate over the length of the lease extension. The City wanted four years and we pushed for one year. We felt it was best to keep our options open. We felt the four year period could be disastrous if the economics went against us. A one year extension with an option would give both sides some quiet time and perhaps some better compromises could surface and allow the two entities to remain together peacefully for some time into the future.

It was not to be. However, after considerable wrangling and somewhat heated discussions, some of which were held at City Council meetings open to the public and under the watchful eye of the press, the option compromise surfaced and seemed to gain acceptance.

It was not all that simple. Our game fees were increased and there were imposed some larger demands made on us in the stadium caretaking area which naturally increased expenses. Jerry had wrung a concession to allow us to construct an office for the manager but it had to be shoehorned into the already crowded dressing room at the football field, and all at our expense. That was allright though because the Giants, which had become our major league affiliate for the 1995 season, was really pushing for that and we wanted to please them.

We actually had considered a move to Pasco in that previous year. It was conceived in a rush and brought about by unusual and seemingly important circumstances.

The first stage of that process occurred in May of that year. Jim Beattie had called. Jim had become the Farm Director for the Seattle franchise. He had been a star college pitcher at Dartmouth College and had attracted the attention of many scouts. He was the number one draft choice of the New York Yankees and seemed to blossom during his minor league career. He was called up to the Yankees and seemed to be paying dividends immediately. The Yankees, owned by the volatile George Steinbrenner, lived with a sword of Damocles hanging over their heads. Steinbrenner had paid good money for free agents and farmhands and expected them to produce constantly, or else. Jim pitched an outstanding game in the World Series but somehow became expendable in the Yankee scheme of things which opted almost always for veteran players over budding prospects.

Jim was traded off to Seattle where he became the mainstay of their pitching staff and did well. Then his arm or shoulder began to hurt and despite everything they did and his courage in trying to pitch through it, his career was over. So, since he wanted to stay in baseball, he took the job as Seattle's Farm Director. He is smart and calculating and his hand on the tiller stabilized and improved the Seattle farm fortunes and improved the main team.

In that phone call, Jim Beattie told Jerry he was coming up to Bellingham for a compliance tour of our facility. We guessed it had something to do with the major league facilities audit that had been carried out but weren't sure. Jerry notified Byron Elmendorf who volunteered to participate in the tour.

Beattie arrived one sunny morning as scheduled and the tour began. They walked the field, tested the sod and the skin part of the infield with their feet. Comments were made about the slope of the outfield part of the warning track which were not complimentary. Even worse comments were reserved for the dugout facilities and the bullpen situation. Worse yet were the comments on the shortcomings of the team facilities down at the football field and the length and dangers in the walk back to the fieldhouse at night. It was pointed out that the lack of a manager's office was a serious flaw and the fact that the team had to share the locker facilities with others was highlighted.

At the end of the tour, Beattie ran down the list of shortcomings, which list was not far different from the items raised by the audit. Jim suggested these matters required urgent attention and very soon. Elmendorf seemed to Jerry to be only mildly impressed. He probably thought the tour had been arranged by us to increase pressure on the City to lay out funds to get the modifications done. He asked Beattie what would happen if the City didn't undertake at least some of those required modifications. Jerry will always remember Jim Beattie's reply:"Well then, Bellingham will just not have Mariners baseball." Elmendorf managed a wry smile. We always thought he felt Beattie was just bluffing as he was convinced we were. His actions following that day certainly reflected that attitude and the event slid into history as if it had never occurred.

Jerry thought differently. He was convinced nothing was done by the Seattle organization without specific purpose. He took the comments by Jim seriously and was able to achieve some things on his own at our expense to enhance the ballpark. Elmendorf, however stuck to his position that the City would not contribute and that any improvements that came would have to be accomplished by us.

As the end of the 1994 season was nearing on August 26,1994, another date that will live in infamy, Jerry got a call from Jim Beattie, the farm director in Seattle. In that call, Jim told Jerry the Mariners were going to exercise their option in our PDC agreement to terminate their relationship with us at the end of the season. They did not plan to make any announcement to that effect until the season was over.

That had happened somewhat routinely in minor league baseball and still does. Many of the major league teams nevertheless eventually re-sign with the same affiliate. They take the opportunity to look at their options to select a different affiliate if any that better serves their needs geographically or weatherwise. Some minor league teams become available through that process just about every year.

Some even elect to exercise the option themselves and terminate their relationship with their major league affiliate. So it is not unusual but it was the first time it had ever happened to us.

However, even without the benefit of experience on that particular type of event, we could tell that there was just something unusual about this happening. Jerry had been told the Mariners wanted it clearly understood they were not expressing any unhappiness with the Bellingham operation, or with us. Jim was almost effusive in his praise of the relationship and the Bellingham operation although he recognized the stadium shortcomings and the difficulty with getting changes made involving big expense without City help.

That position fit in very well with what we had been told over the years after we took over the franchise. We knew they now liked us and we expected it to go on forever. We never thought otherwise. Bellingham was the Seattle franchise's first and oldest minor league affiliation and the relationship truly prospered after we took over. We had found it foundering on the rocks in grave danger of cancellation and had restored it to a very good state where the two parties actually enjoyed each other and appreciated what was involved.

Jim's story in that telephone call explained the action they were taking. He told us nothing being done was intended in any way to reflect on the quality of the Bellingham operation and that everything else being equal, the Mariners would continue the relationship. However, they had just been turned down by the Seattle City electorate in their hopes of obtaining City financing to construct a new stadium in downtown Seattle.

They were convinced the Kingdome, a 15 or 20 year old roof-enclosed facility was no longer adequate. The sport had been switching to new facilities in the open air, encouraging a neighborly feeling among fans. Seattle team executives were convinced the aura of the indoor stadium was somewhat responsible for their regularly low attendance numbers and they wanted to improve.

After all, salaries of ballplayers were disappearing from sight and control. It was becoming difficult if not impossible for teams in small markets with relatively low attendance to compete for the star players, or to keep those they had. This raised the realization that they could never field a winner. Seattle had never yet until that time had a winner. (And still haven't. The best they've done was a division winner in1995 and 1997.) Something had to be done.

The Seattle franchise had just changed hands, having been sold to a group that was selected for its publicly stated determination to not relocate the big league franchise. They like all other small market teams were being courted by other cities which hoped to upgrade their status by being "major league." It was a temptation. The Seattle fans breathed a collective sigh of relief when this group came to the fore and won the rights to buy the team with their announced plan to stay in Seattle.

With the City election results having decided against them, the Seattle Mariners executives had concocted a new plan to obtain state funding for the new stadium they coveted (the election had sought City or county funding of those costs). This new thrust required them to develop clout in the state legislative councils. To do that, they felt they could achieve that by remaking the map of their minor league system. They

were relocating those of  their affiliates they could do
conveniently into larger population markets in  Washington
having the larger number of elected representatives.  That
would give them the legislative strength to sponsor, support
and have enacted state legislation to get the new stadium
accomplished  with state funding.  Not a bad idea.

The way it was put  to us though, led us to believe their
cancellation of our PDC  was not going to be permanent.  We
can't say Beattie encouraged us to reach that conclusion, but
he certainly did  not discourage us.  We labored under the
mistaken  and expressed (to him) belief that if we could
relocate to a larger market, Seattle would retain us as an
affiliate.

We were also motivated by the strong desire to cooperate with
Seattle's plan and to advance it as much as we could.  We
honestly felt that if the Seattle executives thought it was good
for them it would be good for us too.  We were loyal to the end
and expected the Seattle powers wanted it that way.  We were
naïve enough to expect some loyalty coming back our way.

It was under those circumstances and with hopes of retaining
the Seattle relationship that we began to sift our options of
places to which we could quickly relocate the franchise.
Because of the fact we knew of the Pasco stadium under
construction for which they did not yet have a professional
team(we thought) it was THE most logical site for us to
consider.

With only a short time to think about it, we made up our
minds quickly and departed for Pasco with the intention of
asking them for permission to relocate to their new facility.
The area, known as the Tri-Cities  and consisting of a much
larger than Bellingham population base would have been

52

perfect. As we understood it, Pasco, with its sister cities of Kennewick and Richland, had opted to fund the construction of a new stadium in the hope of luring an existing Northwest League franchise or an expansion franchise in our league to play there. It was an ingenius idea and showed governmental guts as well as resolve.

We liked the area immensely. The locale seemed to be thriving and the stadium was under construction in a beautiful area down by the river, just off the highway. The location was ideal and the facility looked like it was being constructed to meet all major league requirements for minor league facilities. We almost drooled when we first saw it and compared its attractiveness to our facility in Bellingham. There would be no more problems with parking space, locker room facilities, vastly improved seating with no pinch-your-fanny seats, and more customer friendly concession areas with no danger of patrons falling over the concrete cracks or gaps.

That day, we met with Curt Lohrs, Assistant City Manager of Pasco, who gave us full details on the plans of the three cities and what they expected to gain from a team coming there. They as much as told us they would love having us bring the Bellingham franchise there and that the stadium would be ready for opening day 1995 . That would be perfect for us since the season was just ending. If we could get a commitment from Pasco in time and get the Seattle executives to accept it and keep us in their fold and get league approval, we could move .We might even make money in the new locale, we thought.

There was one big hitch we were filled in on. The Western League, which was expecting to commence operations in1995, had visited the City and the site and had sent a letter of intent to Pasco to express their stated intention of fielding a team there. Pasco and its sister cities felt it had at least a moral obligation to wait out that "commitment" since they had gotten there first and had expressed an almost unconditional intent to bring a team there. The team would not be affiliated with any major league team and thus would not have the same calibre of play our league had with all its draft selected players.

We saw it otherwise. We felt we were bringing a classier product to the stadium which conformed to the Tri-Cities original expectation in undertaking the expense of stadium construction.

Even though there was really no concrete cause for optimism, we were enthusiastic about the possibilities. On the way back to Bellingham, we used the cell phone to call Beattie. We both apparently gushed with optimism about the prospect of obtaining a spanking new facility. Coincidentally, it just happened to be in a much more populous site, meeting Seattle's requirements for a larger population base, more legislative representatives and thus improved clout in the state legislature on the issue of stadium funding.

Again with the opportunity to turn us off from pursuit of that goal, which we now believe was then doomed anyway, that the die had been already cast, Jim did not do so. He continued to play his options giving us no clue as to whether we should continue to pursue Pasco. Certainly there were no adverse comments about our Bellingham operation. Complimentary all the way. We hung up believing genuinely that we could still salvage the relationship. None of this, the PDC cancellation, the idea of moving, was public knowledge yet.

There was a lot at stake for us if we opted to openly pursue it and word leaked out of our intention to move the franchise. We would suffer severe economic hardship and consequences in Bellingham if the deal fell through afterward, as it was destined to do, we believe. We are convinced the idea could not be kept secret because there was a paramount need for the City fathers in Tri-Cities to tout any progress they were making towards attracting a team since they were out on a limb for the cost of stadium construction. This was a natural and understandable force that would mandate the public be informed, and we understood it. We were willing to take that risk when we thought it was a possible reality. We would not have done so under the circumstances as we now know them. The reader can make up his or her own mind about the propriety of that event.

Anyway, it all became academic. When we contacted the league office to see if they would give us a green light, it turned out they were unwilling to let us proceed further because of the fear of litigation. They would allow us to pursue it if we would indemnify the league against all legal costs. Big deal. As we all know litigation costs often go through the roof and have no cap on their amount. Even meritless litigation, as we are convinced that would have to be, is costly and was beyond our consideration. The League got a legal opinion that there could be a legal challenge to our moving into Pasco and without league sanction, the idea was an impossibility and was dropped. The Pasco franchise opened in the Western League and has thrived so our judgment was correct. The stadium is very nice, too.

As stated before there was really no chance of our saving the Seattle relationship anyway. Seattle followed through on their plan. They relocated their Calgary, Canada PDC to Tacoma, Washington. They awarded our PDC to the Everett, Washington franchise which almost simultaneously opted to terminate its relationship with the San Francisco Giants. Politics had come between old friends and long standing relationships.

The Appleton and Jacksonville franchises were left with their PDC's as they were, probably due to the lack of alternative locations that would be helpful in advancing the Mariners' objectives. The Mariners had achieved their goal. They now had anchors in King, Snohomish and Pierce Counties, the most populous in Washington State. (Actually they only relocated our PDC about sixty miles closer to Seattle but did achieve a much larger population base.)

The strategy was near genius. It paid off in the Mariners getting public financing, partially, for a new stadium in downtown Seattle which was completed in mid-season 1999, and opened as Safeco field. The Kingdome, less than thirty years old, will be demolished.

The Giants were stunned, as we were, by that turn of events. They were quick, decisive and startling to everyone. They were so swiftly carried out after the eligibility date that one had to wonder how much advance work had gone into the switches to have them so easily concluded so soon after that date. We then knew our trip to Pasco would not have resolved our relationship problem.

And so ended our only thought of moving the Bellingham franchise up to that time. It is probably significant on our naivete that we did not think of moving it anyway before for many other reasons, at least before the Pasco/Seattle idea. Later events have made us ruminate on those days and wonder if things weren't already under way elsewhere a long time before consistent with the way events occurred.

The Giants reacted swiftly. Burned by the fact that they had been dropped by the Everett people after so many years and what they thought was a very good mutually beneficial relationship, they contacted us. Brian Sabean, once the New York Yankees president, was now in charge in San Francisco and he was directly involved. He talked to us about becoming an affiliate of the Giants. We knew the Giants to be a franchise with an outstanding history, especially during their heyday in New York City. We appreciated all the lustrous record of success and considered them to be the best of all the alternative options available to us. It took only a little effort for them to convince us to sign on with them with a four year PDC.

As is so often the case with events born of some adverse actions, the move worked out to be the best possible thing for us. The Giants have been very good. Except for 1992 when we won the league championship and again in 1993 when we won the division, the Mariners or Baby M's as they were called were not really a competitive team. They were perennial losers. They produced truly no hitters of significance and home runs by the opposition seemed to far outnumber ours. Even the pitching was only adequate to keep us out of last place in our division. We did have some very good players spotted in here and there. Also, to give credit where deserved, the Seattle climate did change appreciably for the better when Beattie came to town and brought Dave Myers to manage in Bellingham.

Our records with the Giants have been just short of fabulous. We have always been in the hunt right up until nearly the end of the season in each year and we won it all in 1998 as you will read later. The Giants signed their draft picks and sent them to us for the kids' first year. They loved their stay with us and it was a mutual romance. They were nice kids and played well and honored the game of baseball with their presence.

The Giants got what they wanted too. They were able to stay in the Northwest League which was far more accessible to their home base in San Francisco than any other league they could have chosen. It would probably have been a nightmare for them to have to relocate their PDC to the Pioneer League or the Arizona League and have their farm officials journey to Montana or Arizona to see their prize farmhands.

Our franchise also spawned a good family relationship in which the players could easily thrive. We had a record of not having any police incidents with our players and that was important. We were also drawing somewhat better numbers of fans, attributable to our free nights and events, all of which created a far better atmosphere for the players. Those "free" nights were really a mixed bag.

That was why and how we began the 1995 season as a San Francisco Giants affiliate. From the start it was a better relationship and we enjoyed it. The people in San Francisco were nicer and interested, not only in the players but also in us.

It must be remembered, so it is written here, that there was a tarnishing public element to our termination with the Mariners. Near the end of the 1994 season, a flap had opened somewhat publicly between the team and its host families, those people who housed a player during the season. The flap, and that is all it was, somehow got into the papers and a war of words to some extent came about in the press that hungered for a live story or scandal.

Jim Beattie was now angry at us to the core for not "just taking it." The host family flap offered an opportunity for him to avoid looking bad with the people of Bellingham for terminating the PDC for purely political reasons, an action that was not yet public knowledge. He jumped into the host family squabble with both feet. We think he was trying to save face with the Bellingham fans many of whom had regularly journeyed to Seattle to see Mariners' games so the host family flap was made to order for him.

Never mentioning the Seattle political strategy (which we think is still not public knowledge), he tried to put the blame for the lost PDC not on the Mariners or the City, but on our operation. This was entirely contrary to and inconsistent with the many public and private statements he had made before. Beattie proceeded to blast the Bellingham operations and said some very unkind, untrue and inappropriate things about our franchise and its operation.

That was completely out of character for Jim Beattie. We believed it was an opportunistic ploy by the Seattle powers to preserve their fan base if possible. They could rewrite history to escape blame by obscuring the true reason for the action they were planning to take at the end of the season. We never carried through on filing a formal complaint anyway.

We never blamed Jim personally although those statements were publicized and hurt. Unfortunately they reached the press before we announced the end of the PDC relationship with Seattle, a fact we were trying to keep quiet until later. By then, it was too late for the press to consider our statements as anything more than a defensive position, coming as our statements did after Seattle's comments. Our story then seemed only a retort and not a real affirmative statement regardless that it was the true one. Jim was quoted as saying he would never again work with a team associated with Jerry Walker. He will never get the chance.

Jim now seems to have forgotten the incident, too. At the 1998 Winter Baseball Meetings in Nashville, he clearly went out of his way to meet and exchange pleasantries with Jerry as if they were old friends. Bill met up with Jim at the Nashville Airport on his way home and he was friendly then, too. Some people have short memories.

And so we entered the 1995 season newly affiliated with the San Francisco Giants, under a cloud, attacked by the City and the press and with a tenuous relationship at best with our host families organization. It was going to be difficult, and we truly wanted to impress San Francisco with our quality of operation. We were also at the end of our lease and had to commence negotiations towards a new one that we knew would be loaded with conditions and requirements we felt were onerous and unliveable. But we did it as stated above. The negotiations resulted in the one year lease extension with an option exclusively in our discretion for another year.

1995 was a pretty good year given the open hostilities that existed between the franchise and the City. Fan support was only mildly affected but attendance dropped. That was somewhat attributable to the switch in major league affiliates and the need for the fans to acclimate to the new operation we were allied with.

At the end of 1995, the negotiations that resulted in the one year extension we elaborated above were held under stress. Misstatements in the press continued to hammer away on the themes presented to them by the Parks Department through the City Council. The war of words was being lost at the inkwell and seemingly nothing could turn it around. The hoped-for hiatus to allow a restoration of peace and tranquility to reign was not to be. The one year extension meant we would begin 1996 in a quandary. We would be expected to pay more, bear more of the burden of stadium maintenance and either tolerate the shortcomings of the ballpark or undertake the very expensive repairs ourselves.

That was not really acceptable, both from our pride point of view or from a business viewpoint. Sooner or later the PDC could be cancelled on us again. While we might be fortunate then to find another affiliation, we might not be and our franchise would become worthless, or only worth less. We could not risk that. So, facing the prospect of another lost PDC and the option negotiations at the end of 1996, we began to sift through alternatives.

There was no question we were no longer happy in Bellingham with the City fathers. We were happy with the fans but dissatisfied with the stadium as it was. We were even more unhappy with the attitude of take it or fix it yourselves. This was a totally destructive attitude since the City Council and Elmendorf knew of the major league requirements and how far below that standard Joe Martin Stadium was. Something had to be done--and soon, or we would be playing in Bellingham in 1997 on our option year. We had to move.

Happiness is - finally getting the ballpark started

Mayor Roger Gertenrich of Salem "signs in" on home plate

Sam Goesch opened the ceremony with a prayer

Mayor Dennis Koho, who had much to do with the success of the enterprise, addressed the group

Pat Lafferty, consummate professional
emceed groundbreaking ceremony

Jerry Walker then spoke to the attendees

The actual groundbreaking took place - (l to r) Carl Beach, Al Miller, Jerry Walker, Lisa Walker, Dennis Koho, Bob Newton and Jerry McGee

65

Dave Jarvis interviewed the prominent attendees for KYKN - Dan Kerr of Faith Foundation is at far right, in raincoat

The American Way - nothing gets done without pickets

Pat Lafferty also emceed the team naming announcement

The naming ceremony was impressively staged and well attended

Fans signed up for ticket reservations in droves

KYKN was interviewing again

...and again - Mike Frith, station manager, at the mike

Jerry Walker promoted the team at the bowling alley rally

# CHAPTER FOUR: QUO VADIS

It so happened that the league had undertaken and distributed to its members a study of alternate sites available for relocation and expansion if it came as a result of major league expansion. There were not many choices. Available were Vancouver, Washington; Salem, Oregon; Wenatchee, Washington; Victoria, B.C.; Tri-Cities, Washington and a few others. The committee that did the research had done a pretty thorough job. It was led by Bill Pereira who owned the Boise franchise and had constructed his own, brand-new stadium there and was doing well. At that time it was not the newest stadium in the league anymore, Yakima was, but everyone conceded Boise was the state of the art facility with a private restaurant and everything.

Both Bill and Jerry favored a move to Vancouver,Washington. It was an up and coming City across the Columbia River in northwest Oregon. It was really a suburb of Portland and a large number of its residents commuted daily to Portland, a large metropolis. Jack Cain had announced he would move his Northwest League franchise from Bend, Oregon to Portland almost on the day the move by the Portland Triple-A team to Salt Lake City became effective. He carried through on that announcement a year later and has enjoyed outstanding success. If we were to move to Vancouver, it would open up a terrific rivalry. One could envision fans going back and forth across the bridge to see games at either site.

However, calls to selected people in Vancouver failed to produce any positive signs that the move could be made. There was no existing ballpark in Vancouver so one would have to be built. A temporary facility was simply not realistically available making it questionable whether anything could be done quickly.

The supposedly best available site, both temporary and permanent, would be located out at the fairgrounds, which was located out of the central part of the metropolis and a short, but possibly traffic crowded, drive on game nights. Access roads were less than desirable and during Fair times you would have to compete with the Fair for fans, parking space and access. In a schedule that has only 76 playing dates, 38 of which were at home, losing 3 to 5 dates to Fair competition could be catastrophic.

Furthermore, it was apparent there would be no outside or governmental financial help in establishing the franchise there. The notable citizens who were contacted suggested only the state would be likely to help, if anyone. The parks commission which was pushing the fairgrounds site would be happy to have the team but couldn't help beyond allowing temporary quarters to be refurbished at the fairgrounds, quarters which were not really acceptable even after substantial improvement. The likelihood of getting the state to issue bonds or other financial support quickly or ever was really nonexistent.

It was becoming obvious that Vancouver was rapidly losing its attraction for us. If we were to move and be ready for the 1997 season, events and financial assistance would have to fall in line, and fast. There looked to be no possibility that Vancouver could do that. It was almost as if everyone we contacted was interested in having us move there but kept pointing their finger in other directions when it came to any help at all, not just financial help. There was no enthusiastic leader with clout who could step in and lead the charge to get the entire package together, and done.

The league made it academic anyway. Another team in our league had set its eyes and heart on moving to Vancouver, Washington too. Both of us could not do it and, knowing what we did already, we backed away graciously. That other team had different dynamics going for it so the move seemed then to be far more feasible for them than us. Our action resolved on a friendly basis what could have become a thorny issue for the league.

We had always had a soft spot in our hearts in favor of Salem. Jerry had visited the area and found it to be a modern, attractive City with ample population to support the team . Even more, it was the capital of Oregon and capitals were known to be good for baseball, as Bob Zeig, a seasoned minor league operator, always said.

The trouble with Salem, though, was that it was not only the state capital, but it also was the county seat where that government resided and it had its own City government housed there as well. The jurisdictional bobbing and weaving that could go on was awesome if there was no leader of the gang and each jurisdiction would feel the other should bear any cost and expense associated with the move.

There was good cause for concern about trying the Salem area. It had only been a few years since the Salem team had left due to poor support and moved to Yakima where they moved into a brand new stadium. The team had played its games at the Chemeketa College field. It was hardly a suitable field for professional sports, but ideal for college baseball. It had no grandstand, only bleachers. The team that had left had tried valiantly to build up a fan following but could not achieve it.

The concessions were not truly accessible or large and the public facilities were not intended for professional sports use. Access was tolerable but far below acceptable. Parking seemed to be ample, especially with the small crowds they were drawing. That did not seem to be a record of success on which anyone would want to build.

The league report on expansion had given the City good marks despite the recent flight of the franchise to Yakima. Those two things seemed inconsistent and we searched our minds for some way to figure out the answer. What clinched it was the league people, other owners, who were familiar with the league while the Salem team existed. Bill Pereira who had led the league study thought Salem was a good prospect due to all the economic and population factors in its favor. He felt the Chemeketa experience was not indicative of what could be done there. We respected Bill and accepted his opinion.

However, what really clinched it was a conversation we had with Bob Beban. He had taken over and run the Salem team as a favor to the league to save the franchise from failure. He had parted with it when it was sold and moved to Yakima. At the same time, he also ran the Eugene team. He had rendered a major service to the league. He told us convincingly that the only problem Salem had was the venue in which the team played its games. He said the City would support the team especially if it had a new and better facility and it would be a success.

Time was beginning to be an enemy and something had to be done. We resolved to approach the Salem authorities, but with the understanding that a new stadium would somehow have to be the lynchpin of the move and would have to be constructed quickly, at least committed for. So the decision was made. It would have to be kept secret until it was a sealed deal at least until the end of the season.

We had to always be prepared. In early April 1996, Jerry had written very tempting letters to Mayor Roger Gertenrich of Salem, Governor John Kitzhaber and Michael McLaran of the Salem Chamber of Commerce. His letter did not disclose any one franchise that was considering a move. It did mention the league study and the possibility that one team would relocate by 1997 to one of three selected cities, Salem among them.

Mayor Gertenrich was interested but said "...the City government in Salem is not likely to be able to make a direct financial commitment to this effort. That is not to say that we could not participate in some manner to the success of this endeavor." He offered to provide us with statistics and projections and offered his good offices to arrange meetings and further contacts for us. It turned out his grandfather, Louis Gertenrich, had played in the semi-pro Chicago leagues during the early 1900's and in the Federal League in 1913. He wanted baseball to come back.

Gertenrich searched his mind for entities within the government that could be helpful or instrumental in bringing this thing about. He fastened onto the State Department of Corrections as a good possibility. That Department had access to funding from various sources to carry out its mandate to develop inmate programs. It could be a natural for them and he told Jerry to contact Dennis Cook

Jerry never got through to Dennis Cook. However ,Cook's secretary suggested he start with Cook's assistant, Ben de Haan. DeHaan suggested Jerry talk to Steve Ickes who suggested Jerry talk to Brian Beamis. Beamis was enthusiastic and wanted to meet with Jerry immediately. He was the Inmate Work force Development Director and was perpetually searching for opportunities for his inmate work force.

Brian thought it was a definite possibility that the stadium could be built in 1997. There were many bureaucratic hurdles to overcome, but it could be done. First, there would have to be a concept developed to be presented to the Department's independent advisory board. That could occur in June 1996 and a preliminary decision could soon follow. A business plan would then have to be developed and approval of that could take 3-4 months . They were discussing a stadium of 5000 seats that would cost about $5 million. Impressive.

Brian thought he had access to at least 2 million dollars immediately and believed the State Lottery Fund could provide the rest. The Lottery Fund's dollars were intended for economic development purposes and this fit to a "T". The funding of the project was said to be more a political question than a money problem.

Jerry told Bill of the development which looked entirely positive. It was a strange source, seemingly from left field, but Jerry was encouraged by Bill to go down and meet with him which he did. Brian was under a mandate from the state to develop inmate work programs. He envisioned the stadium would be maintained and groomed by the inmates as part of their daily duties. Brian was enthusiastic about the prospect of the tie-in with the team and stadium and seriously thought it would be a superb outlet for inmate work. He recognized it would be a tough and frustrating road to get it done but felt it could be accomplished and on time and was willing to proceed.

Other ingredients made it almost impossible. The stadium would have to be built next to the prison and on grounds already belonging to the state. It was in a relatively inaccessible part of town without good access roads. It was felt the fans would not be willing to make the journey to the facility often. There were several other details that mitigated against accepting the proposal, some of which involved the bureaucratic morass we would have to navigate. We appreciated Brian's enthusiasm which was both genuine and contagious. We owe him a huge debt because he provided a ray of light at a time when we were unsure of the road ahead.

It turned out both Mayor Gertenrich and Mike McLaran would be of immense help to us, too. Whether openly, or sub rosa, word got out, presumably from them, that there could be the possibility of a professional baseball team moving to the area, and soon.

It was not long after that Jerry got a call from a lawyer in Salem named Joe O'Connor. He was the operating force in a company known as Hometown Heroes, Inc. Joe reported his group was supposedly made up of himself and two other participants--Ken Griffey Jr. and Harold Reynolds, both well known professional baseball players and cameo names. There was a holding company involved in his strategy that consisted of Joe O'Connor and others. As he stated in his proposal, Jerry and Bill would turn over a percentage of the team to them to have them participate in the plans he had for the development of a site in Salem. Jerry and Bill would receive a 1% share in the holding company in exchange.

O'Connor said he already had the site selected and in his control. It was in Salem, just across the Willamette River adjacent to Highway 22. It consisted of 33 acres and was planned to include a hotel and conference center, a restaurant, a marina an ice rink, a sports café and a soccer/baseball stadium to be built to hold 7500 fans. It was planned for the stadium to be operated with a removable air supported dome that would allow them to hold events there between October and April, normally weather unfriendly months for outdoor activities in Oregon.

The announcement of the proposed development reportedly had been made by Harold Reynolds at a press conference at Willamette University on December 15, 1995. We understood they already had approval for a motel at the site but were being asked to construct the conference center first. Their presentation was quite professional, a color brochure with aerial photos, artists drawings, maps and statistical data. It just seemed too good.

We actually tried to enter into a confidentiality agreement with O'Connor, and may have. Jerry visited the site and had some problems with its actual location unless highway access was improved.

There were several problems with the idea as we saw it. For one, it violated our standard of total control of operation of the team by ourselves. We never wanted any partners, least of all some we didn't even know, although we knew of Reynolds and Griffey. Secondly, it looked as if the plan was too ambitious to solve our short term predicament. We thought it would probably take years to develop, especially the highway remedy part. That was critical to its success from a stadium point of view, and time was our enemy. We just couldn't spare any.

Last but not least was the money factor. There was no foreseeable financing for any of the project. The stadium would be a difficult sell on its own, but coupled with such a vast and ambitious plan, it would be even more difficult. Then, we felt it would take a good deal of persuasion to keep that group focused on doing the stadium before anything else in the plan. We didn't want our franchise held hostage to the development of so many other things. We knew, as anyone would, that once that group was part owner of what we had, we couldn't get them out. We would be giving up something tangible for some far off dream. We declined.

We liked Joe O'Connor. We later learned he was somehow connected to the manufacture and distribution (sale) of those plastic bubbles. That in itself was nothing out of the ordinary but we then questioned what was driving him. Under no circumstances would that deal have been good for us. We considered ourselves fortunate to have been solicited and to have had the opportunity and good sense to decline. That development never got under way for reasons we never found out. It was an ambitious plan even without the stadium and could have been successful if built. It just couldn't solve our main problem which was time and everything else just mitigated against doing it. Was it DP looking out for us?

Joe O'Connor later did build an arena just south of Salem for soccer play indoors. We went down there one day to meet him and were impressed. Unfortunately for him there were problems with making a go of it and the arena closed. It had been covered by one of those plastic, air-inflated, bubbles he had planned to use at the stadium. It looked good but may have been before its time for stadium use. There were reports the bubble eventually blew over in a windstorm which could make it questionable to use for public events. However, there may have been more to that story and it may not have happened at all. Was it DP again?

We had looked at the O'Connor proposal long and hard which is probably evidence of how serious we felt our predicament was in Bellingham. Now the plate was clean again and we began to search around for other opportunities. We knew we had to make something happen, and soon, if we were to meet our timetable and not be forced to play another season in Bellingham. Our strategy sessions became more intensive. However, two guys with DP in their pockets should not have had to worry.

And so it was that Jerry happened to be sitting idly in his office in Bellingham that hot July day. The team was away and things were naturally slow then. It was time to start the cauldron boiling again so he put in a phone call to Mayor Roger Gertenrich from Salem. This time Roger had a more definite idea for us.

He had just hosted a meeting in Salem City Hall. There were present mayors from several nearby towns, among them one Dennis Koho who was mayor of a City named Keizer. Gertenrich told Jerry that Keizer was a relatively new community, about fifteen years old. It was a bedroom community for Salem largely, but was seeking to shed that image and establish it's own identity. He knew the Keizer City Council was considering building a sports facility on it's own to house some of its sports-active population activities.

The main purpose, though, was to jump-start development of a site near the Chemawa interchange off Interstate I-5 which they called the Chemawa Activity Center. He said they were so nearby to Salem that the school district and many other things were called by the hyphenated name "Salem-Keizer." He felt it could be a perfect fit for us. "And, by the way" he said, "Koho is a real, dyed-in the-wool, baseball fan. "

And so it all started. DP?

## CHAPTER FIVE: KEIZER, HERE WE COME

If you were Dennis Koho, reigning Mayor of the City of Keizer, you were just happy to be back in the cool of your office on that hot and steamy July afternoon. You had just returned from a meeting in Salem with the mayor of that City and the mayors or managers of other cities and towns in the general area to discuss topics of mutual concern and the manner in which those problems could be eliminated. It was not that easy and the discussion was overly long and dry as everyone had a chance to elaborate on the topic.

Koho was not then ecstatic to have his telephone ring almost the instant he dropped into his chair. He answered it politely with all the political aplomb his years in public service had taught him. The voice on the other end of the line was unfamiliar.

"Hello. My name is Jerry Walker. I am on the site selection committee of the Northwest Professional Baseball League. As you probably know, expansion of major league baseball is imminent and those expansion teams will require minor league affiliates at all levels. Our league wants to be prepared just in case the major league expansion team selects the Northwest League to locate it's A-level, short season team here. Am I speaking to the Mayor of Keizer?"

"Yes, Dennis responded, "I am the mayor."

"Do you know or do you think Keizer would be able or willing to allow a professional team from our league to locate there?"

"I sure do, "Dennis said. "I myself am a huge baseball fan and there is terrific interest here in baseball. But how did you get to me and know my name?"

'I just spoke to the Mayor Roger Gertenrich of Salem. You should know that we were persuaded to consider the general area by the attraction of coming to Salem since it was a large City and the capital of Oregon. Anyway, he told me it would be near impossible for Salem to consider that without a large amount of lead time which we obviously would not have. He said Salem was the site of three government jurisdictions in one. They are the capital of the state and have the state government there, they have the City government of course and Salem happens to be the county seat and has the county government there. As a result, he said, it makes it near impossible to do any one thing on a large scale on relatively short notice. He was definitely pessimistic about meeting our time frame although he did say the area had interest in a team and would support it."

"That's ok" Dennis said. "Keizer is a smaller City, not very old and looking to strengthen its identity . I think a baseball team here would help that search for identity considerably."

"Your fame precedes you" Walker said. " Roger told me of your being a huge baseball guy and that you would probably be very interested in such a project."

"Actually," Koho said, "we were thinking of building a new stadium in Keizer anyway. We have considerable undeveloped land and participation sports and all sports are a big thing here. We felt something like it would be needed but we never

81

dreamed of having a professional team locate here. Just how imminent and likely do you think it is?"

"Well, I think it is imminent that major league baseball will expand. They have to open up new vistas to major league baseball and there are several cities eligible. I don't honestly know how likely it is that they will select our league to locate their minor league team but we have to be prepared just in case. You seem interested and I'd like to convey that message if you don't mind."

"You sure can. You can say the City of Keizer is very interested and would like very much to discuss it further. It is a big political process we have to go through as you well know but we can do it and would suggest we get started on it right away."

The conversation ended on that high note. Walker was impressed with the enthusiasm of Koho but had honestly never heard of Keizer before. That evening , in discussions with Bill Tucker he brought up the possible thought of moving the franchise to the Salem area. He stressed that the ballpark would not be in Salem but in the immediately adjacent City of Keizer . He told of the mayor's enthusiasm for the thought of the team coming there and believed it sounded good.

"We have to do more" Tucker said. "We have to get down there and look it over to see just what we would be getting into. Remember we can't leap and then leap again or our team name will be  the Nomads."

"I have been to Salem" Walker said, "back when the league had a team there. It did not work out well principally due to the facility in which it had to play its games. It was at the Chemeketa College field. It was not set up for fans and wasn't terribly fan friendly. It was not entirely accessible either. There were no box or comfortable seats at the ballfield. They only had bleachers so it was tough to sit out a game and concessions were not readily available. Parking was adequate, but only for the sparse crowds they were drawing. It could not hold large crowds comfortably."

"Is that the team that moved to Yakima" Tucker asked.

"Yes." Walker replied. "Bob Beban was involved with the team in Salem and it was eventually sold and the franchise moved to Yakima. You've been to their new stadium in Yakima. It's very nice. They were able to obtain state bond funding to construct it from the state of Washington. I don't know how they did it, but they did do it on short notice and got the stadium built. I have been told by the people in Yakima that it only cost one million to build. In Yakima, they played at a temporary facility until the stadium was finished. Beban was on the committee that did the league survey. He would not have allowed Salem to sneak onto the list unless he fully believed it was properly eligible and would support a team. Of course, he would likely caution against repeating the Chemeketa College experience."

"Well," Tucker replied," we can check that out simply enough. But there's no substitute to making up our own mind by visiting the place soon to determine for ourselves whether it is really good."

Walker agreed. The next available open date, he and his wife Lisa sped down I-5 to Salem    It was a five hour drive from Bellingham. They were enthusiastic about what they saw. They saw it as a successful metropolis with an expanding population base , modern and forward looking. The capital area and the seat of government were spectacular.

Then they drove around to Keizer, only minutes away from the center of Salem. It was essentially a low level City in the sense that there were no tall buildings as there were in Salem. However, River Road which is the main thoroughfare for business was long, wide and well developed. There were stores, offices and banks as well as restaurants and filling stations. One could continue north on River Road to where it branched off Loch Haven Drive which ran east toward the  freeway. There were several large developments of residential housing, relatively new and well maintained.   City Hall in Keizer branched back to the south off Loch Haven and was a single one story office building off the main road.

Jerry was impressed because the area looked prosperous and the City fathers were obviously in an expansive mode, looking to develop  the remaining undeveloped land in the City to expand the tax base.   There were plenty of recreational facilities around and especially the little league fields which were tip top.

They rode around a little to familiarize themselves with the general area and then took the long drive north to Bellingham. It had been a good day.  Totalling it all up they felt they had come up with many pluses and few if any minuses.   It was a little difficult to conceive of the ballpark being in Keizer, and even more difficult to think of the team being named the Keizer "whatnots." It just wouldn't do. The team would have to incorporate the name Salem in its title as the main part.

The next day, Jerry detailed the entire trip to Bill on the phone. We were now into July and the situation in Bellingham had not improved and had even gotten worse. The fan base was beginning to wither away and the press coverage got more and more biting and less supportive. One of the feature writers in the Bellingham Herald wrote a feature piece with his central theme as Bellingham being a City that turned on its sports entrepreneurs with the result that all sports franchises in the City failed. He listed them and told of how their support dwindled after a while and the team either collapsed in bankruptcy or moved. The theme was lost on the Bellingham City fathers.

One of the troubles was that the basic Bellingham fan following was very loyal. They came regularly to games, night after night, and ignored the criticisms (which only related to the field lease dispute) and rooted hard. It was difficult to envision leaving such loyal people behind. However, we were fast becoming inculcated with the idea that baseball was a business , not entirely a sport, and beginning to think in those terms. There could be greener pastures.

Meanwhile Jerry had thrown his support behind a plan which would upgrade the entire area where Joe Martin Stadium was. It would include a skating rink for hockey and recreational skating, an indoor swimming pool and improved softball facilities and little league baseball fields. It was a pipe dream however. It was too big to be completed quickly, involved a major expenditure of money from a City that didn't want to spend any and would leave Joe Martin Stadium with only minor improvements made by large expenditures from us. Bill seriously opposed spending anything on that field. Jerry continued to publicly support that plan although in his heart he knew it would never come to pass.

So that day, in explaining their trip to Salem-Keizer, Jerry did so against a background that the duo had pretty much made up their minds to move the franchise. Eking out a bare living for Jerry in that community while there was a probable good chance of moving and doing much better elsewhere was not the thing to do. They ended that phone call with their collective minds made up to seriously pursue the possibility of moving to Salem-Keizer as quickly as they could. They would have to risk the fact that the thought of their moving would become public knowledge and destroy even their loyal fan base to ruin future seasons in Bellingham while they waited for the opportunity elsewhere to jell, or sold out.

Both of them separately made sure the other understood the hazards in beginning pursuit of the Salem-Keizer opportunity. As of that time, the Keizer people only knew that the league considered the general area as one they wanted to consider to locate a team. Mayor Koho thought it was to be a new team resulting from the expansion on the major league level. At that, he had been sworn to secrecy by Jerry so if he was true to his word, and we later found him to be just that, he would not have communicated the thought to anyone else. Jerry began to scour the papers after that initial phone call and never found anything remotely connected to the interview.

The hazards were too clear. If the Bellingham officials thought we had made up our minds to move, as we had been threatening, and it came to pass we couldn't achieve it, the negotiations for a new or just extended lease would be horrible. They would be properly upset and conclude that we only wanted the extension while the new site was being made ready and they would react accordingly. All the things we opposed in the negotiations would be imposed without any thought of mitigation. Any future seasons under those circumstances would be terrible.

But they didn't believe we would ever move or that we could. It is absolutely certain they didn't believe it would happen as and when it did. They locked themselves into the mindset that the threat to move was a bluff and could not consider any other options. They would never have tried to keep the team anyway if they discovered the threat was real because they were so out on a limb with the correctness of their position they couldn't then get off safely.

So explore they did. Jerry called Dennis Koho again and told him there was enthusiasm over his reaction to the possibility . He asked for a very confidential meeting with Koho and anyone he wished to bring so the matter could be explored further , in person. However, there could still be no news leaks on the idea since it was a very confidential matter and any leakage could endanger the entire proposition.

The first face to face meeting took place in Shari's restaurant on River Road in Keizer. Shari's is somewhat of a fast or rapid food place with a set menu for every day and the food is ample and comes quickly.  It is just the same, a place that gives a high degree of privacy so confidential conversations usually remain just that.

It was July 11, 1996.  It was another hot, steamy day in Oregon and the parties were grateful for the air conditioned sanctuary of Shari's.  Jerry and Lisa came and met with Koho, the City Manager, Dotty Tryk and one of the City Councilors, Jerry McGee.  These people were flabbergasted when Jerry and Lisa launched into a presentation that the Bellingham Giants, a fixture in the Northwest League, would consider moving the team to a stadium to be built in Keizer to serve as the home base of a team to be renamed the Salem-Keizer Something or Other.

It was Tryk's and McGee's first knowledge of anything to do with a professional baseball team, although to get them to the meeting they were probably told it was to be about something connected with baseball.  Mayor Koho had a property in mind already for the stadium the City was thinking about.  So he just changed his thoughts to making that site the probable site for the new professional stadium.  The Keizer entourage was impressed with the sincerity and  frankness with which Jerry and Lisa explained the basis for their wanting to move the franchise and the manner in which they seemed to recognize the many obstacles to overcome and their difficulty.

Chief among those difficulties was money.  Where would the money come from for the stadium?  The City would surely not be able to bear the entire burden and just how much of it the City would bear would be the subject of anxious debate.  What was the general thought about the sharing of costs and could all the parties live up to their financial obligations?

Who were these people from Bellingham? And a guy from Brooklyn! Nobody in the Keizer entourage knew of them and nobody had any line on their financial ability to meet their responsibilities. These were questions that cried out for answers and they had to come quickly. Jerry had laid out a line of achievement that had the stadium question being ironed out by the City Council very soon and the plans drawn and construction started right away. He fully expected the process to only be long enough to allow for occupancy of the new facility for opening day 1997. They had sort of done it in Yakima. Could it be done here? Was he crazy?

"No" he said. "The Yakima ballpark was constructed well within that time frame and cost only one million dollars. They use the parking lot for the adjacent horse race track but it had to be upgraded and striped. The water, electric and drainage were already there. It could be done and with the cooperation of the City fathers and some good weather, it would be accomplished here within that time frame. Everybody has to enthusiastically do their part though and once the die is cast, there can be no stopping."

Mayor Koho disclosed that he was thinking of the site at the Chemawa Exit of I-5, the major north-west arterial highway that runs along the coast. The land on the western side of the highway had some development on it along Radiant Drive. To the north of those houses, there was some acreage that was burdened with huge electric stanchions and power lines that made the site largely uninhabitable for residential use. It was large enough for a stadium and a parking lot  but Radiant Drive would have to be rerouted on the north end to accommodate the field.

However, there were no sanitary facilities out there just yet, no sewer or water lines  and they were very expensive undertakings.  The City had to put them in some day so it might as well be right now while opportunity was knocking on the door, Koho stated. But it would be expensive.  Maybe the ballpark could be the catalyst to further development out there and justify the installation cost.

Dotty Tryk was pensive and obviously mulling over the entire project in her mind.  She generally knew the site but now that it had become the subject of  major concern, she would have to become more familiar.  She was concerned about  the ability and willingness of the City to provide the money for its part of any such project and , even if the Council decided to proceed, just where the money would come from.  To Dotty, who would have to bear the brunt of the practical side of any such undertaking,  it was seen as a huge but very worthwhile project.  It could put the City on the map.  It would give identity, just what the City was yearning for.  She was in favor of going ahead, but  knew it wouldn't be easy even under the best of circumstances.

Jerry McGee was in favor of going ahead.  He liked the project and everything about it and said so.  He would later change his mind and cast negative votes on important Council issues, but for now he was "in."  He was wearing a white shirt with red polka dots that day.  He said he was ready for whatever came. "My shirt was white when I got into the political arena" he said "but you can see I've taken a lot of shots in my time." He thought the time line was a near impossibility though.

Dotty drove out to the site later that day. Standing in the field that July afternoon it was difficult to visualize anything being built there. Off to her left as she looked north was a large cabbage seed farm. Beyond that, she could just see a farmhouse and a road that led down past blueberry fields to the back of the Gubser development. The field was coarse, high grass with terribly uneven surfaces. Water seemed to pool up in spots and the wind blew almost constantly across the open field toward the highway. The highway was something else to think about. That alone could be a serious complication since the stadium lights would light up the area on game nights. Hands in pockets and deep in thought she walked out of the field and went home.

The next day she was right on the job again. There was to be a conference call with her, Mayor Koho, Jerry and his partner in Brooklyn, Bill Tucker. Bill was now being brought into the picture because the entire enterprise seemed positive and likely to happen. He was half owner of the franchise and had to be consulted specially, even though he was known to be generally in favor of moving the franchise somewhere.

July was fast coming to a close. The past was beginning to crowd the future. Things moved so fast nowadays. The group assembled for the conference call. Dotty Tryk knew that all eyes would be figuratively on her. Everyone would look to her for the means for the City to do its part, whatever that was, and to finance that thus far undefined role. But who would check out the financial abilities of the newcomers? Who could tell whether they were for real, could live up to their end of any bargain or whether they were just using the Keizer people as a wedge to do something elsewhere, or as a fallback?

It was getting toward late evening in Brooklyn and Bill sat by his phone as pensive as anyone else involved. He knew the pressure was on and very soon the fat would be in the fire. He knew the dangers that would come if the Bellingham people found out prematurely that the team was really going to move. If that happened and they didn't move, Jerry and Bill would probably have to sell out and get out of the game they loved so dearly. But Bill would trust Jerry's judgment, as he trusted him in all things..

Jerry also felt the pressure, probably more than anyone else. He alone, with Lisa, were bearing the brunt of the hostility in Bellingham. The dispute that began and always remained one of money had begun to take a bigger toll. Jerry had built a home in Bellingham and had then moved into a "holy cow" house on Chuckanut Drive, a fancy part of Bellingham overlooking Chuckanut Bay. That would have to be sold and he and his family would move to Keizer or Salem to be in the area. He was (and still is) a "hands-on" operator and one of the best.

If Jerry couldn't make a go of it somewhere, it must be impossible. He had taken that sow's ear of a franchise in Bellingham and turned it into a silk purse. With a little help from the City , he would have continued to progress and would have really put that City on the map. Now he would have to start anew and do it all again elsewhere. But the sale of his houses would have to come and he was hoping he would not have to do it under stress.

Jerry had placed the call so everyone else had to be brought in by the operator. The marvels of modern telephone were taxed to the fullest that day. Bill was in Brooklyn. Three thousand plus miles away in Bellingham, Jerry had initiated the call which would include people on several different extensions in Keizer , Oregon. Amazing. It was a long-distance triangle.

As the parties were identified and pieced into the call, Bill could not help but think back to another conference call, much like this one. Then, Jerry had told him of people in Bellingham who collectively owned and ran that franchise. Their names were unusual, Casey, Spedo and Rook. Now the names were different, but still unusual, Bill thought. Koho, named after a salmon, Tryk, not a name one hears often identifying a person rather than an act, and the lawyer whose first name was Shannon, the famous Irish river.

Shannon Johnson, City Counsel, had been brought in on the secret by Dotty who felt it would be beneficial to have the legal end covered as soon as possible. After all, if it could not  be legally done the issue would be academic.  Shannon could be trusted with a secret of that or any magnitude and he was an astute municipal attorney, schooled not only in the  law, but also in the practical politics of Keizer.

So the call went forward.  As expected, all parties looked to Dotty to provide the compelling answers.  Where would the money come from and what was the plan to get it. Dotty had the answers. They would have to somehow classify the project as an urban development zone to qualify for certain moneys. The problem was also that several properties would have to be acquired by the City, probably through condemnation, to provide the aggregate of 22 plus acres the project required. It could be done, but all things would need to fall into place just right. The project would require the majority City Council support and have to get past several interim votes to survive and get on the boards. It could be done but it was not going to be easy.

Mayor Koho would be in charge of mustering the City Council support. Jerry McGee was already on record as being supportive and Koho felt there were several other staunch baseball men on the Council who would give him the required four votes for a majority. So the idea already started out, we thought, with half of the required votes needed so it looked like it could get there.

Jerry and Bill agreed they could furnish the two million they thought would be enough to build the stadium, twice as much as Yakima needed to build theirs. Everyone thought that would be adequate.

The City would furnish the land on a land lease, acquire the land to round out the necessary acreage and build the parking lot and fence it in after putting in the electric and drainage facilities and bringing water to the facility. It was a lot to do but Shannon felt it could be done , but with a lot of work and cooperation from all sides and government agencies. The private sector, he said, Jerry and Bill, would have to be diligent and prompt in holding up their end of the bargain. They assured everyone on the call they could and would do it. After

94

all, they probably had the most to lose in the end if the project died at any stage.

Everyone was sworn to strict secrecy after being reminded of the danger involved in a premature leak. If the project was to have a birth beyond just the idea stage, secrecy was an absolute necessity for now. The time for publicity would come and then all could have their public say. Jerry and Bill knew they were putting the political problem on a serious position, but there was no other way, for now. It had to be kept secret. Jerry informed everyone that he was going to have to include the league owners in on the idea since league approval was a vital condition to the idea going forward too. It was not only money.

Thus the call ended, but not everyone was satisfied. They wanted to meet Bill, see what he was all about. He obliged them. He flew out specially and he and Jerry drove down to Keizer to meet with them. It was not one of Bill's routine season trips but the item was of extreme importance and had to be accommodated. The meeting was very worthwhile and everyone now knew each other, face to face, and obviously placed their trust in each other. To a degree, their fates were balanced on the success of the project which would turn on the need for everyone to do their separate parts. The largest burdens, though, were on Mayor Koho, Dotty Tryk and Jerry Walker.

While out there Bill was taken on a tour of the City which included a visit to the two sites that were considered possible locations for the ballpark. One was immediately adjacent to the little league field and was thought to be appropriate because the little league team parents could share the parking field of the stadium. However, that site never really got serious consideration mainly because the other site, close to the Chemawa interchange off Route I-5 was so much more superior. It was in an area where traffic noise already existed so noise complaints from stadium traffic would not be a serious legitimate concern. The highway also provided excellent access and allowed for easy traffic management on game nights, both before and after.

That day however, as Bill looked across the cabbage and alfalfa fields and viewed the heavy truck traffic on the highway, it was hard to imagine the ballpark being there. As the wind blew across their faces they discussed the possibilities. Jerry had it all laid out in his mind already. He could walk to where home plate and the mound would be and point out first, second and third bases. He could visualize and relate the scope of the seating areas and the concessions and skyboxes.

In his eyes it was already there. He was the believer supreme, the one whose drive and enthusiasm would ignite everyone who came in contact with the project. He knew it could and would be done. Bill had such faith in Jerry, he ,too, was convinced it would be done. Jerry would see to that. So would DP.

Dotty, with Mayor Koho's permission and Jerry's consent, now brought into the ever expanding ring Bill Peterson the City engineer and John Morgan the City planner. Peterson was only lukewarm about the project. While he voiced his skepticism, he was a team player and would support the central theme with all his power. He eventually warmed up to the idea and became a full-fledged supporter. Peterson and his staff were exacting and demanding as the project went forward and were the main players in many obstacles that had to be overcome during construction, some very expensively. But nobody ever questioned his loyalty.

John Morgan was just skeptical at first. Morgan had his eye on that site for the construction of an amusement park like one built in England. He thought that would be a huge success and more beneficial to the City. But he was a team player and if the collective judgment of the team thought the ballpark was the best for the City, he would sign on too. He knew the history of the old Salem team and was doubtful a new team could now succeed, even in a new ballpark.

So the project marched onward to the next step and then to the next. Viability was a long, long way from reality and there was much to do. There were many difficult steps to take, much persuasion to be utilized and many obstacles even without considering opposition to the project itself. It would be a test of many human attributes and, most of all, commitment and perseverance. Many soldiers would be recruited to the cause, some of whom had major roles to play and performed wonderfully. Some who started out as partisan for the project would lose their enthusiasm along the way and withdraw their support.

There were others who opposed the project for reasons they honestly believed were right. But the salvation of the project was the large cadre of people who believed in it from the start and stuck to it through thick and thin. They were able in the end to revel in the success of the dream and the enjoyment of the citizens of the Salem-Keizer area who took the team to its heart.

The Dream

The road to the future ballpark - Radiant Drive

Farms along the way

The high tension electricity towers

The cabbage patch - There's gonna be a ballpark here

Disassembling the Labish barn

The workers arrive on the job

The house gets moved as the field is staked out

The digging and grading begin

The buildings getting mapped out

The diamond is staked out

Mud! It doesn't look like a ballpark yet

Now graded, it begins to take shape

Digging and grading for the seating

Building up the ground and forming out the stands

The special infield dirt is added, it looks good

# CHAPTER SIX: GETTING INVITED

Dotty Tryk had faced many hurdles in her time but none would compare to her task she had just signed on to accomplish. She knew that if they were successful and got the civic approvals they required and could get the funding located and the stadium built, it would be the signature event of her tenure as Keizer City Manager and to Dennis Koho's administration as Mayor. This would be their legacy, forever, to the City.

The entire subject matter was still secret as the season in Bellingham was winding down. Now she would have to sell the project, secretly still, to the City Council who would also have to maintain the secret. That in itself posed many problems but they would have to be dealt with and the bonded commitment they had made to Jerry and Bill would have to be honored. Yet in order to make the case, even preliminarily to the Council, she needed to expand her working group in order to include the talents she knew she would need.

Dotty assembled her group, Shannon Johnson, Bill Peterson and John Morgan and added Sam Goesch of the Planning Board and Mary Harting and Wally Mull, the Public works Director to round out the team. Everyone agreed on the need to continue to work in the shadows to keep the project from becoming public knowledge just yet.

The season was coming to a close in Bellingham so the secrecy veil could soon be lifted. Even then it was still risky for Jerry and Bill, however, because the completion of the project was far from being a slam-dunk, in fact it was not even on the floor yet. If it was announced and it failed, their franchise would be sacrificed by having to sign on to a lease in Bellingham, probably for several years, with onerous and unacceptable terms. That could make it necessary for them to sell out. It would be difficult to find a buyer with an onerous lease and declining fan support. Yet, they knew and recognized the need for public knowledge in Keizer as soon as practicable to allow sufficient time for the political processes to play out. So they rolled the dice.

Dotty Tryk laid out the project to her team. The floor was open to discussion and for ideas on how the project could be accomplished within the confines of the City government constraints and the budgetary limitations. This was a set of problems no one in that room had ever faced before. At the opening, there were looks of amazement on the faces of the newcomers that something like that had gone on under their very noses without being detected and pessimistic looks that the secret could be maintained longer or that the project could be achieved.

Dotty would have none of that . She announced this meeting was for the purpose of coming up with the method of having the stadium built. This was no place or time for summer soldiers. They were part of the project and would see it through to a conclusion. She wanted solutions, not naysayers. Their first objective was to figure out the outline of the way to get it done and give the details to the City Council and hopefully obtain their approval to continue to move forward-not fully approve it -yet.

And so the central theme of the project was hatched. They were able in that one meeting to generally outline the extent of the City's undertaking that would be required. Sewers would have to be extended out to and along Radiant Drive, electricity and water would have to be brought to the site. If certain site plans were adopted Radiant Drive would have to be partially relocated. Environmental impact would have to be measured, especially traffic flows with increased vehicular traffic using Radiant Drive and Tepper Lane thoroughfares.

Funding would be difficult. It may have been impossible because the only revenues the City had were from taxes and from special projects. They were limited but project funding seemed a possibility. Nevertheless, that would have never come to pass and the enterprise would have died in its infancy. It was saved by an innovative and masterly proposal nade by Councilman Al Miller.

Miller suggested funding could be partially accomplished by including the site in the City's Urban Renewal Plan. That would give the Council certain extra powers and opened up the possibility of funding the project through the issuance of tax-free bonds, which is what Miller had in mind.

One problem with that was the Urban Renewal Plan had already been finalized and filed. It could be legally amended to include additional areas but they had to be contiguous with and connected to the boundaries of the filed Plan. The Plan had included the entire developed parts of the City but the proposed stadium site was far removed from that boundary. The project needed the bonding capabilities to make the project at least financially feasible and without that the Council would justifiably elect not to proceed.

The Miller proposal was an ingenius solution to the problem. It was proposed to amend the boundaries of the filed Plan by connecting the existing Plan boundary to the stadium site. They proposed the Urban Renewal boundary be expanded by taking in the roadway along Chemawa Drive (where City Hall is located) going north, to Lockhaven where the outline would turn east and take in the Lockhaven roadway up to Radiant Drive where the new line would turn north again and take in and follow Radiant drive to the Stadium site which would then be included.

It was a skillful amount of gerrymandering but it achieved the desired end. It looked like a thin snake running from the main City boundary along roadways only to the stadium site where another big bulge existed. Two large bulging areas connected by a very thin, snaking umbilical cord. If adopted, it would expand the Urban Renewal Plan to include the stadium site, thus opening up the possibility of issuing attractive tax-free government bonds to produce the revenues necessary to fund the City's part of stadium construction and land purchase.

That strategy in itself was fraught with danger. Measure 47 was an issue on the state ballot for the November election. Measure 47 was intended to place a check on governmental spending and incurring long term debt. If the bonds were not issued before the election or sold within thirty days after Measure 47 was passed, that avenue of financing would be forever closed. Without that type of funding available to the City, the project probably could not be done. It was virtually a sure thing that governmental limiting measure would pass since it was heavily publicized and polls indicated it was extremely popular. A similar measure had passed in California recently. It was scheduled to become effective thirty days after the election. Factors beyond everyone's control thus played a major role in the scheduling process.

Beyond that was the need for as much time as possible to construct the ballpark. No plans were drawn yet so the entire architectural phase had to be endured, the bidding and rebidding process completed and the construction contracts and building permits negotiated. Really only two persons truly felt that the entire dream could become a reality by opening day in mid-June 1997. Those persons were Jerry Walker and Bill Tucker who were well aware of the consequences of failure to achieve that result. Playing at the only available alternative site at the old Chemeketa College ballpark was not acceptable. Going back to Bellingham, even temporarily, was out of the question. So we needed a miracle. That was not too much to expect for two guys with DP in their pocket. What was one more miracle?

There was that little matter of the lease situation in Bellingham. The lease provided that unless the team notified the City by the 30th of October, the lease would be deemed renewed for another year on substantially the same terms, except for the setting of payment or rent terms for which a formula had been built in. If the team was reasonably sure it was going to leave, it would have to have the situation reasonably and realistically clear by the end of October.

Then there was the problem of the League concerns. These were genuine concerns because the League had to ensure there would be sufficient facilities for every team to play its games and comply with major league minimums. There was strong feeling among the league owners that the entire process in

Keizer could not be completed and the stadium constructed in time for the 1997 season. Therefore, pressure built to have Jerry and Bill retain alternate facilities somewhere, Bellingham or Salem. This subject is discussed at more length elsewhere in this book but is mentioned here so the reader will have it in mind when focusing on this phase of the process.

The focus was thus on the month of October for many reasons, all important, but not all the concern of the City of Keizer. They were not being asked to bear the entire risk in the situation.

So the outline was prepared. It was general but reflected the positive attitude Dotty had instilled in her team. The memo called for the area where the stadium was to be built to be designated as part of the City's Urban Renewal area. That would allow for the issuance of the bonds if they acted soon enough, for all conditions to their issuance to be cleared and the bonds to be issued and sold. That was an essential ingredient of the successful plan and without it there could be no assurance of success. It most likely would then fail.

Part of the memo indicated the City would be obliged to lease the land under the stadium for a large number of years to Jerry and Bill, probably 30 to 40 in all, with options. The City would have to acquire four properties, probably by condemnation or at least under that threat by negotiation. That would be costly but the end result would be the transformation of an otherwise undevelopable site into a taxpaying unit that could serve as a lightning rod for further development in the area. That possibility justified the investment and the construction of the infrastructure for the site, such as drainage, water and utilities and some road construction. It would also give the City the identity it so desperately craved.

The memo clearly indicated the Council was not being asked right then to fully approve the plan or to commit funds to finance it. The issue before the Council was simply should the City consider moving forward with it or drop it, like a hot and unaffordable potato.

Dennis Koho was out on a limb strongly in favor of the plan and the ultimate construction of the stadium and having baseball again in the area. He knew the road would not be easy. Already there had been complaints from the Gubser neighborhood about the conceptual ballpark the City had thought of building before Jerry Walker had ridden into town. That was only a concept, and complaints had come in. What would happen when they faced the reality of an actual ballpark being constructed there, and on a fast track?

The meeting was informal and the Council members listened intently. The secret had now been spread to a wider group but continued secrecy was still required. They did not and could not mention the name of the team considering the relocation because the season was still under way and early disclosure could jeopardize the public support the team was then receiving in Bellingham. But it was a real team, one they knew about and could want to have come to Keizer. They were enthusiastic about the venture and the secret would not have to be kept secret much longer.

The Council deliberated on the subject and it could be seen at that very early stage, sentiment ran in favor of looking further into the project, especially since they were only being asked whether they wished to pursue the matter further, nothing more. There was no commitment on the part of the City but the parameters and ultimate expectations had been fleshed out. Noone could later say that Tryk's report had not given sufficient detail to allow for a considered vote on the subject, as preliminary as the issue was anyway. The Council voted to proceed.

Now work began in earnest. The Tryk team identified more detail about the site and the land that would have to be acquired. They identified the traffic patterns and noise impact the construction and use of the stadium would have on the neighborhood, not only from the ballgames but also from ancillary uses such as concerts and the like. The early conceptual stadium had proven a good precursor. The complaints that were to come for the new stadium had already been brought to the surface and reaction could be programmed into the plan before the complaints were actually made.

The tract on which the stadium would be located would require six and a quarter acres more or less. The parking lot site with parking slots for 1,500 cars would require approximately fifteen and a half acres. Practical realities would require the acquisition of 29 to 30 acres more or less since people would be unlikely to sell only parts of their land, especially since then the remaining area could not be economically productive. The City would hold the additional acreage for future development.

The four properties that lay in the way of the development were owned by the Deleeuw, Vallish and Labish families. Actually the Labish families owned two of them so only three owners were involved. The Marshal family operated the horse stable business on one of the Labish propeties but had no vested or title interest in that property. Those properties had to be marked for acquisition in order to assemble the necessary total acreage needed.

Acquisition might not be too easy either. It would be far better to be able to arrive at a settlement figure voluntarily since it would avoid all the technical legal maneuvers involved in the eminent domain (condemnation) process. That path required a showing of public benefit to the municipality for the betterment of its citizenry, the details of the development plans and the establishment of property values by experts who testify based on comparable land values and recent sales, hopefully in the vicinity of the property to be taken. It is an expensive, laborious process, costly to both sides of the table and laced with fees for courts, lawyers, appraisers, aerial photographers, stenographers during depositions and the depositions themselves which seem to swallow up time.

In order to avoid the problems inherent in delay, the process allows the earmarked property to be taken by the municipality immediately so that development can go forward. This reduces the ultimate battle in most cases to an issue of "how much". However in projects of the type of the ball park, it is not uncommon for public protesters, usually distinctly in the minority, to raise as many issues as possible, even putting the municipality to its proof on the issue of public benefit. In such

115

situations the opponents almost always lose but they are employing the available tactics for delay purposes and to that degree they succeed.

Almost all public consideration of a project begins by looking at the assessed value of the land to be taken. That is usually a good indicator of the land value if the City's assessment procedures were relatively appropriate and kept up to date. Many municipalities assess at only a fraction of the property's value but the factor by which that is to be multiplied is at hand and well known. Therefore, no matter how the assessed valuation is set forth, the assumed proper property value is quickly established.

The Deleeuw property was the largest of the group. It consisted of 19.11 acres with a building on it assessed at a total of $860,000. Second largest was the Labish property with 8.54 acres with a structure which was the horse barn where the Marshal family operated their business. It was assessed at $360,000. The Valish property also had a structure on it and consisted of a total of 1.85 acres assessed at $360,000. The second Labish property was also small, 1.79 acres, but had no residential structures. The property was used as farmland with an assessed value of $105,000. The total price to the City, if assessed valuations were paid, would be $1,550,000. That at least established the bottom figure for the taking and the bond issue which would also have to have added to it the cost of the infrastructure and parking lot which would be the City's part of the project.

The total tax revenue from the four properties was approximately $6022. That was for the entire 30 plus acres which included extra land the City would retain for future development beyond the stadium structure. If you allocated that tax income to the stadium structure land only, the tax revenue would be only $4360. The project would not eliminate any large income from the City coffers and would likely generate much more income, and even a vast amount more if, as anticipated, it became the catalyst for the extensive development the City hoped for.

On September 6 the season finally came to a close in Bellingham. Despite terrific play by a determined group of youngsters, the team finally dropped out of contention on the last day of an exciting season. The team, with good pitching, hitting and fielding stayed in the hunt the entire season, keeping pace with a very good Yakima team which benefited considerably from the schedule. Attendance, however, continued to be abysmal, especially for the quality of baseball being played and what should have been the terrific excitement of the pennant race.

Since 1986 when the Walker-Tucker team bought the franchise, it had experienced ups and downs in attendance. Beginning the first season when we inherited that woeful program, the attendance was increasing annually. It hit its apex and then began to decline, eventually hitting rock bottom (for us) as the public dispute over stadium issues came to the fore. One look at the annual attendance figures during that period shows how the problem developed and concluded.

| 1988 | 15,015 ( last year of "old" ownership group) |
| 1989 | 31,686 ( beginning of Walker-Tucker ownership) |
| 1990 | 52,515 |

| | | |
|---|---|---|
| 1991 | 60,486 | |
| 1992 | 68,928 | |
| 1993 | 74,900 | |
| 1994 | 71,256 | (end of Mariner affiliation) |
| 1995 | 54,104 | (beginning of Giants affiliation) |
| 1996 | 48,417 | (end of Bellingham era) |
| 1997 | 136,836 | (beginning of Salem-Keizer era) |
| 1998 | 139,980 | |

Those figures have to be considered against the background of the "free night" culture described previously. One would not produce an accurate picture of team revenues simply by multiplying the number of fans counted by average ticket prices because so many attended only on the free nights. From the beginning in 1989 to its season high in Bellingham in 1993 through its precipitous decline to its concluding low, it was a sleigh ride of hope and despair and persistent effort against a background of little official support or appreciation.

We never stopped trying to produce the best possible entertainment for the fans to induce their attendance and enjoyment of this medium of entertainment. Despite the long tradition of Bellingham baseball, of which the City was justifiably proud, we were never able to break through. A culture that exists on free traditions will eventually demand more for less and ultimately reach a level of diminishing returns. That was the Bellingham story reduced to its lowest common denominator.

The day after the season ended on September 6, Mayor Koho, Dotty Tryk and the City Councilors along with Jerry and Lisa representing the team, and with the full support of Bill and Dolores Tucker, called a press conference at the McNary Golf Club. It was a beautiful fall day. About 10AM Mayor Koho

118

stepped to the podium before a newly unveiled banner proclaiming "SALEM-KEIZER Professional BASEBALL Lets Play Ball."

The press conference had been widely advertised. Attendance was good with many people attending. There was an air of excitement since everyone felt an announcement of momentous importance was in the offing. The room was abuzz with the expectation of just what was going to happen.

Many did not know yet. Some did, however, because someone had leaked the secret to one element of the press a short time before. But even that could not dampen the expectation of the crowd or the excitement of the moment.

The leak never had time to spread too many ripples and was probably accidental. Nevertheless, it had been the subject of a story in the Statesman Journal that day headlined "KEIZER COURTS PRO BASEBALL TEAM." Both Larry Parsons and Capi Lynn, the writers, seemed to have many of the details of the proposal accurately but they couldn't just yet identify the proposed moving franchise.

Capi Lynn got it completely right the next day though. She wrote a story under the bannerline "MINOR LEAGUE BASEBALL RETURNS ON FAMILIAR TERMS". It was obvious she had gotten more details and had not only identified the team as the Bellingham Giants, but also had interviewed Jerry Walker. Jerry, however, was not especially forthcoming, preferring to defer to the coming press conference still two days away and to suggest she speak with Mayor Koho. Her story gave a thumbnail sketch of the history of Salem baseball and included a brief discussion of the franchise's motivation to move but the best was still yet to come.

Now Mayor Koho was at the podium flanked by the City Councilors, Dotty Tryk and the Walkers and architect Alan Costic and contractor Cory Redding. Representing the league and attending also for the purpose of lending official stature to the plans to relocate the franchise were Bob Richmond, league president and Jack Cain, owner and operator of the recently relocated (from Bend,Oregon)to Portland franchise and Richmond's immediate predecessor as league president.

The banner set the tone for the conference. Koho proudly made the expected announcement. The Bellingham Giants were planning to relocate to that area. There were many details still to be worked out but the team was committed to the move. The City of Keizer wanted to extend as much encouragement as possible. There was the issue of the new stadium to be built without which the team would not come, and the cost of which would be shared between the City and the team. The stadium land had been identified , the location being a 30 acre parcel to be aggregated just northeast of the Chemawa interchange off I-5. While the stadium would be located in Keizer, the team ownership had made it crystal clear the team would use the hyphenated name of Salem-Keizer.

Anticipating questions on why a team housed in a stadium in Keizer, built on land acquired and improved with the necessary infrastructure with Keizer money, would be only the second part of the team's name, Koho had the answers. "If Keizer were isolated in eastern Oregon, we wouldn't be able to support something like this at all. We couldn't even attract it." he said. "This is something for the entire community" he continued and a hyphenated team name suited him just fine. But the stadium name would include Keizer as the only City involved. There was ample justification for a hyphenated name. Many things, chief among them the school district, bore the name Salem-Keizer. It seemed a logical and appropriate solution to the identity problem.

Walker said the selection of the area was the outgrowth of a league study of available sites. The study considered 16 markets and identified Salem, Tri-Cities, Washington and Victoria, B.C. as "excellent" potential markets. The study factored in the financial strength of the areas, weather, tourism, location and retail quality. It was then a simple matter of elimination by facts. Tri-Cities already had an unaffiliated team (remember the Pasco incident) and Victoria access was only by ferry. That would be less than ideal, but not a difficulty that could not be overcome or tolerated.

But Salem as the capital of the state stood out among all of them. The area was growing, had the population base to support a team and fit in perfectly on the Northwest League map. Had Salem not been in the picture, Keizer alone could not have been considered. In fact, Keizer was not even in the 16 City study on its own. Walker made it clear again and again the name Salem had to be part of the team name. "We feel its important. It is the State capital." Besides, there were many joint name examples already, prominent among them being the school district.

And Mayor Koho set forth what he expected would be problems to come up along the way. He said "I don't want the taxpayers to think this deal is already signed." "It's exciting" Councilman McGee said "but there's still a ways to go. There are a lot of intangible benefits, but a lot of tangible worries."

Koho and Councilor Al Miller expressed confidence that the financial details and political problems would be worked out. That would allow stadium construction to start in January and play to begin there in June. As Koho outlined the details and the tasks and general costs involved, one could read mixed expressions on the faces of those present. They were mainly pleased expressions of support and enthusiasm . He said the four identified parcels that would have to be acquired were in the process of being appraised.

Jerry Walker handed out "Let's Play Ball" buttons and hats and trading cards. It was a clear and professional effort to persuade Keizer residents to support the stadium idea. Jerry Walker was quoted as saying "We believe everything will fall into place, or we wouldn't be here."

And so, it was Keizer, or bust. The secret was now really out, to everyone, and everything was on the line. It would have to be brought to reality or there were severe  consequences to be borne.  There were many sacrifices to be made in time, effort, money now and in the future, with a great deal  at stake.  It would  be no slam-dunk and the next few months would prove to  be extremely difficult and nerve-wracking.  All that lay ahead.

Above (l to r): Dotty Tryk, Capi Lynn, Mike Witenberger;
and the late Ivan Walker

"Hey Beer Man!" Jerry and Bill seated with the Weathers Family,
Hops Growers Supreme

Orville Roth of Roth's Family Markets and Bill Schmidt of Mt. Hood Beverages

Bill with Larry Jansen, former major leaguer

The original Volcanoes - the 1997 team

Even Oregon Governor John Kitzhaber (center) attended

Concrete foundation in place on home team side, note beginning of dugout

Formed out for main stadium building behind home plate

It's a party, Jerry threw regular parties for the construction staff

Preparing forms for concrete to hold box seating on home team side

Framing for foundation footings on visiting clubhouse,
note farmhouse in background which served as temporary office

A rare nice day - setting forms for clubhouse building

Formed out to pour concrete for home team side box seats

Concrete wall to hold box seating on home team side

Preparing to pour concrete for box seating along third base side

A view from home plate to the visitors dugout.   Can you tell it is a ballpark?

# CHAPTER SEVEN:  THE FIRST PITCH

The stadium issue continued to generate comments at the September 16 Council meeting.  Greg Lamb representing the Gubser community dwelt on the subject of the neighborhood associations being snubbed in the stadium consideration process.  He felt the association, particularly Gubser as the area most affected, should have been bought into the process much earlier.  His remarks hinted directly at the theme that there was something surrepticious about the team having contacted the City in July and there having  been nothing mentioned publicly about the subject until two months later.

It did not persuade him that the team had asked that the matter be kept secret in order not to cause a disruption with the players as they were gunning for a division flag.  It was also to avoid damaging prematurely the fragile relationship between the team and its then hosts, the City of Bellingham. They were both good and sufficient reasons for tight security. No amount of explanation, no matter how logical, was able to sway him from his hurt feelings.  Essentially, his theme was one of having been slighted and hurt by the slight.  There was no truly meritorious opposition advanced, except generalities about noise and traffic interference.   It was the eastern NIMBY (Not In My Back  Yard) opposition relocated west of the Rockies.

In some ways, his opposition was understandable.   The stadium was a big matter, it would involve public funds and it would impact his particular constituency.  Nevertheless, there were good motives and ample reason to delay the public entry into the issue and at that it was only a two month delay. The issue was also a long, long way from final decision which was yet to be made so no real harm came from the delay. However, he proposed delay on deciding the issue, a condition that would have made the entire enterprise be reconsidered by the team. The City was not the only one with a stake in the matter.

Manny Martinez was a local activist who was very knowledgeable and one who frequently appeared at Council meetings mainly to oppose proposals. He was hurt by the fact the team had contacted Salem first.(actually there were several other contacts. (See Chapter Four) He conveyed the idea he was upset by the fact that Salem officially passed on it and had bucked the idea to Keizer because he thought Salem did not want to invest its funds in the stadium. Now in Keizer, it was being given a fast track and he felt it should be delayed for a public vote

He also raised the issue of conflict of interest by any of the Councilors, knowing the team had temporarily rented a room in Councilman Miller's office . It was used as a local base from which the public drama could be played out to a conclusion more conveniently for Jerry and Lisa other than having to return regularly to and from Bellingham. It was small, at market rents and was intended to be, and was, for only a few months until more suitable space could be found if the project received a green light. There was no conflict here and every Councilor placed on the record that they had no conflict. The exception was Councilor Newton who introduced a little levity into the proceeding by refusing to say and telling them he was going to let them wonder.

About a third of the way through the meeting, the comments had been almost entirely negative. Those speaking either were against the stadium project or had legitimate concerns from its effect on something in their lives.

About that time, a tall man in the crowd who had been sitting quietly, but impatiently, had his name come up on the list of those who had indicated they wanted to speak. It was his turn. He moved for attention and the right to speak. He was eloquent. His name was Donald Porter. He had been an All-American basketball player at Linfield College. His stature as an athlete had to be outstanding for a tiny school like Linfield to place someone on an All-American team, national in scope. He was an imposing figure.

He was now the proprietor of Porter's Pub in Keizer and thought he had heard enough negative talk. He was all in favor of the stadium project. He felt it was good for the City and wonderful for the kids. It would provide both adult and youth activity and wholesome diversion. It was important to keep families involved and baseball brings families together. What he was hearing was more or less every one's individual issues, few if anyone was thinking of the common good. The future of Keizer and the future of its families and their children hung in the balance. People should recognize that he thought. His speech, which was extemporaneous, came from his heart. It was emotional and called up all the visions of America and apple pie and civic pride.

All the dwelling on whether or not it was to be a profitable venture for the City or whether it would be helpful to future civic development was out of line. "Of course", he said " the operators intend to make a profit. We also will reap a profit from this enterprise. Maybe even a bigger one. And remember--profit is not a four letter word."

Silence. Everyone seemed to breathe a collective sigh. He was right and they knew it. From that time on, the meeting turned around. Everyone else spoke in favor of the project and it was strong and overwhelming support. The entire tenor of the meeting changed from that point forward and heavily favored going forward with the project.

The last speaker was Jerry Walker, himself. Jerry rose to speak to the assembled crowd. There was a deep emotion in his words as he told of his desire to come here with the team to establish a community effort. He told of how he expected to move here to raise his family, grow roots and establish himself as a giving community member. Sure he was bringing a business with him but some businesses produce more than revenues for their owners. Some have exemplary byproducts which improve the quality of life in their fields and baseball was one of them. He was overwhelmed by the spontaneous outpouring of support he had just heard at the meeting and hoped it would set the stage for the Council to get behind the project and give it the life it needed. Tears began to well up in his eyes near the end. He wiped them away, unashamed of the moment and concluded his remarks to a receptive crowd. It was a significant moment. Those speeches would be long remembered.

That essentially ended the public part of the meeting relating to the stadium. Not much moved further on the stadium then and there but the issue was really alive and constantly debated in the public arena. The papers kept up a drumbeat of interest and stories about baseball and the team. If anyone cared to look at the issue from that viewpoint , they would see the prospect of the team coming there and building the stadium had already promoted considerable public interest and democratic debate. The team issue had done more for the news media and the public interest already than had all the routine daily goings on before the issue arose. For the media it was almost like a brand new OJ trial. It was a public success on that score and had an electricity all its own.

In the meantime, the team quietly continued to hawk and sell seat reservations. The number climbed sharply and steadily. The team without a name and without a home had sold about 350 box seat reservations on the first day after the press conference.. Within a few hours it was up to 421 and headed higher. It was a clear demonstration of the team's popularity. "We expected the response to be positive" Lisa Walker said "but this was pretty overwhelming. We're hoping this helps the City of Keizer, and everybody, that baseball is really popular here in spite of the past."

Priority numbers for seat selection were being assigned to fans on a first-come, first- serve basis. Fans with lower numbers would get first choice at the seats. Jim Martsfield of Keizer was among the earliest in line. He plunked down a deposit for five season box seats. "I used to have box seats when the Dodgers were in town, " he said. "I wasn't happy when they left. I've been waiting for this day." The City was really responding.

Everybody's opinion counted. Bob Richmond , president of the Northwest League spoke of baseball's requirements that stadium facilities meet certain minimal standards . " It was better for everybody" he said. "The fields have to be something that the community will be proud of."

Bob Beban, who was associated with the Dodgers before the franchise was sold and moved to Yakima, was contacted. His experience was important. After all, here was a team in the very same league looking to come back into an area where another team had largely failed before, and only recently. "We didn't have a good facility at Chemeketa. The location was bad." Bob Beban said. Bob Richmond gave the reasons for the proposed return of the league to the area "… (the) Salem-Keizer area has the demographics for a team to be successful., but it needs a new stadium. There's no such thing as a bad baseball town."

The stadiums themselves were becoming part of the draw everywhere. Chris Metz, the Director of Media Relations for the Eugene Emeralds, Beban's current team, went on record saying "The quaint ball fields you go to for minor leagues are a lot less intimidating. You're closer to the action."

Still the debate continued to swirl. R.G. Andersen-Wyckoff, former Mayor of Salem said, "Unless you happen to participate in one (diverse sports activities) you don't think it's a sports town." On the other hand , Casey Jones said "People are busy all day and every evening. Everbody is extended. There's girls and boys sports, mothers do Jazzersize, fathers want to work out. There's too much to do."

But the hard evidence might have been to the contrary. The Cascade Surge, the local soccer team, had come to town only two years before and was attracting an average of 1600 fans per game. "A new stadium and another professional team coming into this marketplace is exciting" said Chris McCartney , General Manager of the Surge. "It means Salem is growing up. It can support new teams and it can do well with them."Clint Holland, who had once operated the Salem franchise that eventually left, agreed. Bill Trenbeath almost agreed.

" I think the population base is here to support a minor league team", McCartney added. "We need to get people thinking there are entertainment options ...(here). They don't have to leave." And the statistics supported that view. From 1990 to 1994 the population of the combined cities had increased by 10% and was still rising. (In one of those "small world" events we all love, both Jerry Walker and Chris McCartney had been in the same graduating class from Everett, Washington High School in 1971!)

Dennis Koho was the outstanding supporter of the stadium venture. As Mayor, he was responsible for representing the entire City and had concern for the quality of life available to its citizens and wanted to keep improving on that value. He saw the stadium development as part of a vision to enhance the City's image, improve the entertainment options for its citizens and to spur or jump- start development in the Chemawa area that had been labeled as the"Activity Center." He knew the land on which the stadium was to be built was not appealing to very many development possibilities, certainly not residential or office space, what with the imposing electrical transmission lines that dominated the parcels. Unless the stadium idea was seized for the opportunity it represented, that parcel might never be developed and would serve as a millstone to development around it.

Yet he recognized the reality of politics and the importance of public input and acceptance. In that vein, he and Dotty Tryk accepted an invitation to speak at the Gubser Neighborhood Association meeting on September 19,1996. The meeting was alive with interest on just what was happening with the stadium theme, where it stood and what the effect would be on their quiet, residential neighborhood. This was proper concern.

Koho outlined the entire picture, starting from the secretive (now being considered clandestine by ballpark opponents) meeting at Shari's in July and the need for secrecy and its overriding purpose. He elaborated on the Council approval process that was still ongoing and far from over yet. No decision had been made but he made it expressly clear that he was definitely in favor of the proposal, thought it was an opportunity that should not be missed and which may not come their way again. He recognized the proposal was on an unusually fast track but it was a unique and rare situation and told them they should trust their elected representatives to "do the right thing." The Council's history was not to waste or spend unnecessarily taxpayers money but yet they did have the responsibility to spend it when their judgment indicated they should.

The traffic pattern along Tepper Lane and noise control was one of the important issues with that community. Koho outlined the fact that there would only be 38 regular season games, mostly at night. The stadium would hold only about 5000 people, about one third of whom would drive to the games. They had come up with some traffic control ideas that would minimize the impact on that community and over only a short time sequence of about fifteen minutes following each game. Other events at the stadium would be limited in number, which was unfortunate in a way because City revenues were in part tied to income from such events. However, it was neither realistic nor practical to think such events would be numerous, due to climate and the competing availability of a larger population in nearby Portland. Everyone has to make some sacrifice for the common good and the slight inconvenience that may result from the stadium to the Gubser neighborhood would be relatively minimal.

He asked for their support of the stadium project. It would certainly beat the gas stations, strip malls and fast food stands that greet motorists at many freeway offramps. "The image of Keizer as a residential City will be enhanced." he said. "It says we live here. We play here. And we value our families."

Dotty Tryk further comforted the group on the numbers that had been bandied about as the cost of land acquisition and construction. She detailed the value the City would receive from its investment. The team alone would bring more economic activity to the area and possibly serve to encourage developmental activity at the "Activity Center." There was the possibility of other uses for the stadium such as high school and possibly college football, soccer matches and other community events They would bring total family enjoyment to the area.   The return was going to   be well worth the investment.

Generally , the people in attendance felt the coming of the Giants would be a boost for Keizer's sometimes fuzzy self image.   In the end the meeting voted to support the stadium proposal with provisos on the traffic pattern clarification. The larger question of whether this was a proper expenditure of public funds was not even heavily debated and was accepted as appropriate governmental pump-priming.  The issue had been bared to a representative sample crowd that could be hostile but was not.   That would serve as a barometer for public thinking in the immediate future.

The September 23  Special Council meeting now loomed on the horizon. Dotty Tryk prepared an elaborate spread sheet detailing the steps, procedures and general costs attached thereto for the Council's consideration. She was purposely conservative in the numbers she included, basing them on the investigative results of her team's inquiries.  She was certain they portrayed an accurate picture of what lay in store for the City of Keizer if it proceeded with the stadium proposal .

Dotty wanted that report with the spreadsheet to be responsive to any question that might arise at the meeting, both because time was so important to the enterprise and because that is the way she always did things--complete and thorough and honest. She was always aware a  "no" vote at any time by the Council would kill the project. Both she and the proposal would have to pass many tests or votes, while a negative  vote, or a vote to delay approval, on any occasion would effectively kill the project.

As the days dwindled down to a precious few, Jerry Walker started a publicity campaign to drum up publicly expressed support for the stadium. He hosted a gathering at the Town And Country Bowling Center in Keizer to lay out his plans for the stadium development and the program the team would follow when they arrived. It was well attended and Jerry distributed the now-well-known hats advertising professional baseball. He explained that time was of the essence. Any unexpected delay by the City Council in approving the idea so construction could begin and be completed on time could cause a change in plans.

The franchise was riding on the City Council approval and unless it came within the expected time frame, the team would be forced to relocate elsewhere. Chemeketa was not an acceptable alternative either temporarily or otherwise. Neither would the team stay in Bellingham another year. It was "go" at all cost, whether it was Keizer or another City.

The gathering was well-attended and a huge success. He had selected the bowling alley for the meeting because it was a popular place, sports lovers gathered there regularly, and it was operated by John Preston who also just happened to be active in the Keizer Chamber of Commerce. John would prove out to be a staunch friend and ally and his resourcefulness will be extolled appropriately later in this story. For now , he produced the crowd and helped in disseminating the message.

One of the larger questions being floated locally was the team nickname. Rick Nelson, Vice President of Team Operations, a member of the Giants' entourage, announced that if and when approval was received, and the project a likely reality, we would hold a contest for the public to submit names for the team. It would get the entire populace involved. Jerry Walker had said "It's your team-you name it." And he meant it.

Nelson advertised for people to submit ideas, logos, mascots and colors. "We're looking for something that identifies with the region. From the Willamette Valley and the Cascades to the Pacific Ocean, something the community can associate with." Nelson announced that he planned to enlist the help of the local schools but encouraged everyone to participate. We're going to leave it up to the community" he said, "it's their team." The team had already rejected the name of the"Kohos" (after Dennis) the Mayor had jokingly suggested.

For now it would be a fill-in-the-blanks theme but the team would be literally deluged with ideas. Out of that would come the "Volcanoes", submitted by Bill Lien of Keizer. It was appropriate. You can see snow-capped mountains over the outfield fences. Dormant volcanoes, but some occasionally hissing and steaming. Not long before, one of those sleeping giants awoke and blotted out the sun for a while. Mount St. Helen's eruption was spectacular. We were not hoping for another. Oregon has seven volcanoes in all.

The memo Dotty Tryk and her "team" prepared was distributed to the City Council members in advance of the meeting. The Special Session convened at the Council Chambers at exactly 7:02 PM on that cool Monday evening. Although the public was permitted to attend , there was no doubt this was an official show only and audience participation was not allowed. Mayor Koho announced the sole purpose of the meeting was to discuss the stadium proposal and to consider authorizing a letter of commitment to participate in a public/private partnership for the stadium construction.

The memo outlined the proposal completely. It showed what would have to be done as the City's contribution and what was expected of the team ownership. The memo listed the cost of land acquisition according to the assessed valuation and the cost of developing the infrastructure. It told that some of the development expected of the City would be in advance of expected further development out at Chemawa and some of those costs would be recouped as other development came on stream. We were down to specifics. The memo laid bare the entire cost and case for the proposal, discussed all aspects of its feasibility and found it to be feasible providing certain time lines were met and proposals enacted by the City Council.

Dotty's memo discussed the economic benefit the City would derive due to increased funds generated by the stadium. She included a potential budget which included possible costs of the properties as needed plus the improvements consisting mainly of water, sewer, streets, parking and fencing. She included very conservative estimates of legal and engineering costs. She even took into consideration the use of some street funds to change the alignment of Radiant Drive. The net cost to the City for the stadium would be $2,995,000 with some possible offset by way of assistance from the Department of Economic Development.

She outlined the proposed lease agreement, which then was a long way from being cast in ink let alone concrete, and the revenues the City would receive from participation in attendance income and    parking revenues. There was no doubt there were two lynchpins of the entire enterprise. First was the inclusion of the stadium area in the Urban Renewal Plan which would require amendment by the City Council. Second and as important as the first and dependent on it was the ability to issue tax-free bonds for urban renewal development. That had to be accomplished from dream to sale soon enough to avoid the expected prohibition against debt financing almost certain to be imposed by adoption of Measure 47. If the stadium was to be a reality, time was of the essence.

The Walkers sat through the debate that ensued. The issue was in the balance for the entire three hours of the meeting. The thought would race through Jerry's mind that he might have made a mistake, might have miscalculated the political waters and might come up empty.

The debate was heated at times, and difficult to gauge. Council members who had been thought to be in favor of the transaction asked some telling questions in such a way as to imply opposition. It was a tough night for Jerry and Lisa but they sat in stony silence as the matter progressed. Others witnessing the proceedings also were in doubt as to its outcome until the last minute, some losing track of the technicalities of the parliamentary procedures being followed.

The main concerns were the contents of the eventual lease, whether it was necessary to have a public referendum on an expenditure of public funds of that magnitude and  if the investment if made would prove to be worthwhile. Dennis Koho was clearly in favor of the issue and said it repeatedly.

He stressed the theme that this was a rare opportunity for the City, one that may never come their way again.

To his great credit, he met heads-on the oft-raised issue of why Keizer would not receive top billing in the team name. Koho repeated that Keizer alone would not have attracted the consideration of any team just then and that Salem was considered vital to the marketing of the team by its owners. He had insisted on and received the promise of the owners to include only Keizer's name as the City on the name of the stadium, being careful to state room had to be allowed for the "selling" of the stadium sponsorship to private concerns. It would be embodied in the lease.

"Not every City investment has to be profitable" Koho remarked. "Some City investments have to be evaluated on their contribution to quality of life, opportunities to promote further development and attract new industries and corporations and provide a better image for the City. Identity was important and this will help our identity immensely." Councilman Miller agreed: "This will put Keizer on the map."

Councilman Jerry McGee who had been a part of the initial meeting at Shari's and thought to be on the side of the project, questioned the authority of the subcommittee to negotiate the terms of the lease and expressed his concern about the inability of the Council to then review it. Councilor Newton, as a member of the subcommittee appointed to arrive at a lease, expressed that he understood it was the subcommittee's charge and duty to review the lease terms and identify those items that may be of concern. City Manager Tryk then outlined the specifics of the concepts for the lease that agreement had been reached on with the owners. There were more than twenty of such items and they became the subject of the debate.

Councilor McGee was very active. He stated that he hoped this developer would be treated the same as any other with regard to the placement of the utilities. He stated he was comfortable with the sale of beer at the stadium but was concerned with the sale of hard liquor in the skyboxes as proposed. McGee suggested requiring a performance bond to assure full compliance by the team owners. He reiterated that proposal along with his disagreement with the suggested 30 year term, preferring instead two ten year renewals of the lease. He said the team could remain in Bellingham for an additional year to allow the time for the City to get the voters' approval on the venture. That was his opinion.

McGee also voiced his concern with the data that had been submitted regarding the anticipated costs of the project. He noted the projections did not include the cost of the bonds or other miscellaneous accounting costs or additional staff or police costs. He objected to the use of street funds for this project if they were not to be repaid. He stated his disbelief with the projected costs of the parking lot and thought there would be added cost in providing adequate draining. In the last analysis he thought the initial costs of "jump starting" development at the Chemawa Activity Center were too risky and not a wise investment for taxpayer dollars. He added that he felt strongly that the name of the team should be Keizer-Salem and not the other way around since the financial investment was coming from Keizer.

146

Shannon Johnson, sitting in as City Attorney, responded to some of the issues advanced from time to time. One issue was the right of the owners to sell out, or leave, or to transfer the obligations of the lease. Johnson explained his thoughts on what the lease would contain, prohibiting for at least a period of time, some of the actions questioned, such as selling out or moving out.

Those opposed seemed to fail to recognize the lease was a two-way street. If the contents were too onerous, you could not expect the other party, the team, to accept. They clearly did not have to do so. It was important to protect the investment the City would make, but not to overdo it to the point where the investment would become unnecessary because the team would not accept the overly restrictive lease. There had to be a mutuality to the enterprise. A public-private partnership to a degree. The team's owners were putting in personal funds out of their own pockets equal to or greater than the City's expected investment so they had a lot at stake here too. The team did not "have to" move. It just wanted to.

Johnson separated the covenants of the lease from the Letter of Commitment that was being asked of the Council that evening. He emphasized that it was important for the owners to have that commitment in hand to be able to finance the construction as they expected to do. A failure to vote in favor of the Letter being issued was in effect a veto of the proposal. There was no half-way out. If you wanted professional baseball in Keizer in the foreseeable future, you had to stand up and be counted now.

Jerry Walker had to be sitting there in disbelief over what he was hearing. Jerry McGee had been in on the initial meeting at Shari's and had given the proposal a "heads-up" to continue. That was no firm commitment to stay on the side of the proposal forever but his expressions now were clearly indicative of someone who had become strongly opposed to the project. He had been counted on for support but it was clear that would not now be forthcoming. All his questions deserved answers but collectively they demonstrated a definite philosophical disagreement with the theme of the proposal that certainly had been addressed at the initial meeting. That had not changed.

Councilor Jerry Watson explained his reluctance to sign the Letter of Commitment when many of the details had not been negotiated at that point. He also stated he was reluctant to proceed when an option on the properties had not been secured yet. In the end, he announced he would vote positively for the project as an indication only of his support for economic development, not baseball. He was convinced the return on the investment would be short dollar wise but rich in economic benefits to the community. Mayor Koho mentioned that not every investment by the City had to be calculated to turn a profit, some investments had to be made from time to time to promote growth and family values. This was one such investment and a rare opportunity to achieve so many purposes at once.

John Morgan, Community Development Director, reported that if the Activity Center were to be built out close to what was projected with a mix of commercial and industrial uses, it could reduce current property taxes by about $.42 per $1000.

It was hoped the stadium project would jump-start development at the Activity Center. City Manager Tryk indicated such development would have less of an impact on public services but could increase the City's population which would then increase the demand for City services on the citizens of Keizer. Councilor Newton stated it was his belief the stadium project would not result in a tax increase to the citizens of Keizer.

Some Councilors constantly harkened back to the possibility of holding a plebiscite to get the voters authority to proceed with the stadium project. The procedures inherent in such a move would necessarily delay the process. The delay would be fatal not only to the project but also to the opportunity being presented. If the team's schedule was going to be met, the decision would have to be made at the Council level by the elected representatives doing the duty they were elected for, and now. There could be no passing the buck onto any other or future Council. Mayor Koho was correctly convinced that if the Council did not act positively right now, the opportunity would go elsewhere.

Trying to buy time, Councilor McGee revived the suggestion the team could stay in Bellingham for another year. That suggestion had been repeatedly rejected by the team as was the possibility of playing a season at Chemeketa. It was going to have to be Keizer, and now, or somewhere else. There were no alternatives for Keizer. The issue could not be delayed or passed for just a year. Delay meant no professional baseball in Keizer---for probably a long time.

Councilors Beach and Keller also expressed their feelings. Beach was for the project but was not comfortable with the idea of spending so much taxpayer money without voter approval. He felt the rush of time caused too much pressure to make a reasoned decision and wanted more time to analyze the figures and collect more data. He expressed his concern with the low attendance figures in Bellingham and the disputes he had heard about between team management and that City.

Councilor Keller announced he was not comfortable with the available information to make a decision at that point. He was not convinced the stadium project was a proper expense of public funds. He did introduce the letter from the Gubser Neighborhood Association that gave a limited endorsement to the project.

Councilor Miller reminded everyone the issue under debate was not just baseball. It could provide substantial revenues to the City and jump-start the development at the Activity Center which is what the City wanted. He emphasized the budgeted figures provided by the staff had been fully analyzed and estimated based on their expertise. A cap on the project would contain the City's costs. The land, he reminded, suffered due to the location of the BPA power lines and that would limit development of the parcel whereas this was a chance to develop and add to the tax rolls a parcel not otherwise capable of development. Miller reminded everyone of the comments given at the public hearing and the recent vote of the Gubser Neighborhood Association in favor of the project, with limitations. It was at this point where Keller introduced the Association's letter.

But Councilor McGee continued to raise issues in the apparent hope of delaying the approval which would kill the project. He raised every possible item to attract the support of other Council Members to defeat the issue. From expense, to proper use of public funds, to questioning the estimates and budget figures , to the cost of the bonds, to staffing costs, to the use of street funds that may not be repaid, to his thought the investment was too risky and not a wise investment for taxpayer dollars, and last but not least the civic pride that Keizer had to be named first in the team name.

Patiently, Councilor Newton reviewed previous minutes of City Council meetings dating back to late 1989 and early 1990. The Council established a committee to explore urban renewal at the Activity Center.  On February 5,1990 the committee's report included discussion of extending the Urban Renewal District boundary to include the Activity Center. At that time, they considered putting in the infrastructure (water, sewer, utility lines) out there to serve as a catalyst for development at the Center with no developers on the horizon yet..  Estimated costs at that time were between 3  and 5 million dollars so the cost being asked now seems a viable alternative.  The wisdom of the past would be a guide for the future.

In the end, the Council would vote in favor of the Letter of Commitment. The vote would be close with Councilors Koho, Miller, Newton and Watson voting in favor.  Councilor Watson had started the motion process with a long motion which contained known unacceptable provisions and it  failed to gain a second.

Councilman McGee made four amendatory motions to amend Mayor Koho's motion in favor of the project and the issuance of the Letter of Commitment before a final vote and all four failed of passage. He then made a fifth motion to develop a reasonable, practical method to allow the citizens to vote on the issue before the final decision was made. That issue seemed to resolve itself favorably when John Morgan suggested that they use the process used for renewal plan amendments . He said the next issue of "Keizer on the Move" will contain an article and hearing notice explaining the amendment. While not official, it is mailed to members of the community and they will get the data and be invited to the next hearing.

Almost lost in the process was the motion made as a result of John Lien's report as City Attorney , to have the Council declare the public necessity of acquiring the four parcels on the north end of the Chemawa Activity Center to allow the condemnation to proceed. This permitted the process to be started. Only two Councilors opposed that motion. The meeting adjourned after three solid hours of lusty democratic debate. Jefferson and Madison would have been proud.

The stadium issue was a "go" for now. It had survived its first real test and its proponents could breathe a sigh of relief. However, the slim margin of approval made the matter very tenuous at best and every imminent move would have to  be conditioned on the  proposition that the next test might result in failure. Any one failure in approval or a delay would end the stadium's viability. Those that believed in it , and there were many, would move forward from this day with energy and confidence that it would come to fruition and professional baseball would come to Keizer.

Jerry Walker and Bill Tucker would carefully note the precarious nature of the Letter of Commitment. They really had nothing strong in the way of commitment from Keizer. They would hereafter have to persuade anyone who was to be connected with the project that such a commitment was nevertheless an assurance that the project would be fairly considered and kept alive. Jerry and Bill would have to advance monies and commit their time and energies as well as personal funds to a project that might not be viable after all and everything wasted. With faith in the people of Keizer who had responded so well to the idea of the franchise relocating there and who supported the proposed project, they went forward as if unaffected by the Council split that hung on the strength of a majority of one.

Financing would be difficult under those circumstances. There was another public meeting scheduled for October and even then , if passed, there would be more obstacles to overcome. And the long and arduous process of the architecture of the stadium, the obtaining of cost estimates for construction, the construction process itself and all things in between lay still ahead. The Council issues were only about the City's end of the project. There was still the issue of financing construction of the stadium itself, either through personal funds or through institutional financing which was preferred.

And then, there was the ever-present time pressure. Counting from the September Council meeting, there were almost exactly nine months to Opening Day. If one viewed the situation from that moment, and was aware of all the things yet to be achieved once the political process was completed (and it was not yet completed) and the weather history of the area over which we had no control, you would have to conclude something more than a miracle was needed to make Opening Day on time. The outlook was formidable, but still achievable. Could it be done? Would it be done? It was going to be against all odds but that is the stuff miracles are made of. With DP in our pocket, we couldn't miss.

Sheathing placed on roof of home team clubhouse building

View from home plate towards right field, note special fabric laid out as part of extensive drainage system - dugout floor has been poured

Plumbers laying pipe in frozen turf in visitors clubhouse building

View from right field towards home plate,
note extensive electrical towers which dwarfed site

Progress, progress, progress

Finally, the seating begins to arrive

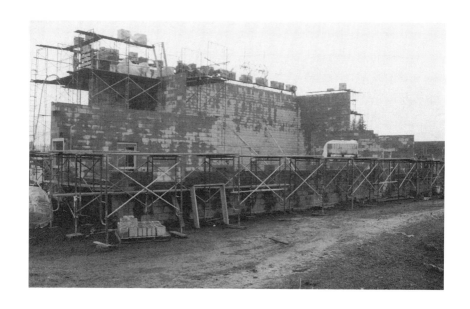

The walls get higher

Progress inside the clubhouses

Making progress on the building

Progress on the outer wall

Framing for the seating and the dugout in place

Even the visitor's dugout got attention

The entire field is graded and the clubhouse is under way

Framing out

Dugout framing in place - ready to pour concrete

View from air taken in April, 1997 - two months remained until opener
with lots to do

# CHAPTER EIGHT: BATTER UP

Ticket reservations kept flowing in demonstrating what the concerned public felt on the issue. The firm of Johnson and Lien along with Dotty Tryk got busy on putting a draft of the lease together . That was intended to and did accelerate the lease agreement process in order to precipitate a final review by the Council. They were armed with notes on the full discussion before the Council and tried to address every single concern expressed at the last meeting . It was hoped that by meeting every such issue head-on, they could resolve any major lingering doubts about the propriety of the project from a public spending point of view and obtain the approval of a broader majority, if not a unanimous one.

In public pronouncements it was clear this stadium and team with its current owners were dedicated to family entertainment connected with baseball. Lisa Walker was quoted as saying: "It's a vital element to take care of the people that take care of us. The way we do that is by providing them with entertainment. When they come to the ballpark feeling they just spent the best $7 they've ever spent, they'll keep coming back. It's important for us to invest in them." It was certainly exciting times for the community in general and they made their feelings very public.

The team was true to its word. Arrangements made or then in the making would include The Blues Brothers, Sport (formerly the Phillie Phanatic), the Colorado Silver Bullets and Myron Noodleman. No Captain Dynamite though.

Best of all was The Famous Chicken originally known as the San Diego Chicken. He came at a steep price, but was well worth the investment. He is a class guy and a big league act. "The Chicken and I are going round and round on dates, but the Chicken will be there come hell or high water" Lisa promised. "Often times when the popularity grows, the demand grows with them. But he's a super guy to work with and a super act. Ultimately it's always worth the money spent. He's faithful to his followers. He will sign every person's autograph." And he does.

Jerry and Lisa were dedicated to the program. "It's real important the first year out of the gate to have some good stuff on our agenda. Some fans want to be focused just on baseball. But my feeling is most fans want to be entertained," Lisa said.

The objective was to offer a variety of programs. There would be nightly promotions, such as base races which feature children driving electric cars from first base around second base to the left field foul line. Giveaway nights would include bat night, ball night and others. Walker and Tucker understood they were in the business of entertainment and reacted accordingly. Promotions and entertainment were constants and fans would be given their money's worth regardless of what the team did on the field. We couldn't control the players or whether we won or not but we could provide an interesting and entertaining evening for our fans.

The Statesman Journal was having a field day every day and kept the stadium issue well before the people. It was the predictable result of a free press doing its job well. The paper set forth the issues succinctly and informed the citizens of what was before them, what lay in store for them and the possibilities of what would happen if the project were built and the team failed. As it laid out the deal, the key elements were detailed as:

(1) The City would buy 20 acres (actually 30) north of Tepper Lane just west of I-5 for a 4400 seat stadium and a 1500 space parking lot.

(2) The City would pay for water and sewer lines and the parking lot. It would also pay to relocate part of Radiant drive and repave it to provide easy stadium access.

(3) The cap on City spending was $2.995 million on land and the improvements stated before. Any additional costs would have to be borne by the team owners who would also foot the entire bill for construction of the stadium.

(4) The stadium would cost at least an estimated $2 million.

(5) The team would have a 29 year lease on the stadium site and an eight year renewal option.

(6) The City gets 5% of the gross ticket receipts for all baseball games and team promoted events.

(7) The stadium would be available 30 days annually for youth sports and other community events.

(8) Tepper Lane would be closed to stadium traffic. (Tepper is the street leading west into the Gubser neighborhood.)

(9) Stadium concerts would be limited to five each year, excluding school band and choir events .

It was as close an enumeration of the conditions as one could get at that time. It was a lease proposal that reflected the concerns of the City fathers, all of them, to protect the City's investment. "The team can't pull out." Mayor Koho said. "We're able to enforce the full value of the lease. If they wanted to buy out the lease and pay us the millions,...we'd have the stadium and all the money back earlier. Regardless of what happens, we still own the land and have the infrastructure."

Koho felt that the location of the land provided for constant increases in value. That only increases the City's security. Councilor McGee acknowledged that. "If it goes sour, we can sell the land at any time and break even" he said.

It was noted that the City had planned long before the stadium idea came up to bring water and sewer lines to a parcel about 100 acres near I-5 which had been earmarked for commercial development. This had been named the "Chemawa Activity Center." "The stadium project simply makes it happen earlier." Koho said. Few if anyone pointed out the parcel on which the stadium was to be built had little developmental value or promise other than for a stadium.

"One of our basic goals  is to give that area a boost, and development will come in faster now." Dotty Tryk pointed out. She said that thus far the City's share of the project was running about $125,000 below budget.  The stadium is expected to have a net worth of about $6 million to the City when the lease runs out and it becomes City property. Tryk estimated the City's share of ticket revenues and parking would   be about $70,000 per year.

One or more of the Councilors  took issue with that.  Those that did  felt the estimates would never be attained. But Tryk insisted the revenue projections were conservative. "It's not a lot of money but we'll still have money at the end of the year." she said.

In the meantime, since everything was working on all fronts simultaneously, the team signed promoter Ken Wilson, flush from his success in Boise, Idaho with the Hawks. He would invigorate the marketing element of the push for the team's acceptance by the City He hyped the growing demand for ticket reservations. By October 12, seat reservations had reached 790 and climbing. There were 15 companies vying for the 13 skyboxes at the stadium which had not yet gotten the green light.

The team also announced it had signed a contract with local radio station KYKN to do every game, home and away, on a live basis. That was a "big-league" minor league element.

Jerry sponsored a support meeting at the Town and Country Lanes on the Saturday before the ominous council meeting of October 14. He drew about 40 or so enthusiastic supporters who would make their opinions known to the Council members. That was the operation run by John Preston, an active member and future president of the Keizer Chamber of Commerce. He was very supportive during the process and continued to be so after the stadium was approved, built and occupied.

Another stalwart and enthusiastic supporter was Mike McClaran, Executive Director of the Salem Chamber of Commerce. He had been extremely helpful from the very beginning, when it was really just a dream, in identifying local banking institutions who might make the loan, locating support for the team and in every possible way. He ran several support meetings at which he served refreshments and introduced Jerry to the community leaders. Jerry would then make what has become for each of the owners a patented speech which ran the entire length of our association, from their first meeting to buying the Bellingham franchise.

Everything pointed to the upcoming meeting on October 14 which was expected to be dramatic. The Statesman Journal had aired the issues and the positions of the various Council members as well as the public. Ticket reservations continued to pour in and nickname suggestions came in abundance. It was obvious the public stood in favor of the proposal. Would the Council feel the same way? At least at the very beginning, at the time of the first press conference, every Councilor had voted in favor of the project by voting to refer the matter to their staff professionals to develop the information needed for consideration. It was a preliminary vote, probably meaningless in the long run, but a vote in favor nevertheless. That unanimity was destined to fade but for the moment it gave major encouragement to the owners.

October 14 dawned brightly and for all practical purposes was a day you wanted to be alive. For Jerry and Lisa Walker, and to some extent to Bill and Dolores Tucker because they were miles away, it was a day of great expectations, fraught with danger over a negative vote of the Council. There was no more politicking to be done. Now it would all be up to the seven Council members to decide whether professional baseball would return to the Salem area, but located in Keizer, or whether the team would relocate elsewhere. That could be attributable to either    a negative vote or    because the conditions under which the item passed were too oppressive.

The City of Keizer was being asked to put up $2.995 million to build the infrastructure to the stadium and whatever future development came to the area. The sum was not being asked of them for the stadium alone. Noone on the negative side seemed to have any faith in the possible additional development at the site.

When analyzed, one could see the proposal involved an approximate expenditure of $159.00 per person in Keizer to construct the infrastructure for the entire Activity Center, not the stadium. That cost was to be spread over 20 to 25 years, or about $7.50 per person per year. Even that was not an immediate out-of-pocket expense. It would be paid by a stretchout of the bond repayment period. It was certainly an investment in their present lives. But it was also an investment in their future, to stir other development at the Chemawa Activity Center which they so badly wanted to provide additional tax revenues from non-residential sources.

On the other hand, Jerry Walker and Bill Tucker were willingly obligating themselves to put in $2.5 million of their own personal funds, or $1,250,000 each out of their own individual pockets.. Their contribution was to be put in up front , immediately, and entirely lost if the venture went bad. The City at least had the collateral to rely on if the team went sour. That alone would be worth its investment, especially after the stadium improvement was completed since the stadium would be forfeited to the City if a default occurred.

There was clearly an imbalance in the risk which should have been easily recognized and appreciated.

The meeting opened promptly at 7:01 P.M. It would prove to be the longest meeting in the history of the Keizer City Council, not adjourning until 3:27A.M. on the morning of October 15. There were a few other items on the agenda besides the stadium proposal but they were disposed of with reasonable dispatch. Several people did offer their opinions on the Chemawa Activity Center, but that issue was truly intertwined with the stadium issue and seemed to resolve within that larger matter.

Besides the full City Council of which there were seven members including the Mayor, the staff was also present. Some of them were from Dotty Tryk's committee but she was not there, having been out of town for a previously scheduled event. Representing the committee were John Morgan, the Community Development Director, Bill Peterson, the City Engineer and the attorneys--John Lien and Shannon Johnson. They would carry the ball at this all-important meeting for the stadium project. Any negative vote at any time would kill the project. It had to survive EVERY vote whereas the opponents just had to muster a majority on any one vote.

The meeting , when it reached the stadium issue, was heavily debated. Some of it focused on the general opposition to the stadium idea, some to the propriety of spending public funds for an enterprise that was at least partially private, and a good deal of time was spent on the terms and conditions of the lease to be concluded. It was clearly the Council's responsibility to go over and negotiate the lease terms and be satisfied with the conditions imposed to ensure compliance by all parties, especially the team, with the terms and conditions arrived at. And they discharged their responsibility faithfully.

The Statesman Journal would say "Much of the meeting had little to do with baseball, some to do with legal technicalities and a lot to do with politics." But nobody on the team side ever believed the opposition was politically motivated. It was almost entirely a good faith belief that public monies should not be used that way or that they didn't want to be rushed into a hasty decision of such magnitude as the expenditure represented for that City.

Neither did anyone on the team's side ever question Jerry McGee's good faith in his position or that it was one of principle. He was not against professional baseball coming to the City, he only opposed the City financing it.

In fact, following the meeting, he made a compromise proposal to Jerry Walker which would have the team purchase the land from the City over a period of 10 years starting with the eleventh year of use of the stadium by the team. Coming as it did in the shadow of the Council vote following such a hard battle, it may not have received as serious consideration as perhaps it should have.

29 of the 33 votes taken that evening were either unanimous or by consensus. By far the vast majority of action taken was by consensus. It was apparent that safety of the City's investment and the propriety of making the investment of this type were the paramount issues.

All the Council members participated over the entire meeting. At times it seemed as if the purpose of suggesting different lease terms was to make them as onerous as possible. Changes were made and the elements of the deal that had been agreed upon with the committee were cast aside and new elements imposed. However, it must be remembered, the project was probably the largest expenditure the City had made to date, and it was being very fast tracked for a private entity to meet that entity's deadline. That alone could create a degree of uncertainty and concern to do the right thing for the City within the short time allowed to do it.

Jerry McGee was by far the most active of the Council members. He spoke at least 39 times on just about every issue that was raised by any member. His comments ran the gamut from performance bonds to the almost constant theme of identity and the desire for Keizer to be first, or alone, in the team name. The latter was a point of pride with him and it did not seem to matter that Keizer alone would not have attracted the team's interest or that it did not even enter into the league's study of possible sites.

In the end , Councilors Carl Beach and Jim Keller, who earlier had opposed the project, switched their votes and voted in favor alongside Mayor Koho, Al Miller, Bob Newton, and Jerry Watson. There was only one negative vote registered on Mayor Koho's motion. The motion directed the City to enter into the agreement with the team for the lease as amended during the evening's discussion subject to the fulfillment of conditions precedent to the signing and effectiveness of the lease.

The motion was seconded by Councilman Al Miller who confirmed the resolution would preclude any further changes in the lease document. However, by consensus the Council immediately amended the Koho motion to include terms to provide for a review at intervals to judge the performance of the parties to the lease and how the terms are working. The motion passed 6 to 1. While it would seem as if the lease issue had been resolved, the facts would turn out to be otherwise.

Nevertheless, at the time, the parties were exhausted and tired of the entire issue. They exited the Council chambers and went quietly into the fading darkness as rays of light from the east were beginning to penetrate the valley. To those still present, John Morgan announced "We're playing ball" The Statesman Journal headline blared "Council tells team: Lets Play Ball."

It had been the longest Council meeting on record. The proposal had ignited probably the hottest public debate in the 15 year history of the City. The political saga seemed ended with the 6-1 vote to commit urban renewal money in furtherance of the project. The Statesman Journal said: "That's a major step for Keizer, a City where providing no-frills government long has been a point of pride."

Several people in the audience had tried to voice their opposition but were not permitted to do so. "I recognize people have strong feelings... but you elected us to do a job." Mayor Koho had said. Jerry Walker had tried to muster support too at the meeting, distributing placards supporting baseball and presenting to the Council petitions in support of the proposal containing 500 signatures. Intended as a final comment on the events, Mayor Koho said" I think the stadium will prove itself. In two years we will look back and see we did the right thing."

The Walkers who had sat through that difficult evening as others were deciding the team's fate, were happy with the results. Their plans could go forward further yet and they could continue to build on the warm reception they had received from the general public.

In reality, it was an outstanding night for Keizer too. It would begin the journey to true identity from that day forward. The stadium and the team would truly be a major credit to the City and the Council and it would establish the legacy of the Koho Administration and of Dotty Tryk, the City Manager.

After a brief respite and long sigh of relief, the Walkers now had to swing into action very quickly. On that October 15,1996 the team stood almost exactly 8 months from opening day 1997. They had a few things to do, such as get plans drawn for a baseball stadium by architects who had little experience in that field, get bids for the construction of the stadium from contractors who had never built a baseball stadium and finance the construction with a lender that had never financed a baseball field before. All this by owners who had never built a stadium before either. And they still had to finalize the lease and get the bond resolution passed and the bonds sold, and survive a final review by the City Council. Could all that be done within that time? "Absolutely," Jerry said.

All the while thereafter , issues related to the stadium would continue to percolate. The Council on October 21  was being asked to pass what was felt to be a houskeeping resolution. For technical reasons, the Oregon Department of Transportation felt that at this late date it was not appropriate to include the stadium site in the Chemawa Acticvity Center Plan. Actually it had only been inserted into the draft of the Plan and not adopted into the Plan itself although the draft had been approved. In effect they were being asked to rescind that approval.

Even there , the opposition sought to delay the action until a later date and, as you know by now, delay was fatal to the project. After the notice was given to Bellingham, delay could possibly have meant disaster. The Councilors didn't seem to realize that failure to adopt the recission of the draft would endanger the success of the Plan but would not really affect the stadium proposal. It was adopted, but not without some tense moments. The worse thing was it gave another opportunity for the opposition to coalesce. The opposition was steadfast it seemed.

On October 16, the day after the momentous Council meeting, the Bellingham Herald broke the story up there. Byron Elmendorf was quoted as saying that the City might end the deal before Jerry Walker did. However, he also said he would wait to hear from the Giants, stating:" I don't know anyone who wants it (Joe Martin Field) so I don't see any reason to move forward and terminate Jerry's deal."

In the meantime the City readied itself for the condemnation proceeding to come as the taking of the properties was a necessary prelude to any construction the City would undertake at the site.

At the November 4,1996 meeting, the Council again got into the issue of the stadium approval. This time, the issue was raised by Councilman Keller who wanted specific clarification of the financial cap on the City's obligation. The debate was shortlived but it reflected the continued uneasiness members of the Council still felt with the stadium issue. Councilor McGee twice reminded the Council in ominous terms that all the issues in the stadium question would come up for debate and decision at a meeting prior to December 31$^{st}$ and should be gone into then. Could they still pull back? What would the owners do then?

That possibility was confirmed by attorney Johnson at the November 18 Council meeting. There was an interchange between the members over retaining the $2.95 million cap in the body of the lease agreement. Councilor McGee felt it expressed the Council's commitment to the community to limit the expenditure of public funds to that level. Councilor Keller indicated he would continue to support the lease agreement with the included section (the cap) on the expenditure limit. The Council confirmed the prior determination to include the cap in the body of the lease and a motion to that effect was adopted. Councilor Keller repeated his expression of support in an unrelated discussion on whether lottery funds would be received for the project. In the last analysis, however, when the last vote was taken with everything on the line, cap included, he would vote against it.

And so the beat went on.

# CHAPTER NINE: YA GOTTA HAVE FAITH

In the meantime, Jerry Walker and Bill Tucker began the process of financing their end of the bargain and having architectural plans drawn for the final layout. Jerry contacted the people at U.S. Bank. A contact had been established through Bill's connections to Manufacturer's Hanover Bank in Brooklyn. The Salem-Keizer project now had national scope and crossed the country in an effort to put the deal together. Through Ken Keller, we were put in touch with the Salem correspondent bankers and eventually with John Burrell III.

This was a difficult process for the Bank. The team was moving from a locale where they had experienced declining attendance. It was also coming into a City where a similar team in the same league had actually failed in the recent past and had to be sold and relocated. It was no comfort to the bankers that there was appropriate justification for that team's failure. They knew little had been spent on public relations and promotions, and they knew the facilities were inadequate to say the least and generally fan unfriendly. It was difficult for them to project the possible success of a new team being relocated there, even to a new facility that would be constructed with both public and private monies.

John Burrell was on our side but our lack of a good track record, or any at all in Salem-Keizer, was a difficult factor for us to overcome, even though John tried mightily to do it. He used considerable imagination in trying to work out solutions but for one reason or another they were either not palatable to us or not possible of full achievement. We felt the higher-ups were just not sufficiently comfortable with the entire idea.

The Bank had absolutely no experience with financing baseball or other sports franchises. Our idea was that we were marketing a stream of income similar to a revenue stream common to public offerings of bonds. We had no history on which they could rely but projections based on new stadia around the country indicated the reality of such projections. That fact, combined with the area's population growth and better than Bellingham per capita income, we thought, should have been sufficiently convincing.

But it wasn't. We spent considerable of our valuable and short time trying to convince the Bank of the quality of their loan should they choose to make it. Many documents such as personal financial statements and revenue statements from the Bellingham enterprise and general data around minor league baseball were presented to reinforce our position.

Patiently, Jerry and Bill kept trying to hurdle the financial roadblocks constantly coming up. It was difficult and almost impossible to comprehend but one had to appreciate the rarity of being asked to finance such an enterprise, especially one that was not robust in its present home and recognized that fact itself, and was coming to an area where baseball franchise failure had been the recent watchword. The Bank never really examined it as a community oriented project and viewed it entirely as a straightforward loan application. Nothing inappropriate, but no flexibility either.

The Bank was not really progressing with the loan approval. Jerry and Bill were concerned that at any time, the Council or the newspaper would begin to question whether the owners could keep their financial end of the bargain. As the franchise floundered without a permanent home or a ballpark to play in, the owners began to fret about the disastrous possibilities that faced them.

It was always possible for them to personally finance the stadium from their own assets. However, that necessitated the liquidation of many assets which would create a huge tax burden. Furthermore, to prove their ability to do so they may have to reveal many personal financial details they were reluctant to do. Nevertheless they were determined to build the stadium, with their own funds if necessary, but they did need help from the City or the Bank, depending on which scenario came into play. They could not entirely finance the project, land, infrastructure and all.

Jerry and Bill kept trying to convince the bankers that the loan was a good investment. There were several layers of approval needed within the bank's procedures. It seemed as if additional requirements were being added at every turn. The owners began to despair of even getting the loan from the bank after the investment of so much time. They began to think of alternatives, none of which would be totally feasible but could be lived with at least temporarily. They could refinance after they established a track record in Keizer.

Through some help from Dan Cardone of the Broadway National Bank in New York, Bill was told of the possibility of the Small Business Administration ("SBA") of the federal government helping out with a federal guarantee. We were able to contact John Safstrom, the person who ran the SBA office in Salem. He was very helpful and enthusiastic. He wanted to do the deal and would do everything he could to make it happen.

As a quasi-governmental agency, it had a reputation for not being very fast on things. However, he got the enterprise into gear and turned things around quickly. The SBA was proposing to provide a federal guaranty of 90% of a loan that any bank they worked with would make. They were very familiar with US Bank and had no problem with doing this transaction with them. The federal guaranty would make the loan less risky in appearance to US Bank and quiet some of their concerns about investing in that type of project. If the loan defaulted, the government would repay 90% of the outstanding loan balance to US Bank which would thus only have a 10% stake. The SBA would get the collateral though.

Despite everything, it began to appear as if the Bank alone, or in concert with the SBA, would never be able to act in time for us. However, we continued to push on both types of loan in the hope that one of them would break ahead from the pack. Everyone working on the loan at either end, the Bank or the SBA, were trying to be as helpful as they could. We were feeling the stress of the pressure to get the financing in place so were probably not as congenial as we could be. We were impatient, but we had cause to be.

That's the way things stood that Wednesday afternoon, October 2,1996, another one of those unforgettable dates. Jerry was sitting in his office on River Road in Keizer. The day was day was uneventful, filled with telephone calls on seat reservations  and the usual public promotion of the entire project, enlisting fan support.  Therefore, the call from the Faith Foundation truly came out of the blue.

The call was from Dan Kerr, the Executive Director of  the Faith Foundation, a  small private foundation created by one Richard Faith, a local citizen who had prospered and was seeking ways to "give something back"  He had many outlets for his charitable interests so  there was no lack of recipients. Dan told Jerry he had been following the saga of our team in the paper and was interested in our plight.  He explained how the Foundation had been formed with its objective to assist in worthwhile activities in the community.  The Foundation had ample assets, kept a low profile and wanted no publicity.  It almost seemed like the "Millionaire" story from television.  It was actually DP at work--again.

It did seem too good to be true.  Naturally, Jerry was skeptical and asked questions about how quickly they could act because time was of the essence.  Having gone down many blind alleys before, Jerry didn't even tell Bill just then about that development.   One of his questions to Dan Kerr was how complex would be the decision to make the loan and how long would it take.

Dan said the entire thing was really up to Mr. Faith.  If it was the type of thing he wanted to do, with sufficient community benefit and involvement of the younger generation, it could be done quickly.  Once Mr. Faith approved participation by the Foundation, a comittment would follow in only a matter of days.  It was an essential ingredient that Jerry meet with Mr.

Faith to tell him personally about the project, its objectives and what it meant to the community.

It was easy to see the approval process would not take long once Mr.Faith approved. Time was of the essence as to every step of the project even though final approval of the City Council of Keizer was still yet to be achieved. Jerry had to be continually moving on all fronts simultaneously and on the basis that all the necessary approvals and preconditions as to every aspect would come through timely .

From that first conversation with Jerry, Dan Kerr tried constantly to connect with Richard Faith. It was difficult to reach Mr. Faith. Dan kept Jerry apprised of his efforts so as not to create any doubt in Jerry's mind that the Foundation and its prospective loan were for real. Finally, on October 7th, Dan called to say he had reached him and for Jerry to call him directly.

Jerry got right on it. He reached him on Tuesday the 8th in the afternoon and the conversation was long and informative. Richard Faith was not really a baseball man or fan and didn't appreciate the attraction of the game for spectators. However, he recognized its popularity  but felt there were probably many other ways to use the Foundation's money better.   Jerry offered to visit with him and to explain the project in more detail  but Faith did not seem interested.

When Jerry started to thank him for his time on the phone, since he felt the conversation was not heading anywhere, Faith suggested they do arrange the visit to give Jerry the opportunity to explain it in person. Still thinking the loan was going to go nowhere, but feeling he had nothing to lose but his time, Jerry began putting a package together with all the information one could possibly want and which was available at that time.

The big meeting took place on October 9th. Dan Kerr was also present. Jerry went through the entire scenario , in more detail this time. He explained the waning attendance problem in Bellingham and how the City fathers there did not want to put any money into the stadium and how badly that ballpark needed improvement. We didn't really fail there but prosperity was not around the corner either.

It was a lengthy meeting. Faith was concerned about what would happen if there were a default. He did not want the Foundation owning a stadium or being in the baseball business. He inquired about the parameters planned for the stadium and the method and timing of construction.

Faith seemed happy both local architects and contractors were to be involved. He was obviously a man of high intelligence with an inquisitive mind. He asked very probing and absolutely correct questions which Jerry was able to answer. Finally, he seemed satisfied he had gotten all the information he needed. He said that if this was something he wanted to do, he would have his attorney prepare a loan commitment within a few days. The funds were available to close the loan if he decided to go ahead. He had a few ideas he wanted to explore first. He seemed to imply we would get the loan.

Jerry and Lisa left, cautiously optimistic now. To their surprise, they received a call from Dan Kerr the very next day telling them that Faith was indeed interested and would make the loan. Dan said they would receive a letter of commitment by that Friday, the 12th. Somehow it seemed unbelievable and almost too easy. They waited anxiously for the letter to come-- and it arrived--on time. It was everything we hoped for. DP?

That was a huge relief. Although the bank and the SBA were grinding forward to what would be a positive result, it was an arduous road to travel, and it may not arrive on time. Then one had to worry about the loan closing and whether that could be done on schedule given the length of time the loan was in process.

Now that didn't matter. The Faith Foundation would make the loan. There were two major conditions. Nobody was to know of the Foundation's involvement. Faith was a man who did not seek publicity and he did his good works almost in obscurity. He was a very private person.

We tried mightily to respect his wishes on privacy. However, the ballpark was a public issue now and the press hovered around almost constantly. They knew the public was vitally interested in our ability to finance our end of the bargain and reported regularly on what they knew of our financing status. Eventually the item had to become public because documents for the loan would have to be recorded and registered and certain taxes paid on the transaction. So it was inevitable.

The news actually did not get out until the closing took place. Despite everything, especially the inquisitive press which was friendly to us, we were able to protect the Foundation's privacy wishes up to the last minute. When it did come out, the news was very favorable.

On January 5,1997, the week before the groundbreaking, the Statesman Journal broke the news with a headline which read:"Charitable Loan Builds Stadium." The article was very favorable and contained some very nice statements about the Foundation and its good works.

For the first time, many people heard of the Foundation, Richard Faith and the Foundation's quiet good works in promoting youth activities and community events. The Foundation, organized in 1993, had quietly made numerous grants to several area charities and organizations. Everything done was done without fanfare or recognition. In a way, it was good to have some news come out about the Foundation even if it was not seeking publicity.

Naturally, the papers were interested in how the talks for the stadium loan got started. Dan Kerr was up front with them. He stated he had contacted Jerry when he learned of our fiscal plight and appreciated the community benefit in bringing our stadium to fruition. It was the type of thing the Foundation wanted to be connected with and they aggressively pursued it and deserve public credit for doing so.

The second condition to the loan being made involved Jerry's real estate assets. Faith insisted on getting a security interest in all the real estate assets Jerry and Lisa owned just to make sure he did not have to operate a ballpark if the loan defaulted. Dan Kerr actually drove up to Washington to evaluate them. He had no interest in New York properties.

To Jerry and Bill, it was a Godsend. It came at just the right juncture in the approval-construction process and put our minds at ease on a major element to ensure our success. Now we could concentrate on the other phases of the process without concern over being able to fund the major part of our contribution. The loan comittment did require us to personally put  substantial equity money into the project but the largest amount of the funds needed  was taken care of with the loan. We needed all the time we could get to concentrate our efforts on the still open elements of the transaction.

So the financing was done.

May 17, 1997 - 35 days to Opening Day - still grading

Grading the left field berm

187

The playing field has grown in well

And already requires maintenance

The scoreboard is finally in - and working

View from above - note absence of parking lot paving and lighting
Cabbage patch is in bloom

Another sky view - the little house at the top of the photo, above the cabbage patch, is where temporary office was

Parking lot paving and striping completed June 9, 1997 -
13 days to Opener

190

The reserved seats in place down the first base line

Framing for the box seats in place and sky boxes progress

The main structure and sky boxes are up-concrete next

Workers pour and "float" the concrete concourse

The scoreboard going in - June 7, 1997 - 15 days to Opener

The right field sign announces "The Volcanoes Are Here!"

June 12th, ten days to the Opener, and lighting is starting to be installed
Installation was completed the day before Opening Day

Voila!  Construction substantially complete - on time
The Miracle on I-5 has taken place

# CHAPTER TEN: THREE CHEERS FOR THE HOME TEAM

The architectural rendering that had been made and presented before the City Council for the September meeting was the conceptual owner's dream of what they wanted. Now, it was the responsibility of everyone involved to bring that into a draftsman's reality. Budgetary concerns were naturally paramount. Only a finite amount of money was available to be spent willingly on the enterprise and the ballpark with all the desired amenities had to be brought in within that parameter. It was to prove a tough chore.

The team wanted to use local personnel wherever possible. It was for that reason mainly that they had gravitated to the Arbuckle, Costic architectural firm. Alan Costic was impressive and conveyed his interest in landing the job for the firm at the outset so no other firms were seriously considered. The Arbuckle firm delivered on time with the initial round of drawings.

Typical of large firms, Arbuckle, Costic assigned the task to Dean Christy, a young associate in the office. There was some concern about that since he was relatively new to the firm and to the architectural vocation but seemed knowledgeable. He broke the drawings down into form to make the first round of bid solicitation and the project took a quantum leap forward.

Similar local preferences made the owners gravitate to the Cory Redding contracting firm. Well established in the area it was an aggressive team run by young, aggressive proprietors. They seemed a perfect fit from age, demeanor and willingness to accomplish everything and seemed to have a good sense of the urgency of time and the scarcity of money. They would win the job as general contractor. They would bid out the job in several segments to subcontractors but they would remain responsible and monitor the subcontractors as work progressed. They would participate in the bidding process although it would actually be controlled by the Arbuckle,Costic firm.

Architect Alan Costic of the Arbuckle, Costic firm had drawn the rendering that had been submitted to the City Council in September. Now his firm had to flesh out that rendering into an actual stadium, measuring and plotting out everything so the parts all fit together.

Construction was planned to go forward on several fronts simultaneously so the pieces had to be jigsawed correctly so that at the end the puzzle could be constructed. There was a time line and a monetary limit, both of which had to be respected. Then, there was still the problem of Measure 47 and the deadline it imposed for the sale and issuance of the bonds. These items were now entirely in the hands of others.

Jerry met with the architects constantly as the drawings began to take shape. The "dream" stadium had all the bells and whistles one could expect. As the construction numbers began to squeeze the available funds, it became necessary to make adjustments here and there but essentially the dream came out alive. Neither Jerry nor Bill wanted to sacrifice on the expected amenities. They wanted to build a stadium to be proud of and to make the City proud of having made the decision in their favor.

The first cut of the drawings for the construction of the stadium was ready in early November. The Arbuckle firm had worked diligently to provide plans at the earliest possible date so that the bidding process could begin. Time was getting as short as money and every day counted and had to be used properly.

Now, with no final commitment from the City yet, with no financial support yet from the local bank, the project was let out for the first bids. The first round of bids in any construction project is almost always a "best estimate" by the subcontractor. There are usually many questions to be clarified between the plans as submitted and the subcontractor's understanding as gleaned from the plans. They are usually somewhat close and some are very accurate. For this reason, Dean Christy had drawn a 200 and 100 level set of drawings.

The first bids confirmed Jerry's and Bill's worse fears-the 200 level plans could not be achieved. Dean took off on a trip to visit other stadia in the area to determine where "value engineering" could be applied in the most effective way with as little impact on the 200 level as possible. It would prove to be time well spent.

The first bids were really out of sight. They were almost double what funds we had available above the loan amount. However, the first set of plans were really a dream stadium. They had a second level of seating that ringed the infield and extended out down each foul line. There was a restaurant and amenities some new major league stadia would envy. We were hoping against hope that would not happen but were truly not surprised when it did. We did not really want to run a restaurant either.

The value engineering ( a/k/a "cutting costs") almost immediately eliminated that second deck or tier of seats. However the skyboxes remained as part of the plans even though they were scaled back somewhat. The same number, 13, were included. We insisted on that amenity.

Construction of the second ring of seating involved a considerable amount of above ground level construction. As a result, it was quite expensive in and of itself. With that eliminated, we were essentially within range of the 100 set of drawings with a few changes here and there. We insisted on keeping the elevator as a symbol of our intention to construct a state of the art facility to the extent possible. It now leads from the field level seating to the skyboxes as conceived and may be the only elevator in our league and possibly in the stadium of any A-level team anywhere.

If we could get the plans as set forth in the revised drawings at our price, it would be something to be proud of. However, the contractors' bids still came in above the level we were hoping for on the second round and we had to really think long and hard about what could be done to make it work within our bounds.

From the beginning we were very much concerned about "extras" which would come up after the bids were accepted and construction was under way or nearly complete. It seems to happen often in construction projects and sometimes can put the owners behind the eightball. When an extra occurs, the contractor usually says it was something that was omitted from the bidding plans or so unclear as to allow for a wrong interpretation or was a change from the original plans. The theory is that such things were not included in the original bidding process and courts look with  favor on  the bidding contractor. So you have to pay.

At all times, we kept the emphasis on the shortage of additional monies and the need to avoid such "extras." We wanted a guaranteed cost contract but it was not to be. If we had had time to shop around or could have shopped it to different contractor organizations we might have been able to better both the numbers and a few other things. However, we were committed to using local people and by that determination limited our choices and our scope of price opportunity. It is always better to have the widest possible choice but we were willing to stand by our determination, and did.

Working with the contractors to hammer on their prices was no joy. It was difficult work since they did not want to underbid and then come out on the short end themselves. We didn't want that either since many of them file bankruptcy which can stall a project for a long time and still end up unfavorably. The bankruptcy rules are very owner unfriendly and getting unfriendlier all the time. We wanted the project to be a joy for everyone anyway, so we didn't want any one contractor to just come out even or below. We had learned from Don Porter, if not from our own experience, that "profit is not a four-letter word."

We had planned red theatre seating for the box seats, with just a little narrower theatre seat for the reserved seats, but in orange. In the redraft of the plans, we had to go to bench seats for the reserved seating, but with seatbacks. It was still a good arrangement for the fan but not exactly the grand style impact we wanted to make. That was to be one of the changes we had to accept but it was not a huge concession. The strange part is that both the architect and the contractor were constantly telling us our expectations were not out of line. They reaffirmed regularly that our budget should be adequate, but in the end the concessions we made to price were what brought the ballpark to fruition.

In the long run, however, their affirmations and our expectations were wrong. We eventually had to resort to removing several large items from the overall cost and leasing them. This has become virtually a customary process in construction projects nowadays. That procedure allows you to lower the overall cost of the project by removing the cost of large items from the cost by arranging a lease of them. It does reduce the construction cost but then impacts cash flow as you have to make regular payments on the leases until they are fully paid. Jerry and Bill felt they could handle the lease payment as they went forward, out of their own pockets if necessary. They were really committed to this stadium, now, in Keizer.

Leases require a financial inquiry all their own since they are in effect a borrowing of some sort so they take time to exchange all the necessary papers. All suppliers and contract vendors are used to it so it moves relatively quickly. The problem is they finance the leases themselves through banks which want sufficient paper documentation as if they were loaning you the money which in reality they were. Time.

The architects, Arbuckle, Costic and the contractor, Cory Redding, were very helpful. They were totally on our side and did everything they could to get the job priced out right and built to produce something with sufficient amenities to have everyone proud of their involvement in the process. We would badly need that esprit de corps as the job went forward and they came through with flying colors.

Thus far, nobody had made any mention anywhere of the weather. It had begun to rain almost daily in Salem-Keizer and the lot on which the stadium was to be erected absorbed a vast amount of water. Rain was an almost daily occurrence now and sometimes it was a real drenching. It was if a monsoon season had begun. Jerry and Bill watched the weather reports and results daily to be able to judge just how much of a problem water runoff might become. It would be a factor.

We signed on with the Arbuckle, Costic firm officially on November 16, 1996. That date is actually misleading because they had been on the job some time already. They had prepared the rendering that was produced at the September and October Council meetings and were present at the open meeting with the citizenry at which an opportunity to speak was afforded to all those who sought it.

They had been enthusiastic about the project from the very beginning. In fact, it was that enthusiasm that suggested they be retained without any further shopping. The architects saw the project as one of huge civic benefit and realized they wanted to be involved if possible. They did considerable work, were present at the press conference and at every meeting, hearing and event from that day forward.

There is no question their professionalism contributed mightily to the stadium coming into being.  Significant too was their willingness to work for a fixed fee that was only a portion of what they would ordinarily charge .  It was their first stadium, would be a feather in their cap, and would likely , and did, lead to further sports facility business so in a way it was an investment in their future too.  The role of Arbuckle, Costic in the stadium drama cannot be overlooked or taken lightly. (The stadium design later won an architectural award .)

We did not sign on with the Cory Redding construction firm until January 10,1997.     That was four days after groundbreaking day .   While it seems late in the process looking back on it now, they were also involved much earlier. Actually, it was all Redding's tools that were used in the ceremonial groundbreaking.  They were his shovels, his rakes, his  picks and, for photo opportunity purposes, his hard hats.

Cory Redding was extremely helpful in the design,  bidding, value engineering  and rebidding procedures.  Redding himself spent considerable personal time working on details of the proposal and generally helping everything along.

It was Redding's absolute faith in the project that helped us through many down periods when the Council debates seemed to be running contrary to our expectations or hopes as well as overwhelming public opinion..  This was his first stadium too but unlike the architects, he did not look forward to additional business coming in through the stadium construction job.  He was a local contractor and would stay in the general area which would be unlikely to build many, if any, other sports complexes.

Therefore, his contribution was in its entirety a "contribution" in the fullest sense. His time was valuable and since the three ends of the equation-owner, architect and builder, were all rookies never having designed or built a stadium before , a great deal of personal time was involved. It was the relationship that sprung up between him and Jerry that kept the procedure going once construction started and had many things going on simultaneously.

We eventually got the bids within some type of acceptable cap. When it was done, all the documents were signed and the project could go forward. We geared up for a relentless vigilance on prices and extras since we had little room for error without applying some alternative methods to produce funding from our own resources. It was touch and go but Jerry with the help of Redding and their clerk of the works managed well. We were planning to put in about $400,000 of our own funds once all the "value engineering" had taken place and the costs seemed capped within acceptable limits.

At the eighth meeting of the construction team on December 30,1996, ten days before groundbreaking, the meetings monitored by Arbuckle's Dean Christy, we were hit with a staggering blow. The Gelco firm stated that it had revised its bid on excavation and site utilities. It had been increased by over $190,000. In effect it wiped out all the value engineering savings we had achieved. The basis was they had not had final or complete information at the time they formulated their original bid and we would have to accept the revised bid almost as if it were an ""extra". We now had to concentrate on the additional  funding  now required.  Bill and Jerry between them actually put in over $600,000  of personal funds to build the stadium.  You can understand their pride in the achievement.

At that meeting suggestions began to seep in about possibly postponing construction until the summer.  It would save us close to a half of a million bucks but it would mean no playing on that field in 1997.  Alternates would have to be used.  That would involve  either a temporary retreat back to Bellingham and negotiation of a one year lease and shabby fan support or go to the Chemeketa College Field which was the site of the prior franchise in Salem.

Nothing was worth trying either alternative.  Bill and Jerry had resolved to build this stadium in Keizer, now , and would see it through to the end in time for play in 1997.  It would take a miracle to retain the cap level on costs even where it now was, but we had to do it.  The entire exercise would prove to be exasperating and trying but the end was beginning to come into view then, and it looked real good.  Especially helpful through all these trying times was the fan support we were receiving.  The people in the Cities of Salem and Keizer were showing their support in many, many ways and it buoyed the spirits of Bill and Jerry throughout the ordeal.

So, here we were, over budget, with the important individuals in the construction process counseling delay, and there had not been one shovel thrust into the ground yet.  We looked forward to an experience we would long remember, but went forward bravely, with more courage and daring than intellect. It would be built and we would play Northwest League baseball there-in 1997, or bust.

# CHAPTER ELEVEN: SWING?  DECISION TIME

The most momentous decision of all still had to be made by the two team owners.  Had the City Council voted negatively, nothing much would have happened except there would be no baseball in Keizer for a long time to come.  The team would have to endure another sub-par season in Bellingham.  They could have used the following year (1997) to locate another venue and try to accomplish there what they could not get done in Keizer.  However, now they had to be sure that the stadium could be financed and built within the time allowed.  It had to be brought in within their monetary limits with little room for extras that consume vast amounts of money.  They had to be right on the amount the City had limited its investment to or pay the additional themselves.  They had to roll the dice on those decisions and come up with sevens or the consequences could be staggering.

Now they had to put their franchise and financial necks on the line.  Demonstrating faith in the City's commitment to them thus far was all-important but so was the safety and stability of the franchise.  No team could fiscally survive a nomadic existence for two or three years with uncertainty as to the final stop still in doubt.  In fact, the league would be unwise to allow it and probably would not.  So the decision to  be made by the two owners was whether to put their faith in the City fathers.  The spirit of the public debate on the issue, sometimes contentious, left room for consideration of the possibility that the enterprise might fail to gain the necessary support at the next Council meeting, or the next, or the next.

This decision had to be made privately by them. Perhaps few knew or even fewer appreciated the gravity of the decision they faced. Most people probably thought the issue had been resolved and the most important decision made, but it had not. It was a major decision to cut the ties that bound them to the City where they were ensconced and risk uncertainty as to all facets of the baseball franchise at a time when several important elements still hung in the balance.

Jerry and Bill were committed to moving the team to the Salem-Keizer area. With absolute trust in the correctness of their decision to do so and fully aware of the consequences if they failed for any reason, , they resolved to give the City of Bellingham the necessary notice to terminate their relationship. And so it was that Jerry prepared the notice to the City of Bellingham to be delivered on the 31$^{st}$ of October, 1996, the last day on which notice could be effective for that purpose. The notice read as follows:

"To  Byron Elmendorf
City of Bellingham
Department of Parks and Recreation Director

From: Jerry Walker
Sports Enterprises,Inc.
In accordance with item II.TERM: section lll (B). of the facility use agreement  between the City of Bellingham and Sports Enterprises,Inc. dba Bellingham Giants Baseball Club, the Bellingham Giants do not desire to extend the agreement through 1997 or thereafter.

We understand our current agreement will expire on December 31,1996 and we plan to remove all team property and equipment before this time.

Thank-you very much for the courtesies extended to the team during our use of the Stadium. We enjoyed our time in Bellingham and wish the City well on their future endeavors. "

It was short and only slightly sweet. They had crossed the Rubicon.

That momentous notice never really got out into the public forum in Salem-Keizer. Jerry was quoted in the Bellingham article as saying"... we're certainly not happy to leave behind the friends and relationships we built over the years. Life's full of changes. This wasn't one we were necessarily seeking out--if things had been different we might not have ever left town."

He mentioned the then overwhelming Council support in Keizer. Citing the construction deadlines, he said "We have a fast track schedule. But it's not unusual or something that hasn't been done before in the Northwest. Yakima built their new stadium in 93 days."

Bellingham's official reply was equally succinct. Two warring parties had eliminated all the possible venom from their systems and had exchanged polite correspondence over an issue that was momentous to both. It put an end to the entire fiasco but was hardly reflective of the difficulties they had endured and the hard feelings the battle had engendered.

Later historians would be confused by the friendly end to the paper trail. Byron's letter ended with the sentence " You can take pride in the growth of professional baseball in Bellingham due to your efforts. Good luck with your new stadium and program in Keizer."

Thus ended the Bellingham saga.

# CHAPTER TWELVE: HOME RUN -LEAGUE APPROVAL

While everything else was going on, Jerry had to deal with the Northwest League officials. They had a vital interest in the goings-on because schedules had to be planned and they involved some degree of travel information. In anticipation of making the move, even without Council approval yet, Jerry had formally requested permission from the League to approve the move. Jerry had always kept Bob Richmond, League president, fully up to date on developments, good or bad. Bob was always a true and fervent supporter of our making the move since he was very familiar with the Bellingham story and knew all the problems. More importantly, he also knew that franchise was about tapped out income- wise and felt there were greener pastures for us.

Shortly after the Council meeting on October 14, Jerry and Bill together felt it was time to formally approach the league for approval. After all, we were now committed to Keizer or moving the team somewhere. We were on the verge of giving the final notice to Bellingham. We had faith in our projections that to us demonstrated the stadium could be built within our budget and the team would be supported by its fans. If we had any doubts they were minimal.

The League, though, did have reservations. Not on the City or the ultimate success of the franchise but on the timing of the completion of construction and the cost. Jerry kept repeating the Yakima experience in construction both as to time and cost. It was not fully persuasive, especially since the matter was receiving such a mixed reception at the Keizer City Council

The League ,expressing their concern over the timeline for construction, requested that we come up with a contingency plan. It was even suggested that we should renew the lease in Bellingham for 1997. Then if we couldn't get the Keizer ballpark finished on time, we could play in Bellingham again. If we did get the Keizer ballpark finished by opening day l997, we could play in it and just make the lease payments to Bellingham without playing there.

Nothing doing. We were not going back to Bellingham under any circumstances. We contacted the Chemeketa College authorities. It was possible to play games there, at the same old site where the other team had failed, until the stadium in Keizer was built or a new stadium was no longer an option. We really did not want to play at Chemeketa either. It was a fallback option only.

In smaller municipalities such as Keizer, the newspapers furnished substantial informaton to the populace. In Keizer the Statesman Journal and the Times kept everyone well informed. There were hardly any secrets. They knew about the Keizer deal and all the ins and outs that had appeared so regularly in the press, and we wanted them to have the full story.

Jerry actually did call the Bellingham Parks Department anyway. They expressed a desire NOT to have us return there. They really did not want us back. They seemed relieved that pressure on the City Council to invest huge sums of money into the stadium would be eliminated if we didn't return. They said they were going forward with plans to use the stadium as it was for public sports and activities, no professional baseball. It later became clear they really wanted professional baseball but without the pressure to make stadium improvements. We weren't coming back anyway--no way.

Our application was actually made to the National Association of Professional Baseball Leagues, Inc. which is the governing body title for the minor league baseball organizations. The Giants wrote a letter of support on November 5 as part of the approval process. It was a brief three sentence letter, no frills, but it was sufficient . On November 13, the Northwest League formally gave us their written approval for the move. That phase was done.

# CHAPTER THIRTEEN: THE FINAL SWINGS

The bonds and lease still awaited final approval from the Council. Much had happened since the meeting of October 14 which had sort of rocked the boat on how different the various positions were. There was concern that they may have become polarized simply by having to defend or advocate their respective positions. However, the Council and its members, separately, were performing exemplary democratic debate and standing up to the awesome responsibilities of their elected positions.

The Councilors and the Mayor had to be truly committed people. They had to stand for public election and have parts of their private lives fully exposed by the close scrutiny of a local press searching for issues to report. None of them were paid a single cent for their work in their elected capacities. They served for really altruistic purposes , to advance the commonweal and contribute as much as they could to the development of their new City through governmental involvement and concern. None of them had any special interest axe to grind. They gave of their time and services willingly and freely, doing an elected job, no matter how difficult it may be from time to time.

The stadium issue had really brought them to the fore and reached down into their respective core of principles. Every one of them brought to their respective seats their special input from a lifetime of experiences, most of them different from each other's and all of them from very different economic backgrounds and present circumstances. This was to be a test of democracy and they were to be the actors on a public stage with their own friends, neighbors and relatives as the audience.

Each Councilor and the Mayor had a somewhat different expertise to contribute. So it was that Councilor Watson took a particularly deep interest in the wording and effect of the various clauses of the lease. The lease as submitted for consideration of the Council at the October 14 meeting, although it was not submitted for approval then, seriously bothered him. He decided to take a personal hand in the matter. He is a practicing attorney.

Still uneasy with the state of the lease wording following the October 14 meeting, Watson convened a special meeting of the City attorneys, the City Manager and the team representatives. For literally hours they pored over the various clauses of the lease, singling out specific areas to change. Not everyone agreed on the changes being proposed, particularly the team representatives, but the meeting ground forward and taxed the concentration and patience of many present.

At the end of the day, Councilor Watson seemed pleased with his efforts and what had been accomplished. As an attorney he came from an experience level in such matters above all the others except the City attorneys. Much of what he proposed was thought to be acceptable or necessary legally or was accepted by the assembled group to just close the subject and the meeting closed in that vein. He had suggested substantial revisions, many of which were adopted into the final language of the lease, so he was thought to be proud of what he accomplished. However, in the end , with the lease approval on the line, he would vote against it despite his substantial input, time and attention and revisions he had made. Go figure.

The regular Council meeting on December 2 was preceded by a meeting of the Urban Renewal Agency board which consisted of the same individuals as the Council, except Dennis Koho was the Chairman rather than the Mayor. It was expected to be a short meeting based on the 6-1 vote in favor of the stadium issue at the October 14 meeting. It was not to be so.

The Urban Renewal meeting was intended to authorize the issuance of the tax-free bonds to finance, among other things, the purchase of the properties and the cost of construction of the infrastructure for the stadium. Therefore the stadium issue was front and center in the minds of everyone present. There were some other, smaller , projects that would be deferred or eliminated to provide sufficient funds for the stadium project. That was sufficient justification for debate and concern and kept the passage of the required resolution in doubt to the end.

Dotty Tryk had anticipated the difficulty that would be encountered. With her customary preparedness, she had developed packets with information in them that would serve her well. All the questions asked that night were answerable from the packets of information . Some of the questions were very complex and required complex answers which not only had to be right, but had to be so well phrased that the answer would be understood and accepted.

This was Dotty's show and she was up to the performance. She was well prepared. She had digested the material so well that she could not only state the response but also tell the questioner where in the information packet he would find the support for her answer. Dotty knew full well that the approval had to be obtained that night, no delay. Measure 47 had passed as expected and there was only a small window of opportunity to obtain approval, get the bonds issued and then sold before Measure 47 forbid doing that. The bonds had their own deadline, irrespective of the deadline imposed by the reality of time it would take to complete stadium construction for the 1997 season.

Dotty Tryk was up to the task. She constantly pressed the theme that delay would be tantamount to voting down the stadium proposal. The decision had to be made here and now, once and for all. There could be no postponing, no footdragging, no delay. The buck stopped right there, then. It had to be faced and everyone for the proposal had to stand up and be counted or the opportunity would slip beyond redemption. If it failed of passage that night, there would be no professional baseball in Salem-Keizer in 1997 or in the forseeable future. They had to do their elected duty.

The same principles enunciated before by the several Councilors as reasons for declining the proposal were advanced again. This time they felt they had ammunition in the form of specifics in the bond proposal and a rationale for passing on the project because of its effect on other projects planned or on the future wish list. Not one of them if passed for now would not be there for future consideration. Only the ballpark fitted into the category of now or never. None of the others would impact the quality of life locally either to the extent the stadium and the availability of professional baseball would.

The proponents of the project certainly stood up for it. To the concern of whether it would prove out to be profitable for the City, Mayor Koho would reemphasize that not every thing undertaken by the City was properly expected to turn a profit. If the projections of income did not prove out, the benefits immediately and ultimately to the City would still make it worthwhile.

Al Miller stood tall in the project's favor. He pushed the arguments for proceeding and with the wisdom that evidenced his vast experience he advanced the idea that the proposed use of public funds was both proper and appropriate. He felt deeply that baseball by itself would be a good thing for the youth of the City and their families which benefit would be augmented by whatever other events were able to use the stadium facilities. And in the end, the City would own the stadium. If everyone else was unwilling to recognize that the ballpark could serve as a catalyst to bring about the development of the Chemawa Activity Center, he wasn't.

Bob Newton also clearly favored going ahead and now. His was the voice of quiet reason , calm and cool, focusing the debate on the proper foundation whenever it tended to stray. Many items floated around the hall that night and he was able to balance the equities  so that the merits of each of them would be fairly considered and assessed.   He grasped the importance of the moment to the project and the project to the City.  He had decided the benefits of the stadium outweighed all the other arguments collectively, as persuasive as they may be.  The ballpark gave the City everything it wanted.  Youth activity and role models, family life, entertainment at prices everyone could afford, grist for the mill of the media and at the same time delivered  a major push for the identity everyone was seeking.  The stadium had to be built.

Questions ran all over the lot.  There were so many, that after a short while of solid, able questions, it became apparent they would have to interrupt the meeting until later.  The regular meeting of the Council was scheduled for the evening and there were citizens present to testify and hear the debate on the published calendar events.  It would not be fair to keep them waiting.

No sooner than the regular meeting had been convened that the stadium issue came up.  Manny Martinez was back, this time claiming that the proposal for the ballpark violated the Oregon Constitution.  He quoted from Article 11, Section 9 which, he said , prohibited any county, City town or other muncipal corporation by vote of its citizens or otherwise from raising funds for or investing in any private entities.  He wanted the issue deferred until appropriate  legal opinions and answers were given.

It was not long in coming.  Shannon Johnson put the issue to rest immediately.  While he did not pretend to have researched the legal precedents on limits on spending public funds for private purposes, he did have some background on the subject.  He stated that over several decades the judicial gloss on this doctrine in Oregon had been defined broadly.  Public-private transactions were allowed and were common.  He cited the Portland Rose Garden as an example, virtually stating the examples were so common that it was beyond question anymore.

Other, more mundane issues were then taken up. There was some degree of public testimony on those subjects and they were treated with the dignity they deserved and the consideration to which they were entitled. Then, as expected, the meeting turned again to the stadium project.

This time the issue came up in connection with the map amendment proposed along with a change in zoning to allow for the site to be used for a stadium. Public testimony again cropped up, but only a few , some of them household names to some degree on the issue locally.

At the close of the public part of the meeting, the Council took on the major element of the issue. There were questions about whether the properties needed had been taken yet in condemnation and over the zoning issue. One Councilor mentioned that the zoning should be agreed to be changed back if the stadium project was not approved or could not be built. After tacit agreement to do so, Mayor Koho moved to approve the zoning amendment and Miller seconded the motion. Anticipating the issue would be moot if the Urban Renewal Bonds were not approved, Mayor Koho sought and received unanimous consent to defer debate and a vote on the motion until after the Urban Renewal meeting.

The Council then turned to some other matters under consideration. However, one could sense a level of anticipation of the debate and vote yet to come and it seemed to permeate deliberations. Everyone seemed on edge, itching to get back to the prime issue, one that involved the largest expenditure by the City in its short history. The evening was getting near midnight and people were tired, tense and concerned, but vitally interested and alive.

As the clock had  ticked close to 10PM, the Urban Renewal Agency meeting had been reconvened. It had resulted in the anticipated spirited debate. Several Councilors raised objection and several posed questions that still troubled them about the issue. There was at least one who stood on the issue of principle to not forego previously committed or planned projects to do the stadium.

There were questions of the accuracy of the projections in the spreadsheets Dotty's committee had provided. Not one of the questions or questioners were prompted by bad faith. There were principles involved that some felt overrode any possible public benefit to be derived from quality of life improvements or anything else the stadium would generate. The pride in the City identity did not seem to arise according to the minutes.

Dotty Tryk was masterful. The stadium would be the legacy of her and Mayor Koho to the City for at least  half a century. She would not be denied. She met every challenge with sharp, well thought-out answers and responded quickly showing her complete grasp of the entire issue which had many facets. From the less tangible benefits of professional baseball to everyone, to the precise statutory condemnation procedures, to the menacing prohibitions of Measure 47, to the construction of the infrastructure and of the stadium itself, she demonstrated a professionalism and character of outstanding quality. She handled everything thrown at her and hit it back.

Finally, Dennis Koho made the official motion. Now the fat was in the fire. It was time to fish or cut bait. It was the end to the postponing the ultimate question , the moment of decision had arrived. The project would face the acid test. It would stand or fall on the next vote which was imminent.

There had been much nose counting in anticipation of the meeting. Everyone knew that Koho and Miller were in favor and believed Newton could be counted on too. All other votes were still toss-ups because so many questions had been asked and so many statements made throughout the life of the process that it was hard to tell where the other four Councilors stood. Some could be predicted rather well but not for sure.

Councilman Miller, who had been a proponent of the proposal from day one, was sure the Council in the end would vote in favor of the project. He was convinced the popularity of baseball and the idea of professional baseball coming back to the area, and being located in Keizer, would be such a persuasive force that it could not be denied. As he counted the votes, he was sure it would pass.

On the way to the meeting, he had looked in on Jerry Walker to buoy up his spirits. Those spirits were lagging at least a little by now. After all, the owners had cut the umbilical cord to Bellingham based entirely on the reception they had received locally from the fans. The team was now without a home. If their decision proved out to be wrong, it could be disastrous.

Despite all the commitments the owners had made by way of franchise relocation, their borrowing and the cash they were going to put in from their own pockets, there was still resistance from the governmental area. Sure it was a huge expenditure for a City with so little history behind it, but the City's commitment would be less than that of the individual owners. Was that not enough to convince the Council with or without consideration of all the other benefits to be derived?

As Al Miller saw it, the decision should be considered as in the bag. He was confident his colleagues would in the end exercise their judgment properly in the discharge of their elected responsibility. So, as he passed Jerry's office on his way to that fateful meeting, he said "Jerry, if I can't bring this one in I wouldn't be entitled to be called 'Big Al' anymore."

At precisely 11:24PM, Mayor Koho recessed the City Council meeting and reconvened the Urban Renewal Agency meeting. The chips were on the table. The time to debate and question was over.

Dennis Koho pressed his motion to vote. There were some parting shots, but the vote was called and taken. Councilors Koho, Miller and Newton voted in favor as did Councilor Carl Beach. It had passed 4-3. The bonds would be issued and the stadium project could go forward.

The decisive vote was short and sweet. It was almost disappointing in its quickness. This part of the Urban Renewal Agency meeting had taken a mere two minutes, give or take, and the momentous decision was made. Nobody could have predicted the way the voting finally fell out and it surprised almost all present. Despite the closeness of the vote, it was firmly believed the Council would now close ranks and all of them would pull for the success of the project near and long term. It was to be expected from men of good will and principle which all of them certainly are.

Now the meeting reconvened as the City Council meeting to complete its unfinished business. However, with the bond issue being assured, the issues were a foregone conclusion. Mayor Koho moved the motion for the City Council's approval of the bond issue and it was passed with the same vote. Then Mayor Koho moved for the zoning change and it passed with the same vote too.

However, since the zoning would have to be changed back if the stadium did not get built for any reason, Mayor Koho pressed for a unanimous vote on that resolution and got it. There was another housekeeping issue to be dealt with relating to the properties being acquired and that was handled with dispatch as Councilor Watson joined the majority.

It was almost done. The dream could be fulfilled. The vagabond baseball team from Bellingham could find a home after all. It was now a definite possibility there would be professional baseball in the Salem-Keizer area in 1997 and if it was up to the owners of the franchise, it would be in a brand new ballpark in Keizer, Oregon.

Larry Parsons of the Statesman Journal heralded the results of the meeting under a headline that stated :"Keizer OKs stadium bonds." His article detailed the precise problem that faced the elected representatives that night and all those that favored the stadium. Mesure 47,having been passed , meant the bond approval would have had to have passed then or it would have had to be submittted to a public vote several months hence in which at least 50% of the registered voters participated.

Dotty Tryk stated such a vote could not come before May of 1997 at the earliest. The stadium was expected to be ready for opening day baseball in June of 1997. Those two dates presented a serious conflict, so the bonds had to be approved right then and there, and were. The bonds were actually sold on the next Wednesday, two days later, with Bank of America purchasing all of them for resale to other investors sometime in the future. Measure 47 took effect that Thursday so the deadline was both real and menacing.

Measure 47 would also have reduced the amount of money the City could have raised through the bond process. Those predicaments were avoided by the Councilors' courageous enactment of the bond resolution. "We don't expect even a lot of rain will slow us down now" Jerry Walker said after the meeting.

Season tickets were selling well. 900 of the 1500 available had been reserved and "..we expect the demand to increase between now and Christmas." Jerry said."Construction is scheduled to start January 6 and the stadium should be ready for play by June."

Only the issue of the lease remained. That came up for final consideration at the regular December 16 meeting of the Council. It was debated fiercely and the opponents of the project hung tenaciously to their positions and worked the lease proposal over very carefully. This would be their final opportunity to challenge the whole idea and they would try to make the most of it.

Even Jerry Walker got into the act. During the lease deliberations, the Council continued to chip away at the rights of the owners as tenants on the land. There came a time when a line in the sand had to be drawn. There was a point beyond which the lease and the entire deal would not be acceptable and they had to be so informed.

Jerry rose to the occasion. Speaking emotionally and with an air of desperation, he informed the Council that there could be no more changes on the area then under consideration. Nothing more could be compromised. The lease was well past the point where it had been agreed upon and yet they continued to try to hammer down concessions. It had been a unilateral exercise which he had to witness, but now he rose and informed them--no more.

The issue was over public use of the scoreboard during public events. Jerry was convinced that use of that finely tuned and very expensive piece of equipment by untrained and inexperienced, people, with no money of their own at stake, just could not be allowed. And Jerry told them so. It was then accepted as it existed in the lease draft and the meeting quickly moved to a close.

There were a couple of aborted motion attempts to make changes in the lease format or to change the parking lot formulas. These were the last gasps of an opposition clinging to their dwindling hopes of killing the project. Those motions either died of lack of a second or failed by a 4-3 vote although the composition of the majority changed slightly.

Mayor Koho moved the acceptance of the lease in substance and the motion was seconded by Al Miller. The motion was carried with a majority of Beach, Koho, Miller and Newton voting in favor. It was over.

It had been a hard fought battle and we had won, but barely. The precarious thread on which the success of the stadium construction project hung would have to be carefully managed to avoid future collisions. One would never really know if any deep seated hostility or anger remained after the vote had put an end to the quarrel. If it was as it is supposed to be, the people had spoken through their elected representatives and everyone should close ranks to work for the success of the project. That was the essence of the democratic system and as it should be.

The meeting had consumed another three and a half hours. The Councilors should have been, if they were not, tired of the issue and the adversarial nature of the meetings on the subject. Both sides of the issue felt deeply in their respective positions and clung tenaciously to them as it metamorphosed from the letter of commitment back in September, to the approval of the bonds and lease in December.

It had been a difficult four months but there were really no winners or losers on the Council. The beneficiaries were the people who would enjoy the stadium , baseball and whatever events were held there. If the stadium got built, they would reap the benefit for over thirty years, long after any then member of the Council was likely to serve. It would be their legacy to the City, each and every one of them, no matter how they had voted.

Both the bond issue resolution and the lease approval resolution had passed by the slimmest of possible margins. It was tenuous. "In baseball, it doesn't matter if the score is 7-0 or 4-3, it's still a win," Jerry Walker said jubilantly after the vote. Dennis Koho, who had led the Council's majority to approval said "This is one of the best deals we could possibly have made." From the outpouring of fan support and the enjoyment and civic pride the team seemed to produce, Koho's words would prove prophetic.

The process had worked and the pros and cons of the issue were heavily debated in open meetings before the eyes of their constituency. Now the next step was seeing the matter through to construction and completion. That was no easy task under ordinary circumstances, but nearly an impossible task in just a short six months. As it stood that evening when the Council members and the spectators filed out into the chilly night, we were almost exactly 180 days to opening day. Was there enough time? Could it be done? Jerry Walker and Bill Tucker had no doubt. They had DP on their side.

The red box seats going in - it looks like a ballpark now

View from the parking lot - looks good

Fans start the seat selection process

More fans in the seat selection process

229

"Is it something I did?" Jim Martsfield checks out his seat

Another bird's eye view of the Opening day scene

We got recognition on the highway - with Carl Valentino

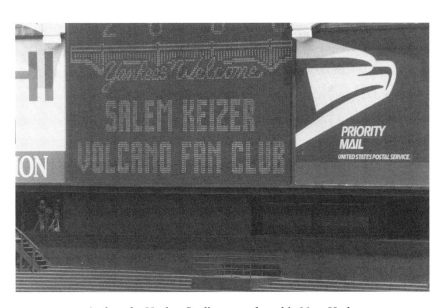

And on the Yankee Stadium scoreboard in New York

Great fan and supporter, Dale Emery on the left

Mayor Dennis Koho (center)

On left - Katrinka Rau, field operations manager supreme,
Kim Spicer on the right

Bill and Jerry with loyal fan Jeanette Welty

Nate and Lois Holeman

Don Porter - "the man from McMinville"

Friend Carl Valentino visited from New York

...and some went east - (l to r): Bill Tucker, Al Miller, Mike Tewell;
and Don Porter at Yankee Stadium

# CHAPTER FOURTEEN: HOME PLATE GOES HERE.

The deadline had been met and passed. The year of 1996 faded into history, unceremoniously. The team still had no name but its presence was felt everywhere. It had been a hectic and eventful year for the owners, but now all the politicking and pressuring had ceased, at least momentarily. Now, all that faced them was the construction of the stadium on a fast track in order to be able to have the park ready for play on Opening Day. That's all, simple as that!

The existence of the stadium now seemed, at least to the public, to be a reality. To the owners, the path ahead was still treacherous. Construction could bounce many ways. There was always the problems associated with uncovering ground no one really had dug in ever before. The underground could contain many surprises, almost all of which would be likely to increase the overall cost. There was little true tolerance for extras that would add to the cost.

Then there was the construction process itself. It would have to click and continue to click like a well-oiled machine without let up until final completion. That alone was difficult to achieve as contractors usually have more than one job going at any time and like to show progress on each so as to placate each of their clients to some degree. The danger of having any of the building trades pulled from this job to another for that reason was real and had to be watched.

There was also the problem of scheduling the various trades to get them in on schedule after scheduling them in such a way that one would not impact upon or clash with any other tradesman doing another job. Ever-present was the possibility that when the job was ready for some tradesmen they would not be ready to come to the job. Or vice versa. When the tradesmen were ready to come in, the job may not have progressed up to where they could effectively work.

Next in the line of worries was the delivery of various ordered equipment that was being fabricated elsewhere just for this project. Other fabrications of equipment that were not custom made were also problematical because of what could happen along the way. Factory scheduling had to be just right and interruptions due to union activities in the fabricator's plant or in the plant or mine of any supplier of raw materials to that fabricator could wreak havoc with the job schedule. It could throw the entire project into disarray and make delivery of the completed ballpark difficult to achieve on time.

We were also subject to the vagaries of the weather which in Oregon during the Spring promised to be an adventure in itself. It rained very frequently and the site where the ballpark was to be located took on a lot of water. If it was the Titanic, it would have sunk again. Neighboring home owners worried about the existing drainage from the site and were even more concerned about what the drainage would be like after the stadium was constructed.

This was a daily concern of Bill and Jerry. Rain could cause a disruption in the continuity of the work which could be disruptive to progress and ultimately the completion of the entire project. We did not have the luxury of having any latitude on that score. We had to have it built and running when the team came home from its opening 5 game series in Spokane.

The league had generously made up the schedule for 1997 having us on the road for the first five games to allow us as much time as possible to complete construction. There were many doubting Thomases among the league owners so they figured it was prudent to do it that way. We agreed and appreciated that favor. It turned out it was not needed but the availability of the extra time took some of the pressure off to some extent.

Another cloud constantly hovering over us was the possibility of one or more of the tradesmen or suppliers failing and filing bankruptcy. That is such a traumatic event that it could put the project into a hole from which we could not recover. Bankruptcy is a huge consumer of time. The law grants an automatic stay to the bankrupt which holds everything exactly where it was on the date of filling. Nothing gets done by or to the bankrupt while that automatically imposed stay is in effect and everyone in any way connected to the bankrupt just has to mark time. We could not afford that.

Adding to the problem is what happens to the money you may have paid to or deposited with the bankrupt firm. That becomes the corpus of a debt which the purpose of bankruptcy is to arrange for the payment of, usually on a percentage of value basis (such as 10 cents on the dollar), or to write off entirely if the bankrupt has no assets and tons of debt. The concept of bankruptcy is to give the bankrupt first time to catch its breath without being hounded by creditors, and then to give the bankrupt a fresh start by wiping its slate clean of old debts it had found impossible to pay. The law pays no attention whatsoever to what that status and the effect of the laws do to other persons. Its sole concern is the bankrupt.

In our case, many of the suppliers demanded deposits before they would consider fabricating or shipping anything. We had no track record with them or in the construction industry so they properly treated us as unknowns. Also, we were using the funds of a construction lender so we were paying interest on funds advanced from time to time. There was no cap on the amount of interest to be paid (although the interest RATE was fixed.) Interest had to be paid every day on every dollar outstanding at any time. Naturally, we didn't pay interest on those dollars remaining in the loan amount until those funds were actually spent. Any delay was extra expensive in our case and we tried to avoid that consequence like the plague.

Then there was always the hurdle of change orders and extras which could be caused by anything. Sometimes they resulted simply from not liking what you saw when it was translated, or about to be translated, into reality as opposed to imagining how it would look from the plans. Extras and change orders meant extra costs, without fail, and put a huge drain on our available funds. We were working diligently to preserve those committed funds for working capital and needed it badly.

Some extras occur almost naturally in just about every construction project of any size. They seem to be almost beyond anyone's control. For instance, once the excavation got under way, without anything even constructed yet above ground, there was noticed the accumulation of a large degree of water from the unfortunate unusually heavy rainfall the area had experienced. We naturally wanted a field that drained well, especially in Oregon where rainfall was anything but rare.

We consulted with drainage experts and even imported an outside expert in the highly specialized field of drainage. It was decided to add substantially more crushed rock base to the field. That meant not only extra rock we had not figured on importing , but also the removal of about an additional foot of soil from the entire field surface. We could not begin to count the cubic yards involved. You can bet that entire process was expensive.

All that was still in our future but they all came to pass in this project.

The real estate needed for the stadium and parking lot still had to be acquired by the City. The four parcels had been sporting rather modest assessed values up to the point the stadium project came along. For instance, the Labish farms were assessed at $80,690 but due to the stadium being conceived, the City had to pay the price of $625,000. The Valish properties consisted of two parcels, one with a house on it and the other vacant land. The latter was assessed at $43,010 and the occupied property was assessed at $124,000 before the stadium effect was considered, but the City, presumably paying market value, obtained both for $390,000.

The Deleeuw property was the largest, consisting of nineteen acres. The assessment pre-stadium was just about $ 96,100. The City paid $860,000. The proposed stadium was already increasing land values in the area significantly even before one spade of earth had been dug and long before it was reality. With those numbers, it is impossible to believe anyone thought it would not be productive for the area.

The firm of Johnson and Lien (a relative of Bill Lien who submitted the winning nickname, "Volcanoes") was in general charge of the legal aspects of the land acquisition. It was necessary to actually condemn only one property and all the money was paid into court on December 31, 1996. They had to evict some mobile homes before construction could be started. It was all accomplished in good time.

January 6, 1997, appropriately Little Christmas, was a raw, windy day with rain blowing down from the western mountains. The rain was not one of those pelting rains, but one of those that just seemed to wet one down over time. It stopped and started and stopped again from time to time. It was not an "outdoor" day to say the least.

Heavy construction equipment and blocks and girders and steel reinforcement lattice had been transported to the site and more was arriving daily. About 10AM some sixty people huddled in the open field , just off Radiant Drive for the groundbreaking ceremony. They were bundled up against the cold and stood in the general area where the main grandstand would eventually go, and waited. There had been a large sign erected for the occasion proclaiming "Northwest League Of Professional Baseball" and sporting the traditional NWL logo in large red letters. The Salem-Keizer Baseball-Let's Play Ball sign, used at the press conference the preceding September, leaned against a table set up for the occasion.

Over the signs, in the background, a large yellow backhoe loomed and blue and white balloons were tied in bunches all over. A portable microphone had been installed for the festivities. It was a relatively somber setting, due mainly to the weather, for such a momentous occasion. Trucks passing the scene on I-5 probably thought they were witnessing a burial ceremony of some type.

Present were the team representative group of Jerry Walker and his wife, Lisa, and Rick Nelson. The Mayor of Salem, Roger Gertenrich, who had started the entire process with his phone call referring the owners to Dennis Koho and Keizer, was front and center. Mayor Dennis Koho and City Manager Dotty Tryk were there as were City Councilors Al Miller, Bob Newton, Carl Beach and Jerry McGee. The entire City Council of Keizer had been invited.

Pat Lafferty was the master of ceremonies as he was frequently, and really the "master." As the balloons flapped in the almost constant breeze, Sam Goesch was enlisted to open the ceremonies with a prayer. Then Lafferty introduced the dignitaries, those holding shovels of various sized handles, and invited several persons to speak.

First, of course, was Dennis Koho. He had been the first, firmest and strongest supporter of the project. He spoke largely about how he felt the stadium would bring both identity and progress to Keizer. Nothing could be accomplished, he said, in a democratic system without open debate, full disclosure and the airing of all views, both public and elected officials. Sometimes that brings out protests , he said, but that is our system, the best in the world.

242

He waxed nostalgic when he spoke of how he was disappointed when the Salem Dodgers packed up their duffel bags and moved to what they thought were greener pastures in a new stadium in Yakima, Washington. " I used to attend on occasion" he said. " I grew up in Bend , Oregon, three miles from the baseball stadium. My older brother was scouted by the Giants. He was killed in Vietnam and never got to play, but he passed along a love for the game to me, if not the talent."

Then Jerry Walker spoke. It was a dramatic and eloquent speech, just right for the occasion. It had to be brief because the cold was now getting to the attendees and they were anxious to get on with it and conclude the ceremony.

When Jerry finished speaking, Pat Lafferty called attention to the semi-circle of personages holding the shovels. They were Carl Beach, Al Miller, Lisa and Jerry Walker, Dennis Koho, Bob Newton and Jerry McGee. The ground was hard underneath but the topsoil was wet and heavy. They pushed the noses of their shovels into the ground and turned over the ceremonial spades of earth. It was good that they would then turn the job over to professional workmen because they did not move any large quantum of earth with their spades. The ground was wet and soaked with water.

The ceremony was then complete. From beginning to end it had taken about twenty minutes but it would have a lasting effect. From that day forward there would begin, and eventually be, a ballpark there. The scene would become a beehive of activity and out of the empty barren ground and over several sites where once a house and a horse barn had stood, huge grandstands and a green baseball diamond would be erected.

There young people would come and go for seasons in the sun, some to go on to big things in the major leagues and others to just play one or more seasons before moving their lives on to other jobs. They would supply needed entertainment to the people of Salem and Keizer, many of them, and they would come in droves to appreciate and enjoy the games and the players. Something new was being started that day, something good. Everyone was invited to sign a home plate supplied for the occasion . It became a memento of the day, to be treasured by the team for all time.

Among the gathered crowd there were at least four protesters. They were principally from the flood-weary Country Glen subdivision. One of them, without a sign, was Rick Frey. He said they weren't really protesting the stadium but were expressing concern that water runoff from the stadium and other planned development near the Interstate I-5 Chemawa interchange would make Labish Ditch even more flood prone.

A young lady stood behind a sign that shouted" Put your citizens 1st before we float away". Of course, she was interviewed by the TV station that covered the event. She probably got as much air time on the tube that night as the entire ceremony did. The media has a way of equalizing everything, even if they are not actually equal in status.

The protesters were truly concerned about water runoff and flooding. Another sign read poetically, "Say, Hey, Koho,

Where's the water going to go". Answering back, Mayor Koho said "It would have been nice to have this (the stadium) in existence already because with it comes two water detention pools that would have reduced the flooding in the area downstream from this." He would prove to be correct. Flooding would not be a problem thereafter.

Also among the attendees was Mike Witenberger, season box holder and enthusiastic fan. He said " Today, it looks like just a field. But I'm looking forward to having baseball back in Salem after seven, eight years." Mike would be the first fan through the turnstiles at the new stadium when it opened.

"The stadium will be more than just a ballpark" Jerry Walker said. "It will be used for football and soccer and other public events. It will be an event center that all of us can gather around." Bill Tucker got into the act, even if not present. "It's going to be the nicest ballpark in the league" he said. Dave Jarvis, who covered the event for the Volcanoes' radio sponsor KYKN, interviewed everybody in prominent focus that day and made it the highlight of his show the next day, and many times thereafter.

It was now really a race against time. The stadium construction would begin and it had to be completed on schedule. The test was now. "It is a realistic schedule" architect Dean Christy of Arbuckle, Costic would say. "We've accounted for inclement weather, factoring in that we would have some delays. The contractor feels comfortable we'll be able to get it done. We've seen others built in four or five months. We have almost six months for this one."

Kevin Monaghan of Gelco Construction of Salem, the excavators who were the first of the contractors to come to bat, said "It's got to be done by June. There's a lot of work to be done." An understatement if there ever was one.

As the crowd dispersed into the gloom, one could hear the roar of engines as bulldozers and shovels cranked their engines. Shortly thereafter, they moved onto the site to begin. There WAS going to be a ballpark here. We were then approximately 175 days away from Opening Day.

The house that had sat on the one parcel was going to be moved to another site. Equipment and personnel to achieve that unusual event came onto the scene and labored alongside the excavators and surveyors. The horse barn was carefully disassembled to be reassembled elsewhere. All people being relocated from anything as a result of the land condemnation for the stadium were treated properly as well as being fully compensated.

In a day or two, wooden stakes about two feet high began to appear protruding from the surface of the land. There were little red plastic ribbons flapping in the breeze from the tops of those stakes. With a good imagination and a view from above, one could make out the outline of the ballpark to come, almost like tracing the Zodiac signs in the heavens, like connecting the dots.

Rain continued to be a problem. Water soaked into the land and made the lifting of any appreciable amount of earth very difficult. Even the large machines were taxed to perform up to their customary efficiency. But perform they did and earth began to be moved into larger and larger piles and holes in the surface where forms would go and concrete be poured began to appear here and there. There was a method to all of this activity although it did not look as if there was too much control. Actually, Dean Christy and Cory Redding were in constant attendance monitoring the progress and issuing orders and decisions to guide the workmen.

Also present, about twice each day, was Dotty Tryk who came and went almost invisibly, to see what was going on and to make sure it was continuing on schedule. The City had its own project out there to be done and she oversaw the progress on that score. Even in this day and age it was unusual to see a woman on such a job site, especially one who had expressed unusual savvy about the construction process and what was needed and had to be done.

Back in her City Hall office , she interfaced regularly with her activity committee and City experts who monitored both projects to make sure construction met City and other governmental standards. She also acted as a buffer between the bureaucracy and the contractors making sure that rigid enforcement of the regulations did not smother the project and cause extra work where safety and good construction did not require it.

As construction was getting under way, the Statesman Journal beat a constant tattoo of stories concerning the ballpark, the owners and baseball in general. The media was still enjoying a news gusher such as never before had been seen after the formation of the separate City of Keizer.

Now, the articles began to focus on the owners. The history of these two guys from opposite coasts meeting and joining in partnership was always an unusual tale. Now it took on a new life as Capi Lynn was assigned to do background pieces on the parties. Photos of Jerry and Lisa in their office on River Road adorned the papers and Capi found substantial human interest in the husband and wife team working together in the unusual baseball field. They even published a photo of Bill Tucker , revealing then to the general public for the first time what the "other guy" looked like.

People may not have been fully interested in the story but they got it anyway. The detail of how Jerry and Bill met, became friends and elected to get into their "dream" business of baseball together IS truly a magnificent story. It has been told and retold and even chronicled in their first book "DP-Or Billy And Jerry In the Promised Land." That is the fullest recanting of the story and there is a fast synopsis of it retold at the beginning of this tome. Enough is enough. You shouldn't continue to beat a dead elephant. Or is that a horse?

Capi was doing her homework. Her article entitled "New team will nurture big-league dreams" told of the Salem-Keizer history of stars in the making. Mike Piazza, Chuck Finley and Dante Bichette and others had launched their big league careers right there. That was before the team deserted Salem in 1989 to go to Yakima for a new facility. Others would now have a chance to add Salem, and Keizer, to their resumes and follow in their footsteps.

She told of how many players had passed through the Bellingham franchise on their way to the big show. She mentioned Ken Griffey, Jr. but there were many others, about one hundred in all. Before its move to Salem-Keizer, the team had been affiliated with the Los Angeles Dodgers, before the Dodgers switched their PDC to Salem, and was the first minor league affiliate of the then newly minted Seattle Mariners. Now it had come full circle and was moving in locally as an affiliate of the San Francisco Giants.

Jack Hiatt was the director of player development for the Giants and he spoke enthusiastically of the move from Bellingham. San Francisco had only this one A-League short season team, unlike other major league franchises. The kids who were to come to Salem-Keizer would likely be new to organized baseball. It would be their first stop on the professional baseball ladder. Hiatt said, "The key is the draft in June. Eighty percent of the team will come from that draft. The players you do get, a lot of them have an excellent chance to make the big leagues. You used to say if you got two out of a draft, it was good. Now, you're hoping for five, six, seven, eight to make it."

The drafts and subsequent signings had been productive in the past. In 1995 the Giants signed 18 of their top 20 draft picks. They all were assigned to Bellingham which then proceeded to win the Northern Division title. In 1996 the Giants signed 17 of their top 20 picks and they all were sent to Bellingham. That team almost repeated as Northern Division Champs and would have except for a swoon in the last five games. Yakima still only beat them out by a slim margin. One will never know how much the atmosphere of hostility between the team and the Bellingham City Council added to that late slide.

The owners were happy with the Giants. They were interested in winning as much as development and that made for exciting games. The teams were traditionally very competitive and stayed in the hunt up to the end. "We met with San Francisco at the winter meetings in Boston and they assured us all of the top draft picks would be sent to Salem-Keizer," Walker said. "Their commitment is to make the Northwest League squad as powerful as possible."

The team was enjoying immense popularity. By early January, at the time of the groundbreaking, about 1,000, or two-thirds, of the box seats had been claimed for the season. Twenty two customers were vying for the thirteen skyboxes. Ticket sales were averaging about ten per day. Christmas sales had been brisk with gifts of half season and nine game packages being stuffed into many stockings.

"We do plan on selling out the stadium before the season starts" said Tom Buckley, director of ticketing services. Still, a good number of seats would be held out for sale on game nights for walk-up customers. It was intended to promote the idea of spontaneous decisions to attend a game any evening, knowing you could get in. Ticket orders were ringing in from not only Salem and Keizer, but also from Lincoln City, Silverton, Woodburn, Dallas and Independence. Some even came in from Portland.

Jim Martsfield said he would use his box seats for friends and clients. "It's a lot of fun. You see a lot of people you know, have a drink, eat peanuts. It's worth it. It's good entertainment." He said. Frank Hoevet was a big fan of minor league baseball. "I'd rather see a ballgame in person than see it on TV. It's just small-time baseball but you never know when you are going to meet a rising star." Certainly the new team on the map was a rising star, even without a name yet.

There was still some rehashing of the debate of pro or con for the stadium idea. The Statesman Journal said "Faster than a speeding basestealer the baseball stadium went from wild idea to reality." The question was posed: "Is the City taking a wild swing-and jeopardizing its financial stability-for a baseball stadium? What's the City's risk if minor league baseball flops, as it has before in the Salem area?"

"There's little or no risk," said Mayor Dennis Koho. "I can't see in the long term how this can fail." But Councilman and President of the Keizer Chamber of Commerce, Jim Keller, saw it differently. "It's all so speculative," he said, "There's certainly a risk, but the only way we are going to find out is in time."

City Manager Dotty Tryk was more positive. "We built the agreement to protect the City in as many ways as we could." She said. "The key is the City isn't putting up money for the stadium, someone else has to make a go of that," Koho chimed in. Jerry McGee, probably the most staunch skeptic worried out loud that if the owner's money for the stadium runs out, the City would be under an awful lot of pressure to "chip in." There was no question the City was hoping for a "hit" with the stadium for Keizer.

But the City was well protected both by security in the land and its improving value (see above about land acquisition costs and post acquisition assessments) as well as the completed stadium either at the time of default or at the end of the lease. The City was also doing just a little more than what it had planned to do for some time. It had long planned to bring water and sewer lines to the more than 100 acres near the freeway that had been marked for development. The stadium was simply the catalyst to push that plan into activation. In addition, the stadium did not use up the entire land acquisition. Many acres would remain in the City's hands undeveloped for the time being. That future development would benefit from the infrastructure being installed because of the stadium.

No matter which way you saw it, the construction project at the Chemawa Interchange was big news. Even the Oregonian from Portland got into the act. It chronicled the fact that Keizer, as Oregon's newest City, was expecting much more from the stadium than just future big leaguers. The paper told how boosters of the project were counting on it to be a catalyst for future development out there and that it would provide inexpensive family entertainment. It mentioned how Keizer boasted rightfully of one of the strongest Little League programs west of the Mississippi.

The Oregonian quoted Mayor Koho as saying, "From the start, I thought it was an excellent way to really give a jump-start to the Chemawa Activity Center." The paper also quoted Councilman Jerry McGee more at length though, giving a somewhat negative flavor to the article. He said, "In between the 10th and 15th year (of the lease) they'll (the team) give us the sad news that the stadium will have to be dramatically upgraded or they'll have to go someplace else."

McGee was concerned the City's agreement regarding the taxes on the stadium was setting a dangerous precedent. He was not impressed either that the City will just about have doubled its investment at the end of the ballpark lease. Not impressive, he said. He also continued to object to the fact that Salem would be included in the team name saying the people of Salem "scorned us" for wanting to incorporate. He felt the City could have stimulated growth at the Interchange by simply extending sewer and utility services to the area for about half the cost, $1.5 million.

Dotty Tryk was again typically more positive. She felt the project "keeps the City whole" and would spur development out there. "I think it will make a big difference. It's something very visible and attractive. A sewer line isn't going to do that." All Keizer residents would benefit when the urban renewal district was fully developed. It would pay more of the cost of City government. That would help reduce the tax rate when , it was said, Keizer already had one of the lowest tax rates for a City its size.

To top it all, the Statesman Journal dredged up the Bellingham situation all over again. In an article headlined "Bickering Forced Walker Out-Politics and an outdated stadium cost Bellingham its baseball team" the paper rehashed that story. It came out the same as ever, with the major leagues requiring ballpark upgrades for compliance and the City not being willing to pay for any.

It discussed the problem with the Seattle Mariners pulling their PDC, but only from the Mariners end, which, as stated above in detail, is far from the full story. The flap with the host families was included  but overall, the good things Jerry and Bill had done in Bellingham shone through.

The article did tell about the stadium improvements the ownership had made and the installation of that state-of-the-art scoreboard with graphics.  It also revealed correctly that the owners were faced with a big bill to upgrade someone else's stadium which it used less than twenty percent of the time, or move, so they moved.  Not a bad article, but timing was questionable.

Bill Tucker came through town on a business trip on February 28.  He had with him three other lawyers from his firm, Antonia Donohue, Susan Persichilli and Maryanne McCarthy.  They had been visiting west coast clients and drove down to Keizer for a look at the construction progress.  It was not a good time to come.

Bill and his group arrived at the construction scene in the midst of a typical western Spring downpour.  The field looked to be a quagmire of mud with mud puddles everywhere and appeared depressing.  Holes had been dug but forms for the concrete had not been worked in.  The entire site was muddy and it bore little resemblance to a baseball field in the making.  There had been grading of the land surface carried out and the surveyor stakes stood out as evidence that there was a plan to that madness.  It took deep faith in the dream to believe that from that day, with only 112 days to Opening Day, the field could be installed and the stadium completed.

Jerry was waiting in the construction trailer with the Cory Redding group.  Jerry definitely exuded that faith.  He bubbled with enthusiasm and alluded to an expected shift in the weather and construction progress to come to make the deadline easily.

Jerry had arranged a radio interview of him and Bill jointly on KYKN during the Dave Jarvis show. We were to be on for an entire hour less commercial time and Jarvis worried about whether we could keep the conversation going for that time. He needn't have worried. When Jerry and Bill got to talking about the theme of baseball, time meant nothing. As always, Bill gave Jerry the major credit for the things that had been achieved and were being accomplished. It was a fan club of at least one.

The chatter covered the general subjects one would expect but it also allowed an opportunity to again thank the citizens of Keizer, particularly, for their faith in the project and in us. We thanked the people of Salem too for their support and generally expounded on the benefits to be anticipated from the stadium and the team coming there. Those benefits were numerous. At the end of the hour, Dave had to cut off the conversation.

After the show, Bill and his troup left to drive back to Portland for the trip back east. They flew home literally on a wing and a prayer-Delta's wing and Bill's prayer for success on the project. Despite the stage of the project that day, Bill believed completely in Jerry's judgment and Jerry believed it would get finished on time. That was enough.

But there were gremlins ahead. The fabricator of the seats filed for bankruptcy. This negated the careful shopping and negotiating Jerry had done to get the best seats for the least money.

Now shopping and negotiations would have to begin anew. It would be complicated by the fact that now time to do the fabricating was even shorter than before, a new supplier needed to be located, and that the fabricator would know we were now in difficult straits and would drive a hard bargain. Costs would definitely go up, and they did. Time was the main factor at this point so we had to pay the price to save the time. We had already swallowed the increased price from the excavator and had little latitude left. Fortunately a new supplier was located who could deliver and within the necessary time frame. An even larger gremlin lay right around the corner.

It was Easter morning and Jerry Walker was making his daily inspection of the site. Jerry's daily inspections sometimes occurred two and three times each day. It was normal for Mark Rudolph, who was the project manager for C.D. Redding, and Jerry to be the first to the site each morning, arriving many times before day break. They would discuss the daily work schedule and what was needed to keep the project on schedule.

Many decisions had to be made on-the-spot. There wasn't time to "think about it". In any construction project of that size unforeseen problems will develop. The best possible solutions then available had to be quickly identified in order to keep the construction moving. A huge challenge, one that would jeopardize the entire project's timeline, was discovered that Easter morning.

It was a sunny and bright Easter morning. A ghostlike quiet pervaded the construction site. Workers were enjoying Easter with their families. Jerry arrived at the site and was basking in the tranquility of the moment. In this fast tracked project seldom was the site without workers.

Jerry took the opportunity to examine the seating placements and the sightlines that fans would be able to enjoy. He made an unbelievable discovery. It appeared, from the foundations being set, that the concourse between the reserved seating area and the box seating area was very narrow. It appeared to be less than two feet wide. Something was clearly wrong. Fans would have to be skilled tightrope artists to navigate that type of setup. Obviously something was askew. Jerry rushed to the trailer and checked and rechecked his measurements thinking that he must have overlooked something. Certainly he wished for everything to be correct. It wasn't.

If Jerry's measurements were correct, he had discovered a huge potential problem. He rushed directly home to call the architect and the contractor to get their input on a problem only he at that time had perceived. Could he be correct? If so, had he discovered it in time?

The Easter holiday made it especially difficult to reach anyone but finally Jerry reached Dean Christy at his home. He was the lead architect assigned to this project for Arbuckle, Costic. Dean immediately recognized the urgency of the situation and agreed to meet Jerry at the site right then to evaluate the situation.

Dean brought the plans and measured off the site as closely as possible. To his disbelief, indeed, something had been done incorrectly and there was not adequate room for the concourse between the two seating areas! Dean said he would contact the contractor and review the problem. Later that night, Dean reached Cory Redding. They agreed to meet first thing the next morning at the site to study the situation.

Bright and early the next morning, that small group gathered at the site. It was apparent that indeed there was a BIG problem. The next few minutes and hours would decide the fate of the entire project insofar as timely completion was concerned.

Everyone gathered in the construction office at the site. Cory Redding took the lead. "We don't have time to figure out how this happened or who is responsible.", explained Redding. "If we are to stay on schedule, we must spend our time to identify how to FIX the problem - we can figure out responsibility later," said Redding. No amount of finger pointing at this moment would do anything to help. That was a separate issue and could be determined later. To determine responsibility, would require surveyors to be called in and engineering specifications calculated. It could take 'forever' to figure this out. All that could be done later.

The group's focus had to be on fixing the problem while maintaining the quality of the project. Any idea from any source that could possibly be effective to correct the problem had to be considered. In short order the group determined the best alternative.

The best alternative naturally turned out to be an expensive one. Responsibility for the error would determine who would bear the expense. If we weren't going to stop now to figure out who was responsible, we had to determine the party willing to accept the burden to advance the monies to pay for the mistake.

Cory Redding volunteered to do so. "C.D. Redding Construction will accept responsibility for whatever the costs are," Cory said boldly. "We have enough faith in our relationship with all the parties involved that once the responsible party or parties are identified we feel they will step up and pay there respective share(s)," said Redding. At that point no one even knew exactly how much money would be involved but everyone knew it would be expensive.

C.D. Redding's decision to 'back' these new costs kept things moving. The decision to do so was a brave one on his part and he deserves credit for doing so. The remedy decided upon to 'cut' the first two rows of the reserved seating sections in all areas. This would allow for the concourse to be the necessary width. It would also mean almost 200 fewer seats. To counter that, new seating sections would be added. One new reserved section and two new box seat sections would make up for the lost seats. It was a wise solution.

As it all turned out we were never able to sufficiently identify how the mistake happened or who was responsible. Surveyors were called in and precise calculations were made, but it was still not entirely clear exactly who 'messed up'. So much happened so quickly to make the project's aggressive timeline possible it was hard to know for sure.

Cory was right about ultimate responsibility and his relationship with all the parties involved. The Stadium was complete and the first season was winding down when Cory suggested a financial solution to the big problem that occurred months earlier. He suggested that the architect, owners and contractor split the cost of the mistake. It seemed a fair way to handle the expensive solution.

Certainly the owners who had hired and relied on experts to do the work weren't responsible in the slightest. However, Jerry and Bill agreed to Cory's suggestion and split the costs with him and the architects. They felt it was the right thing to do as it was a fast track project and everyone did their best and had good intentions. It was an unfortunate event. Jerry and Bill didn't want to burden any one party with the obligation to defend themselves or bear the entire cost, especially people who had worked so hard for them.

Rain continued to be an enemy. To keep the project rolling forward, when it rained Jerry would hold a cookout on the grounds for the construction staff. This kept them from closing out the day the minute the rains came and they stayed around to go back to work when the weather cleared. These cookouts eventually developed into Friday night parties which made the construction site one happy place to be.

Then there was the City oversight responsibility for its own construction end of the project as well as monitoring the private contractors. Bill Peterson, the City engineer , had his assistant, Preston Van Meter, in constant attendance, since he was the project manager for the City. He was regularly making suggestions which seemed like orders, some of them requiring debate and some caused changes in the work. Many of these were expensive in time and cost but had to be made. Some of those things are natural occurrences when plans are translated into reality and when actual conditions at the site are faced for the first time.

Often, it was easier and faster to comply than to argue about the suggestion. That is really the essence of bureaucrat power and they know it and wield that power relentlessly. Fortunately, Van Meter and Peterson were working with us in good faith and wanted the project to be "right" when finished so their presence was looked upon as a contribution.

Then, on March 17, St. Patrick's day, while Bill was celebrating the occasion in New York, events which were not favorable were unfolding in Keizer. Suddenly and without warning, Dotty Tryk announced her resignation as Keizer City Manager. It was a bad blow to the owners who had now lost one of their most stalwart friends and supporters in Dotty.

Dotty was the one who had the strength and courage to stand tall at those Council meetings and to the press when the opposition was vocal and held important positions. She, almost alone, mapped out the method by which the City could get the stadium project accomplished without affecting taxes and with little detrimental effect on other pending projects. Dotty had the idea of stretching out the term of the debt so that the City taxpayers didn't have to pay a nickel more in taxes any year, but they had to do it for a few more years. It was Dotty who understood the complexities of the Measure 47 problem and the nature and mechanics of the bond issue financing. She had discovered the formula for the success of the enterprise and advanced it with a will and devotion not common under such circumstances.

We would owe a lot to Dotty, then and always, for her ability to foresee the good the completed project would do for the lifestyle of the City's residents and for her unswerving loyalty to two strangers who suddenly thrust themselves into her life. She would remain a good friend and we were determined that her name and position would be prominently displayed on a plaque somewhere in the ballpark to honor permanently the feat she accomplished.

We wanted to have an everyday reminder of what she did for us. It was for that reason we decided to create the plaque that hangs on the outside stadium wall. Dotty was sorely missed thereafter. We never found out why she left. Wally Mull took over her position with the title of interim City Manager, but no one ever took her place.

Bill Tucker swung through Keizer again in late April and the entire atmosphere had been vastly improved. There had been considerable progress and cement block walls had been erected for the concession stands and players clubhouses. The structure in which the team offices were to be built out and on which the sky boxes would be located had been poured and the surfaces of the concrete finished. You could climb the stairs to the sky box level and see the constructed outlines of the planned units, but they were far from finished. The elevator shaft was in but the elevator itself was nowhere in sight.

The field itself had sprouted a bright green cover and the grass was filling in well. You could tell the finished product would be a ballpark. But when? At that point we were 52 days from Opening Day using the full grant the league had given us by allowing the team to open on the road. We were getting dangerously close to ground zero.

To Jerry, it didn't matter that there were huge amounts of concrete to be poured. He still exuded confidence the entire package would come together in time. The miracle worker in him kept telling him it could and would be done.

The concrete had been poured for the box seat area but the long plates for the aluminum reserved seating and the bleachers were still stacked up in the area behind the visiting clubhouse. None of the red box seats had been installed and there were whispers of a problem with their size or fittings that would affect their placement. The dugouts were still in the form stage awaiting their pour and the light stanchions and the light housings for the field were not even delivered yet. You really had to believe.

While the beehive at the field was going forward, the City was fulfilling its end of the bargain. Workers had begun grading the parking lot site. Sewer and Water and electricity had been brought to the site although they were still exposed and had to be filled in or buried as the case may be. The parking lot still had not been covered with the asphalt blanket and the striping and curb cuts still had to be laid out after that was done.. The fencing to go around the perimeter had been delivered but lay in huge silver rolls stacked up amid clusters of piping waiting for installation.

There was obviously a whole lot left to do but the workmen were on the job and getting to it every day. Scheduling of material arrival was becoming a testy situation and a major concern. Timely completion required that all materials be available when needed or wanted. The seats arrived shortly after Bill left to go back east. The aluminum seating was in a storage shed being assembled for installation. A major missing element was the light towers and lights that would be the lifeblood of the stadium, giving the teams the power to play baseball in the darkness.

Late in the afternoon, the City's contractors moved onto the site with a vengeance. The gargantuan job of paving the large parking lot finally was getting under way. It was just 35 days to Opening Day and the task before them was formidable, even without the time bind. It was a job that had to be done, but truthfully, the ballpark could have opened without that being finished.

During the last ten days in May, the workmen began installing the 1600 red theatre style seats in the box seating area. Now they had to grapple with the chaos caused by either the irregular placement of the seat sockets or the extra width of the seats or failure of design. We never knew what caused the problem with finger pointing going in every direction. However, blame didn't matter, we had to solve the problem and get on with the construction business. Time was our major problem. And it was solved.

Jerry was very much aware of the cost problem and the limitations of our funding. He tried to save every penny he could without sacrificing the amenities we had wanted for the stadium. One of his cost-cutting ideas was painting. He and Rick Nelson undertook to paint the inside walls of the structures at the ballpark. They did it at night, after their regular duties during the day. They would leave Jerry's house at about 6PM and paint almost until they dropped, way past midnight , well into the early morning. They painted through the darkness since there were no lights because electricity hadn't been brought to the buildings at the site yet. They used flashlights to see, often holding them in their mouths while continuing to paint. The entire scene must have looked strange. It was tiring and backbreaking work but they got it done.

Then we received another blast of upsetting news. Dean Christy, the architect so closely associated with the project, had been lured away by a California firm. It was disturbing but not fatal. As it turns out, architects have done the major percentage of their work once they have drawn the plans. The supervision of the construction progress and the decision making en route to completion were not as major a part of their contribution. Arbuckle-Costic, a resourceful firm, appointed someone to take his place and the effort continued uninterrupted. Dean was missed but we got along.

In the meantime, the league had other fish to fry. The league president and Bob Beban had come by to see for themselves the miracle that was unfolding at the Chemawa Interchange. Jack Cain from Portland swung by too, possibly to inspect, but also to act as cheerleader and promote confidence that the project would beat the deadline. The league was really behind us.

With the stadium in Keizer becoming a reality, it was natural to look at the status of the league organization. After all, the Bellingham team which was the northernmost, had suddenly become the second most southerly team in the league. It made simple sense to consider realignment to save time, mileage and expense for everybody.

A study was undertaken by Bob Romero, the General Manager in Yakima, to consider the various options open to the league. One option was to move Portland into the Northern Division with Salem-Keizer moving to the south, where it should be. A second option was to move Boise to the Northern Division to replace Bellingham which we had moved to Salem-Keizer. The travel issue shaped up this way:

| team | 1995 miles | 1996 miles | Boise in north | Portland in north | proposed 1997 |
|---|---|---|---|---|---|
| Salem | 6524 | 7092 | 4200 | 5000 | 4200 |
| Eugene | 5826 | 6818 | 4450 | 5130 | 4476 |
| So.Oregon | 6926 | 7480 | 6830 | 7200 | 6824 |
| Portland | 5266 | 6659 | 4300 | 4900 | 4244 |
| Boise | 7729 | 9316 | 8660 | 8900 | 6996 |
| Everett | 5534 | 6538 | 6340 | 5700 | 5914 |

| | | | | | |
|---|---|---|---|---|---|
| Spokane | 7126 | 7530 | 7280 | 7400 | 6321 |
| Yakima | 5557 | 5634 | 5230 | 4900 | 4895 |

Salem-Keizer would opt to commute daily for games with Portland and Eugene when scheduled, and Portland would do the same in reverse. Eugene would commute for 1997 but not thereafter. The mileage in the study was based on traveling to each team in your own division twice and only once to teams in the other division. The 1997 draft schedule was done with Boise in the north. That provided the most mileage savings to everyone and thus was adopted. For 1997 and thereafter the league would line up as follows:

| Northern Division | Southern Division |
|---|---|
| Spokane | Salem-Keizer |
| Yakima | Portland |
| Everett | Eugene |
| Boise | So. Oregon |

Medford ( now known as Southern Oregon) had already announced it was moving to Vancouver, Washington. That would place it right next to Portland. They had seen the same advantages we had seen. With the new realignment, the league could absorb the So. Oregon to Vancouver move without any further change in realignment. That would give the appearance, at least, of a steadier league. As of the season end in 1999, however, So. Oregon ownership has not effectuated its move, and it has now become more complicated.

With the new alignment, every team except So. Oregon and Everett would save almost a thousand miles, some closer to two thousand. So. Oregon would achieve only a slight mileage reduction. Only Everett would experience an increase, and only 500 miles at that. It made simple business logic to make the change and implement it.

The league officials were becoming believers. The stadium could be ready for the season opener, at least on a delayed basis by virtue of the scheduling break they had given us.

And it WAS coming together. The last few days were tedious and worrisome but it seemed that everything was falling into place. The City actually completed paving, striping and curbing the parking lot. The perimeter fence went up and gave the entire site a finished look. Construction and field work had been completed. We had retained a soil specialist for the grass and the construction of the mound on the field as well as the mounds in each bullpen. It was an expensive but necessary item. The infield dirt had to be trucked in specially to meet major league standards. The warning track that ran in a fifteen foot swath around the inner perimeter of the field itself was made up of the same composition.

Our new sign was already blaring the "Welcome to Keizer" message. The scoreboard was functioning and Jerry's nephews, Gary and Philip Knudson, were cranking it up and practicing to be able to play it during the game. Jerry's brother Jim was tuning up our music facility and the loudspeaker system was being tested. That all was happening on the day before Opening Day, June 21.

On that same day, a huge crane moved into position and lifted the tall towers with the assembled light housing. They were moved into place, bolted and electrically connected. They had to be tested, and would have to test out just right to be usable for the game. They were. It was fortunate, because the light towers, so essential an ingredient, were going in on the next to last day possible. If that one last but very important item had not been installed or tested out properly, the game the next day could not have been played. It was tightrope walking to the nth degree.

Every one was awed by the fact that the miracle had been achieved. From dream to reality, over every kind of obstacle imaginable, weather, political, monetary and construction, it had taken just over 5 months. From the first shovel full of dirt being lifted on January 5, 1997 it had taken just 144 days. The stadium was substantially complete. There were punch list items to correct and a few remaining small things to get done, but it was basically complete, ready for play. Most people were impressed, all should have been. It was just one more miracle. DP had done it. Again.

## CHAPTER FIFTEEN: THIS BABY NEEDS A NAME

Rick Nelson had started the naming frenzy at the original press conference back in September. He had announced that the team would be named the Salem-Keizer something or other and that it was up to the public to give it a nickname. It was, after all, "their team." That day, a contest of sorts was announced that would produce the name for the team. Included in the quest for a nickname was the idea for a mascot and team colors.

It was emphasized the team was a community and regional team and that suggestions which identified with the region and the geography would be most likely to succeed. There was much to choose from. The area was rich in geographic landmarks, was historical being known as the Lewis and Clark expedition terminus, and for the Oregon Trail pioneers. It had mountains ,valleys and volcanoes and the vast Pacific Ocean on its shoulder, all of which could contribute to or constitute a nickname. The central theme however,was it was a community team and the name would be a community name.

The idea took root and the contest was well received. Proposed nicknames poured in. There were literally hundreds of them. Everyone had been encouraged to contribute and the Statesman Journal and Times played their parts too. With the Council debate going forward at the same time, the program to name the team and select its colors and mascot received good press play and regular attention.

The name proposals were pure genius. One group was the names of animals similar to the Detroit Tigers. So some of the submissions included the Black Lions, the Black Sheep, Bobcats, Bulldogs, Cool Cats , Frogs, Grey Fox, Hound Dogs, Kangaroos, Mountain Goats, Mountain Lions, Ox, Purple Panthers, Rabbits, Raccoons, River Rats, Stallions, Tigers, Wolfpack, Wilcats, and Wolves. Someone even submitted the name Kow Flops!

Then there was the bird group of submissions a la the Baltimore Orioles. These included the Blackbirds, Canaries, Eagles, and Golden Eagles,Hawks, Horned Owls, Katbirds, Kestrels, King Fishers, Krows, Mallards, Meadowlarks, Red Hawks, Red Robins, Skyhawks, Skylarks, Starbirds, Sparrows, and Woodpeckers.

There was a Bigfoot and a Sasquatch and Beetles and Flycatchers, and HOP-ers in the groups. There were Carnivores, Fighting Opossum and Fighting Sow Bugs as well as Home Runners, Gamblers,Frontiersmen and even the English Rounders. Also included were suggestions like Kamikazes, and Ambassadors, Mavericks, Farm Boys, Fighting Lawyers, Senators and Thundereggs.

There was a fish category too as in the Tampa Bay Devilrays. These ran the gamut from Orcas to Steelheads to Chinooks to Katfish, to Suckerfish. There were Bandits, and Bad Boys and Bongos and Krauts as well as Lobos, Loggers, Rain Drops and Vampires. Someone, we can guess who, submitted the nickname Kohos.

There were hundreds of them    Almost all showed creativity and imagination and considerable thought in an effort to link the theme of baseball with some primarily local icon.  The letters received reflected the entire population, children and adults.  Some told of the process by which they arrived at their proposal and they were creative.  All were appreciated.

A contest like that though, has its own life.  As names would be received, some were clearly not going to be chosen for one reason or another.  Much had to do  with the marketability of the name and the ability to identify it with a logo that would not only capture the theme but also capture the hearts of the fans.

However, others were very appealing and from time to time different ones reigned as The Choice, until others were received which would start the turmoil all over again.  It is impossible to list all the names proposed or all the names that were selected to serve as the team's nickname at different times.  Suffice it to say, all the submissions received considered attention and were the subject of much discussion, nothwithstanding some were ruled out at the first reading.  They all had a chance , however.

The entire committee consisting of Bill and Jerry, Dolores, Lisa, and Rick Nelson worked the list over and over and then did it again,and again.  The importance of the selection was not lost on them.  From time to time each of them opted for different selections and promoted their respective choices to the other committee members.  It was not like congressional lobbying for votes, but rather the outgrowth of an honest effort to select the name that would be best for the team for the future. It was easier to name our children.

Special invitation tickets were sent out to all fans who had made season ticket reservations. There was going to be a team naming gala on February 5, 1997 and two tickets were included in each invitation packet. Nobody really knew how many guests would show up but there was the attraction of a free lunch to follow the ceremony. The real attraction though was to be in on the historic announcement of the team nickname, the colors, logo and mascot choice.

They would not be disappointed.

On Wednesday, February 5 ,1997, the clouds seemed to part as if on a signal from Heaven and the rain that had been falling intermittently, ceased. The sun broke through at about 11AM as the crowd started to gather in the Elsinore Theatre. To some it seemed as if the abrupt weather change was a message from on high. It was the largest auditorium in town and between 600 and 700 invited guests piled in. The Elsinore was historic in Salem and had seen other historic events, but this was the cap to them all.

Seats were at a premium. As the crowd filled the theatre, the organist provided a lively atmosphere by playing baseball and other jaunty tunes. Pat Lafferty, the Volcanoes' radio announcer, took the microphone to speak. Pat is a real professional. He is big league in every sense having served as the radio man for the NBA Portland TrailBlazers for years. Everyone recognized his voice immediately and knew and liked him. We are fortunate to have such a distinguished man of class with us.

The program was well choreographed. Lafferty launched into a narrative on the historic nature of baseball as a game,a sport and as America. While he went through the presentation, the screen in the darkened auditorium flashed scenes of baseball events and great players of baseball history. Babe Ruth, of course, topped the list, but was followed by many other baseball Hall of Famers, flashing reminiscences of them and their records and statistics and how they played the game.

The narrative began with the 1926 season which preceded the greatest sports and events year of all time,1927. That was the year of the Dempsey-Tunney heavyweight battle, the year Lindbergh flew the Atlantic alone and the year of perhaps the outstanding baseball team of alltime- the 1927 Yankees. It was also the year the Babe slugged the historic 60 homers to set an alltime recod for everyone to shoot at.

Lafferty was at his best, ad-libbing without a script but calling upon his vast knowledge of baseball and baseball history. His presentation was overwhelming. If he had written it and then rehearsed it repeatedly, he had done it well. The presentation came out perfectly without a pause or a hitch and was very impressive. It was delivered in grand style and may have been the performance of Lafferty's career, certainly one of the best.

Then he stylishly introduced a movie clip from "Field of Dreams", the movie about a dreamer who builds a stadium to lure back ghosts of long ago players to give them a diamond on which to play their games. The baseball field gets built in the middle of a cornfield and actually does exist in real life.

The theme for the movie was "if you build it they will come." James Earl Jones made the oft-quoted speech in his deep voice "People will come, yes....people most definitely will come." The movie was memorable and the film clip shown fit in perfectly.

That was the theme for the ballpark then under construction at the Chemawa Interchange off I-5 in Keizer. We were going to build it and we hoped "they will come." The theatre sound rose in crescendo as the closing scenes of that film clip rushed across the screen

Lisa Walker was called to the podium as she was acting as the sales representative for the team. Expressing gratitude for the reception the team had received from the fans, she proudly announced that all the stadium box seats had been reserved and were considered sold. All 1500. It was a momentous announcement and was roundly aplauded.

Jerry then spoke to thank the staff that had worked so diligently to accomplish that feat. He wanted the public to know them and consider them as friends. Several were from the local area and were probably known to most of the fans present anyway. They were to be distinguished by their association with the team.

Next, speaking on behalf of the entire organization, and on behalf of Bill Tucker who was not able to be present then, Jerry launched into the announcement of the team name. As he paused for effect, a smoky fog began to emanate from somewhere in the theatre and to circulate around the screen. Suddenly the house organ burst into a loud rumbling noise and it seemed as if the entire theatre shook.

Then the screen was alive with images again. The name "Volcanoes" appeared on the screen in large letters. The word was out, the announcement was made. The team would be called the Salem-Keizer Volcanoes. The theatre erupted in applause.

One by one in somewhat rapid succession, the logo images raced across the screen. They were each applauded roundly in turn while the organ blared out the tune of "Take Me Out To The Ballgame."

The logos were important to the team image. First the main logo with the artistically blended "S" and "K' sloped against one another to form a volcano with the appearance of smoke emanating from the top of the volcano-like letters met everyone's eyes.

Next came the alternate logo of the "V" in a large red letter with a fiery faced baseball protruding between the arms of the red "V" . It , too, was a huge success and received loud applause. Next, the different uniform emblems shot onto the screen amid more applause. The theatre was really alive by now and the crowd enthusiastically responded to everything.

It had been truly real theatre, dramatic and effective. The staging had been well conceived and carried out. The announcement of the team name had been long awaited and anticipated. It was a tribute to those involved that, once chosen,the secret could be kept to that moment.

The Statesman Journal headline roared "Volcanoes Explode On The Scene." They called it a "ceremony worthy of Hollywood." And it was.

Capi Lynn wrote:" More than 600 people flocked to the Elsinore Theatre on Wednesday for a different show. This was by no means a big-budget film, but there were special effects. Music rumbled and smoke swirled on the stage. That's when Jerry Walker and company splashed the minor league baseball team's new name and logos on the screen in lava red, obsidian (a black volcanic glass) and ash gray. Those would be the team's official colors." The mascot would be named "Crater."

"We want to come into this community first class and try to stay that way," Jerry Walker said. He went on,'"Our goal was to come in and be as close to major league as we could be. You people deserve that."

Capi's later story was even more expansive. Citing the fact that Oregon has hundreds of volcanoes, of which seven had erupted in the past 300 years, she lauded the name selection. She went on to say that the positioning of the new stadium then under construction would afford fans a view of majestic Mount Hood on the horizon over the centerfield fence.

Capi noted how the name was selected partially with its marketing potential in mind. "It's an easy one for promotional purposes,"said Blanche Conat who was already a box seat ticket tholder. "At the games they can go with a big volcano puff when it's a home run."

Jerry had already thought of that. He was already looking into the possibility of installing a scoreboard that would erupt every time a home team home run flew out of the ballpark.

The name and logos were very well received. The uniqueness of the name was also noted. "As far as we know, no other professional sports team has ever used the nick- name. It is reflective of our team's makeup--full of power, energy and explosiveness" Jerry Walker would say.

The name obviously had regional appeal. That was probably what motivated Bill Lien of Keizer to submit the winning entry. He was shocked to learn that he had won and was pleased to know that he had won a prize and has been immortalized for a long time to come. He could not attend the festivities.

The lobby of the Elsinore was filled with tables of food and drink. It was a good opportunity to preview the quality of the food that would be served at the ballpark. Everyone was invited to join in the luncheon festivities and enjoy the food the team's concessionaire had prepared.

Out in the foyer, Volcano hats and t-shirts went on sale. Dennis Koho bought the first of each and was quickly followed by Dave Day and his son Darreon. All the merhandise proved very popular and was sold out in a big rush. Now the hats and shirts went out into the public arena and would serve to advertise the new team name even more.

It had been a memorable day. Even the weather cooperated. The event was launched about 11 AM on a sunny Wednesday morning. It had been a rainy January and February up to then but the clouds seemed to part to help the event and the sun broke through. It signaled good things to come.

It was a day of anticipation and joy and launched the new team to a new level. From that day forward the name "Volcanoes" meant only one thing in the area. It was the team, their team, forever named for history. The announcement gave a permanence to the team. No longer the "Salem-Keizer What's Its Name", it had an identification as an entity and identified with the region it would make its permanent home. We belonged.

Jerry was ecstatic. He had hit a proverbial homerun. The staging of the announcement had been expertly choreographed by non-experts. It was pure genius. Everyone involved, Jerry and Lisa, Rick and, last but not least, Pat Lafferty, deserved high praise. They had done a magnificent job from beginning to end and had achieved a memorable event. That day would be long remembered by those in attendance. They could be proud they participated in the launching of the new team nickname. One thing was missing--noone thought of taping the event so it marches into history as a memory, subject to recall only.

Greg Jayne would write in his column that the name was indeed hot. He gave it high marks for originality but only a passing grade for its regional impact. He apparently did not think "Volcanoes" truly represented the area, he said, because most of Oregon's volcanoes had been dormant for thousands of years.

He gave the team name a failing grade because it has nine letters . It would be a headline writer's nightmare he claimed but his own headline that day  said, among other things, "Volcanoes Are Hot."  It looked pretty good.  Over all, he gave the new name a 'thumbs up.'  The fans gave it several thousand 'thumbs up.'

Father Pius from Mount Angel Abbey blessed the new ballpark

Everyone spoke - (l to r): Dolores Tucker, Lisa Walker,
Jerry Walker; and Bill Tucker

Mayor Dennis Koho cut the traditional opening ribbon

There were plenty of dignitaries - (l to r): Jim Keller, Al Miller, Jerry McGee, Dawn Meier, Garry Whalen; and Jerry Walk

283

Dotty Tryk made the trip back to the Grand Opening

There was a Marine honor guard presenting colors

The Post Office issued a special Grand Opening postmark

Alyssa White, Karima Olson and Lauren Carter, all from Salem, became the first persons to sing The National Anthem at the new ballpark

Bill Tucker spoke - Dolores Tucker and
Pat Lafferty enjoyed

**First Pitches:**
Top (l to r): Wally Mull, Bob Newton, Jerry McGee, Dawn Meier
Bottom (l to r): John Morgan, Jim Keller, Garry Whalen, Al Miller

Dotty Tryk throws a strike

Mayor Koho arrives by helicopter with "first ball"

But we didn't play - note umbrellas in crowd

Grand Opening Day from the sky - you can see the "committee" assembled for decision by second base

# CHAPTER SIXTEEN: (GRAND) OPENING DAY

The additional time the league had given us by allowing the team to open the season on the road was used and every hour proved to be needed. The season was five days old and still no player from professional baseball had set foot on its virgin infield or outfield grass.

Actually, Jerry Walker and Al Miller had sort of christened it unofficially. One rainy day they ventured out to the untouched outfield grass and tossed a ball back and forth. That didn't count though. Only professional players counted. None of them, including the manager and coaches, knew what to expect either from the ballpark or the town that would  be their "home" field. .

That was not unusual for an A-level, short season team. Every year the entire team, almost, turned over and the newly drafted and signed players would come in.. A few would come back from the prior year, held over due to injuries or the lack of opportunity to show what they are capable of. Everything at this level is based on promise. The coaches and farm directors have to evaluate the talent based on what they see but projecting their thoughts forward to imagine what those players would be like in the next several years. Prospects were prospects though, and those to whom a large bonus had been paid would get plenty of opportunity to make it, even if they were not having any immediate success just yet.

So the people coming in to play as the first players for the Volcanoes, would be coming to unfamiliar ground anyway.

They were coming to a spanking new stadium that nobody had played on before. There was no way they could know the idiosyncracies of this ballpark, nor could they be expected to. It would be the same, however, for them no matter where they were sent, new ballpark or old one. They never had any home field advantage at the outset.

Even worse, the team had gotten off to the poorest of possible starts. It was actually limping back from a disastrous series in Spokane where it had lost all five games. Some of them were close but it was not the kind of record you would really want to bring to the festivities that awaited them as the new ballpark was christened. With the Salem-Keizer area being asked to adjust again to professional baseball, Jerry and Bill had hoped the team would hit the ground running and come home with at least a winning record, or at least a win. But it was not to be.

The team consisted of about forty players so there would be a weeding out process to locate the players who would contribute the most to the team effort. There were prospects to be considered since they would play most games regardless of their success. There would be no home field advantage they could count on to break their skid. They saw the stadium for the first time as they got off the bus after their long trip from Spokane. "It looks real nice," outfielder Brett Casper said. "Everybody kept talking about what a facility this is , and they're right."

Young fans, like Zach Tatman, Nathan Holstedt, Chelsea Mattson, Alison and Adam Peulen were excited to be there. Some of them had never seen a professional baseball game live before. They were hoping to mingle with the players a little, get autographs and maybe catch a foul ball. But there were some who had concerns about the very newness of the stadium.

"It's almost uncomfortable" Shane Turner, Manager of the Volcanoes, groused. "There's not going to be an advantage. These kids don't even have a bed." The bed comment was a reference to the host family program the Volcanoes management was working on. They did have beds, though, at the Quality Inn in Salem. Turner's reference was to the fact the players had not met their host families yet.

The host family program was a real good thing for the young athletes. Those that elected to participate would be assigned to a family that had volunteered to have one or more players live with them during the season. It was successful because the families really took them to their hearts and made them feel at home. They could come and go as they pleased, but mostly the family atmosphere kept them on the straight and narrow, focused on their jobs in an effort to make the most of the rare opportunity they had been offered.

Setting up and effectuating the host family program was just one of the many hats Lisa Walker was wearing those days. It was no easy task to be a host family. It took commitment,patience, and considerable sacrifice of time and effort to make the idea work. "It takes a lot of flexibility " Lisa Walker said. "Your summer months will be disrupted." The season ran from June 15 (although our season was starting five days later) to September 3. You had to be there all that time .

A typical host family had to have a spare bedroom for the player. Their home had to be reasonably close to the stadium or accessible by public transportation without difficulty. In smaller cities like Keizer, it was important that such public transportation be available during late hours since almost all home games are played at night and can get over as late as 11PM some nights.

Kari Naughton of Keizer had volunteered to be in charge of the host family program. She was experienced in that she and her husband had been hosts to several players when the Salem Dodgers were in town. It was her task to seek out the families willing to "adopt" a player for the summer.

Prospective host families really had to want to do it. There was a formidable questionnaire to be completed. It asked such questions as to the number of bedrooms in the house, the number of bathrooms, whether smoking was allowed and whether there were any pets. It was also important to know if anyone spoke Spanish to any degree since several of the players came from the Caribbean or South America. The players would contribute $150 to help cover room and board, but they got far more than that back in convenience, assistance and love and affection. Host families would feed and house their player, doing his laundry and providing transportation when needed. It was and is a good deal for everybody.

"You don't want to put a smoker in a nonsmoker's house, or a player who's allergic to cats and dogs in a house with pets," Kari explained. She was very successful in getting volunteers. She compiled a list of 30 to 40 families that wanted to participate as hosts so the sifting of the volunteers to find the most perfect "fits" became very important. She didn't want to disappoint or discourage any volunteers.

Kari had enjoyed her tenure as a Dodger "mother." "It was fun for us because we used to go to the games anyway." she said. "That just gave us more of a reason to be involved. The hard part was at the end of the season when it was time for them to go home."

They have been able to follow their adopted players throughout their baseball careers. Henry Rodriguez now with the Montreal Expos and Rafael Bournigal now with the Oakland Athletics were two who stayed with the Naughtons while they were in Salem. Many of the host families have stayed very close to their players, visiting them at their other stops on the ladder to the big time, and even visiting them there after they had made it. The host atmosphere produced a relationship of love and affection that was very strong.

Probably no one knew what to expect. There had been no shake down cruise for the field or its facilities, so to speak, because work had "finished" actually on Opening day. Even as fans were coming through the turnstiles that evening, workmen were diligently at work completing some things and correcting others. That effort would continue for some time to come.

Least of all, the players and manager did not know what to expect. "I've seen an overhead picture faxed to me. I could make out a black circle with something that looked like a field," Shane Turner said. "It's almost uncomfortable. We don't know the field any better than anyone else in the league.

Is the field slow or fast? When does the ball carry and how's the wind? Where's the sun field?"

The team knew they would have to learn as they go. It was much like being on a road trip for the first home series. But they would warm up to it as the day grew longer. Then they tried on their new home uniforms and sported about wondering how they looked in the spiffy white, gray and red with slanted numbers on their backs.

You had to appreciate what had been before to fully appreciate what we had now. "The guys who weren't in Bellingham don't know what we're coming from," Shane Turner said. "But some of the new guys are coming from state-of-the-art facilities in college."

Nine players on the roster had been in Bellingham the year before. Third baseman Art Baeza said "Bellingham wasn't that good. The clubhouse wasn't even near the field." Shane Turner agreed. "It was underneath a track stadium. It was always damp. Our uniforms never dried.. There was no circulation. It wasn't very nice," he said. The clubhouse was over 400 feet from the stadium across a parking lot.

He expounded on the other faults with the playing field. In particular, he spoke of the generally inhospitable conditions and the sharp wire on the outfield fence. "I had to tell my players if a ball was close to going over, don't go for it. It really killed me to say that," he said.

They had to love the new ballpark when they saw it and love it even more after playing there. Fan support would be nothing short of stupendous and the field and facilities were clearly the best in the league. Shane Turner grew to be an outspoken supporter of the field, the fans and everything about Salem-Keizer in general. Who wouldn't?

Everything was up to date. The locker room facilities, both home and visitors, sported spacious locker facilities, a separate trainers room, a managers room and coaches lockers with a private shower stall, a weight room and ample showers. The lockers were spacious in themselves. The stadium had been built so that if anyone else used the field while the season was on, they had their own separate locker facilities and the team's private possessions could be locked safely away.

There had not been ample time for Jerry and his staff to move into the office facilities at the Stadium. That job had been pushed to the end of the line to exert all available efforts to completing the field and the public parts of the park. As a result, the operations end was located several hundred feet away, across a cabbage field and a grass seed grower's field in a small farmhouse. A huge crop of alfalfa was in bloom on the corner where Radiant Drive joined Tepper Lane. And a ballpark was going in there and a reasonable facsimile of a baseball team front office was digging in to field questions as mundane as seating and tickets and all the logistics of serving a large number of fans for the first game.

Last minute tasks were being completed at the ballpark, even while construction workers labored mightily to finish their jobs. The lighting was being installed and that was a sight to behold as the cranes swung the entire lighting fixtures into place in the various locations around the field.

Seat directions, listing the box and sections numbers were just delivered and would not be installed until opening day. Pat Lafferty had volunteered to put the seat numbers on the reserved seating. It was no small task since each seat had to be done individually and correctly. If not, we would not know about any error until the chaos of the fouled seating arrangements struck on game day.

About 2PM on game day another distraction took place. The Salem-Keizer Volcanoes, resplendent in their brand new practice jerseys, took the field for batting, infield and general practice. Pitchers and catchers worked out on the area behind the bullpen and the coaches from the Giants' system eyed them carefully. Everyone everywhere inside the park stopped to catch the event. After an eight year hiatus, professional baseball had come home to Salem-Keizer. They WERE back-- to stay now.

Jerry and Bill walked through the cabbage field to the ballpark to catch the momentous event. It was a sight to behold. Young players, just getting to know each other now, were getting to know the new ballpark. It was their home field for now and they were going to get used to it. The crack of the bat hitting the batting practice pitches sounded like heaven to those two owners as they sat in back row red seats to watch the proceedings The first professional players ever to set foot on the new ballfield were out there cavorting and strutting like newborns. It was historic and the relatively few people who caught the event would rightly treasure it forever.

Over in the farmhouse, however, chaos had hit. There was trouble in the seating arrangements and the ticketing procedures had been badly snafued.

About 3PM the farmhouse-office was a mass of hysteria. Office staff raced from phone to phone, trying to satisfy callers about ticket inquiries or the location of their season or package seat tickets. There were several rooms in the farmhouse, each of them now dedicated to some element of the ticketing process. Upstairs, Rick Nelson sat quietly ensconced, away from the hullabaloo going on downstairs, trying to make sense out of what had happened to the expensive ticketing system we were so proud to have purchased. It was a time-consuming and exacting process.

Meanwhile the phones were ringing off their proverbial hooks. After many rings someone would run from one phone to the ringing one to answer it and try to help out the caller with whatever information they had. Staffers kept running in and out of the building, up and down the wooden porch steps, and racing across the cabbage field to the still unpaved part of the stadium parking lot to the ballpark itself . There, they began a frantic hunt for the answer to whatever question they had brought with them, hoping to get it and return to call back the caller. Viewed from above, the farmhouse probably looked like an ant farm with staffers scurrying in and out, always in a big hurry. The inside of the farmhouse probably more aptly resembled the interior of a beehive.

Then, suddenly as if a bell had rung or someone had called every one out of the farmhouse, the staff had all disappeared. Everything went silent except for the phones which kept ringing incessantly. People would show up and bound up the porch steps looking for someone in particular, someone they might have spoken to on the phone. Bill and Dolores felt, and were, helpless to do anything. Answering the phone brought almost instant frustration as there was nobody available to answer whatever question had been posed.

But they did answer the phones hoping to somehow prevent a public relations debacle in the team's new surroundings by having the fans become frustrated and turned off by not being able to get through at all. Messages were taken, as complete as they could be, for later handling by the staffers who presumably knew what was going on.

Eventually, they were able to figure out that everyone had just left for lunch. Having flown in just that day from New York, they were still on east coast time and were neither hungry nor aware of the local habits that they now came face to face with. No one told them what was going on and, suddenly, they were alone with the ringing phones and aggravated fans. They were fearful of a public relations debacle before the first fan had entered the ballpark. Bill and Dolores were both very much mindful of how public relations problems could undermine all the good work that had been done. Those fences take a long time to mend and they were very concerned about it.

Actually, something really had gone wrong, terribly wrong. Specially developed lists and indexes created to keep track of the seating and the sales, either got lost, or proved less than useful in the process. The ticket manager Tom Buckley, who had shepherded the ticket arrangements from the beginning was befuddled by the mess at the end, stating, "I estimated there would be an error in one out of four seat assignments." He resigned near the end feeling he would be blamed for the snafu, but he never really was. Buckley said that the time constraints and limited staff made problems unavoidable. He claimed not to have a computer available to keep up to date records of sales or accounts.

The ticket snafu actually only impacted about 150 people detrimentally. Those fans who incidentally benefited from the snafu never mentioned it. Most of the fans who were affected were understanding, knowing it was the first go-round of a new situation, selling seats in a ballpark no one was familiar with. The mess was correctly described in the Statesman Journal but the emphasis was overdone on the dimensions of the problem. Newspapers always try to seek out the human interest element for a story and gravitate towards the loudest complainers. That is almost Journalism 101, and it was no different here.

Rick Nelson tried to save the process but the absence of records and the failure of their applicability frustrated such efforts. Eventually, he remained locked away upstairs, insulated from the ringing phones and the visiting fans, trying to mend the fences as best he could. Jerry also jumped into the fray full time, closeting himself in a room with the computer and printer, pounding out tickets as he was able to straighten out each situation.

The stabilizing force in the entire process, though, was Kim Spicer, a young local gal with a good head on her shoulders. She bridged the gap between the callers and those who came to pick up tickets, intelligently being able to figure out what had happened and what needed to be done. Her patience and temperament were just what the doctor ordered. She began to impose sense into the chaotic scene and the hubbub began to die down.

Regardless, the day moved along despite the anxious moments, frayed tempers and lost patience. The bus with the visiting Yakima players aboard pulled into the unpaved part of the parking lot. You could see from the farmhouse porch how the players gawked at the new ballpark as they exited the bus one by one. It was an historic moment for everyone and they would earn a place in the annals of Salem-Keizer baseball by being the first opposing team. Actually being the visiting team and batting first, they would send up the first batter ever in that new structure.

The day was somewhat cool and cloudy at times, and then clear. In between, it was sunny and everyone felt we had been blessed with good weather for the grand opening. Everyone.

Lisa Walker had arranged for a priest to visit during the afternoon and bless the ballpark officially. Bill had seen many such blessings bestowed by Catholic priests of various ranks on many things before--fishing fleets, planes, houses and many others. Since this was the first official opening he had anything to do with, he suggested it would be a good idea to have it done here. Lisa arranged for Father Pius, a monk from Mount Angel Abbey nearby, to swing by and officiate at the blessing and thank God for His help and support in getting the ballpark finished on time. It was a wonderful little service and Holy

Water was sprinkled around. It undoubtedly had a major influence on our success.

We then had a ribbon cutting ceremony. Mayor Koho cut the ribbon and it was then official-- the stadium was open for baseball business. It was a time to revel in the success that had been achieved. Jerry turned the ribbon-cutting ceremony into a full blown party and invited all the members of the City Council, the City staff and others, including the local newspapers, to join in. There were refreshments served and we all had a good time, recognizing the goal had been met, the stadium was a reality.

Like the true gentleman he is, Jerry McGee came to the party and looked the place over. At the completion of his inspection, informal as it was, he walked up to Jerry and congratulated him. He said, "Jerry, this construction far exceeds my fondest expectations." Jim Keller, another sometimes supporter but final vote opponent on the City Council, quietly voiced similar sentiments.

Somehow, the time passed and before long it was approaching 5PM, time to open the gates. The crowd was gathering outside the fences, anxious to get in and see, and experience this new event. Cars were streaming through the parking lot gates, steadily, and the flow seemed endless. Ushers, ticket takers and parking lot attendants were resplendent in their bright red shirts and aprons. The entire sight was impressive and even the naysayers would have to be impressed. It was a grand night for Salem-Keizer, it was a more outstanding night for the City of Keizer, and an even a bigger night for Bill Tucker and Jerry Walker.

At 5PM sharp the gates were opened for the first time. Mike Witenberger, the barber from downtown Salem, had the honor of being the first fan through the gate--ever. He did not seek out that honor, it was just the result of his being so anxious to see baseball   back in town. He was and is an outstanding baseball fan.

Now the weather started to become a little less cooperative,. It was still warm but clouds continued to gather and pass  by with greater frequency. Oregon will never be known as "big sky" country but this was unusual. All of us, those connected with the team, those connected with the architect or contractors and the City officials all felt rather certain the weather would stay as it was. We certainly hoped so.

Meanwhile, fans flocked into the ballpark. You could tell by the way they looked it over and admired the surroundings that they were pleased with both the thought of the team and stadium coming, and the now accomplished fact we were here. To stay.

It was going to be an epic night attendance wise. These fans loved their baseball and were decidedly put out by the Salem Dodgers leaving and leaving them flat with no professional baseball at all. They enjoyed it and wanted it back, and now they had it again. They wouldn't lose it this time.

There were a lot of festivities planned for the evening and they all had to be brief and concise. The ball game was the event of the night and you couldn't delay it too long without risking fan impatience. The fans would allow you some degree of leeway.

After all, it was a big new event, this grand opening, in a brand new stadium. They recognized we all were proud of it and how it had been accomplished but they didn't pay to see us bask in our success. They would tolerate some, but not much. They wanted to hear the umpire yell "play ball."

Pat Lafferty served as Master of Ceremonies. He moved the program along very rapidly. First he introduced the two owners and their wives. Jerry and Bill each got an opportunity to say something to the crowd, probably something very corny, but heartfelt. Then Pat called upon two of the ground crew to bring forward a huge bronze plaque which memorialized the accomplishment and the names of those connected with it. That plaque now hangs on the wall outside the stadium just to the side of the office entrance. It was presented to Dolores and Lisa.

Then Al Miller, a City Councilor who supported the stadium theme from the  beginning, spoke representing the City government. It was a very moving speech  reproduced in full later in this volume. It was just another of those  moments.

Next, the City Councilors attending were called to the mound to throw out a ceremonial first ball. All of them-- Al Miller, Bob Newton, Jim Keller, Jerry McGee, Dawn Meier and Garry Whalen, together with Wally Mull and John Morgan, all gathered there and, one by one, threw their ceremonial baseballs to Manager Shane Turner in place of the Salem-Keizer catcher. Many were strikes.

Then Dotty Tryk came to the mound to be honored. She was very deserving and we owed a lot to her. We were proud as she wound up and tossed the ball into the air towards home plate. It was a strike no matter where it landed. We were very happy she decided to come back to us for the evening and participate in the ceremonies marking the opening of the stadium which could not have been built without her. It was the crowning of her legacy to the City of Keizer. She had given the City a gift and it rightfully owed her a debt of gratitude, as we did.

Following the ceremonial baseball throwing, the players and managers and coaches on both sides were introduced. They lined the first and third base foul lines between home plate and third bases as they were called out of the dugout. It was impressive to see these young athletes decked out in their brand new home uniforms which were being seen in full for the first time by the spectators. As they stood there, three young ladies walked out to the microphone set up behind home plate and crooned the national anthem. They were good.

But where was Koho? Everybody was silently turning that question over in their minds. He had been such a huge factor in luring the team to Keizer and a major force in weaving through the political process to get the deal done for the stadium. It was surely a moment for him and he should not miss it. But where was he?

Suddenly, a helicopter was approaching the stadium, still a good distance away. Then it started to come in closer, towards the ballpark, over I-5. The fans speculated it was a television news helicopter trying for spectacular photos of the opening day ceremonies. But it was coming closer still, closer, closer.

Then it started to descend as it zoomed over the highway and over the outfield fence. It set down just behind second base.

Out tumbled a figure. As the person straightened up after getting out of the orbit of the helicopter rotor, everyone was able to identify the person. It was Mayor Dennis Koho. He began jogging toward the mound as the loudspeaker blasted a welcome to him and announced he had in his possession the first ball to be thrown from the mound for the first game ever at the ballpark. The crowd went wild. Koho, somewhat naturally shy, waved back to the roaring fans. As he approached the mound, the helicopter roared away. To the applause and roared approval from nearly five thousand throats, Dennis heaved that first pitch in to the waiting catcher. It was now official. The game could begin.

But could it? The ominous clouds had gathered now directly overhead and started to give off a light sprinkle of rain. That light sprinkle quickly advanced to an all out rain, then to a heavy downpour. Everyone was dumfounded as they watched the infield absorb the rain and the dirt portions quickly turning into a muddy surface. How long would it last? Nobody knew and everyone hoped it would end quickly and the field could be put back into playing shape for the game.

The downpour, however, became heavy and the clouds did not seem to move eastward as they should have. The rain had drenched the entire field which had been uncovered and both the infield and outfield grass were hardly in playing shape. The first professional baseball game in the Salem area in almost a decade, and the first in Keizer in recorded memory, was in grave danger of being washed out by rain. Rain! It had plagued us all through the construction process and was still dogging our trail. Would it happen?

The players were scurrying for cover and retreating to the dryness of the dugouts. They were donning their team jackets for warmth. They didn't know what to expect next, the rain had been so sudden. They peered out from under the bills of their brand new home hats expecting the rain to go away as they had wished in that old children's jingle.

We did not have a tarpaulin to cover the infield but it would not have been adequate anyway. The rain in such force had been so unexpected and so heavy, that we could never have gotten it spread out in time to do any good. It became decision time. In the minor leagues, the umpires make the ultimate decision as to whether to play under the circumstances. This was indeed a difficult decision for them.

They didn't want to reach either decision, to play or not, on their own. After all, it was a record making game what with the baptism of a brand new ballpark and a brand new team in a new City, and all those people. A large crowd. What to do?

They were "minor league" umpires too. Nothing in their training suggested a course of action under these circumstances. An ordinary game during any season subjected to these conditions was far different. There was no difficulty with that. Here all the special circumstances present made the approach to the decision different--far different.

The umpires called out the two managers. They in turn decided to call out the owners of the home team. Jerry Walker responded and joined the huddle. Then Bob Richmond, league president here to attend the festivities at the new ballpark, was called upon to join the huddle. Now the gathering was somewhat larger. Decision   by committee.   They walked around the infield now that the rain had stopped completely. They tested the outfield grass.   Would it tolerate game conditions?   Even more important, could anyone get hurt because of these conditions?   Nobody wanted to risk that.

You could see, even at long distance, that Jerry desperately wanted the game to go on.  His face reflected his confidence in the field  that had been constructed and prepared to handle just this type of unexpected situation.   Early in the construction process a decision had been made to accept a large 'extra' and install additional drainage for just such occasions. Now that was supposed to pay off. Would it?

The committee decided the risk to the valuable playing talent was too much.   If anyone had sustained an injury that abbreviated their career because of the playing conditions, everyone would have felt bad.  Nobody wanted that to happen. Balancing that risk against postponing the game for another day mitigated in favor of a rainout. And so it was announced. Game postponed on account of rain.

The crowd accepted the dictate.  However, they didn't just file out like an ordinary crowd after the conclusion of a game. They had been enthused by the festivities and the history being made.  They were in a party mood and they continued to talk and converse with the people they met there, some they knew before and friends they now met for the first time.  Friendship is the name of the game.

The game part of the festivities would be played the next day if the weather cooperated. In the meantime, the fans enjoyed the camaraderie of the event and had consumed considerable amounts of the refreshments offered by the concessionaires. They sang songs, visited and in general had a time. It was an old-fashioned get together.

Bill and Jerry thought that after all the pain of the political process and the concerns during the construction stages, they had been dealt a poor hand on what should have been a spectacular day. But it was something you had to accept since there was nothing you could do otherwise. However, they could and would be content in the knowledge that they had accomplished what they had set out to do, on time and in grand style. No one could fault the aesthetics of the stadium and the turnout, even if heavily sprinkled with the one-time curious, signaled public acceptance and approbation.

On balance, the night was a success from almost every viewpoint. In the end, even Manager Shane Turner became a convert. He was quoted by the Statesman Journal as saying, "I'm as excited as they (the players) are. I love playing baseball. It could be a cow pasture. But when you have a nice field, a nice setup, you can enjoy coming to a game more."

Dennis Koho was particularly disappointed. There was no question his legacy as Mayor, whenever he left office, would be inextricably tied to the success of the stadium. As James Bennett wrote in an article in early January, "The stadium will stand for decades as a monument to the City's vision for the future and Koho's belief that it will be an economic boon for the community." It would measure Dennis Koho's stature in the history of Keizer. He was the one who, in the face of budget cuts that would be imposed solely as a result of Measure 47, and against a civic credo that forbade everything but necessary spending, stood tall to support the stadium idea. He made it happen when many others were running for political cover. "

"I was not concerned about the political aspects of it," he said, "I was doing what was best for the community. I'll let the politics take care of itself." Koho was the glue and fabric that made the stadium deal float and he kept it afloat though all sorts of counterweights. He had to satisfy real public issues such as flooding concerns and the perils of urban growth as well as cost tight City government where spending as little as possible was the motto from it's mission statement. Yet he shepherded the motion through that would have that very City spend almost $3 million, the largest single expenditure in its history to date.

It was Koho's tenacity, his belief in the dream,his loyalty, his unbounded determination and unswerving support, aided and abetted by his four horsemen-Tryk, Miller, Newton and Beach, that more than anything, made the stadium a reality. He had a vision. "The larger question is economic development. That area is one of two urban interchanges on Interstate 5 that is undeveloped. We expect the new stadium to attract business, maybe a new hotel, and provide jobs and benefits for our residents beyond a baseball season", he said.

Into our third year it has begun to do that with room for much more. Fans now have been able to see an Oregon Ducks

Spring football game, the USA Olympic baseball team, a USA World Champion soccer star, high school graduation, country singer Patty Loveless in concert, and the Nike Baseball World Tournament, all of which would never have come near Keizer but for the stadium.

At the end of the day, that day, the tribute that actually happened, since no game was played, was a tribute to that Lone Ranger, Dennis Koho and his sidekick Dotty Tryk. That was perfectly appropriate under all the circumstances that had gone before. The game could wait for another day.

The 4,901 fans did not seem to want to leave. The rain had stopped and the interplay between them appeared destined to carry on into the night. However, after a while, they began oozing out of the ballpark they now knew, adopted and loved, into the early evening shadows. They were pleased and happy. They now appreciated, if never before, the tenacity of those champions of the dream that had achieved such tangible results. It was for them, the fans, the people of Salem and Keizer and all neighborhoods in the general vicinity and their quality of life, that the fight had been fought and won. They now had a team and quality, wholesome family entertainment to enjoy for them and their children. Life was good again.

Outside the ballpark in the parking lot, the Statesman Journal distributed its special edition souvenir issue of the paper. Aglow with photos of first day activities and bulging with stories and data about the team and its players, it marked the success of the evening for all time. It was an historic occasion and in an era of television news which seems to drone out of tv sets all day long, the event was being marked for memory by and in an era of television news which seems to drone out of tv sets all day long, the event was being marked for memory by that old fashioned method of an "extra" by the local newspaper. That in itself was newsworthy.

So the day passed into history. All the worries about the stadium getting completed on time were now forgotten. Gone were the league concerns about having to play some games at the Chemeketa ballfield until the new park was finished. Gone were the doubters who tried to convince those who would listen that the stadium would never come to pass. Gone were the naysayers who felt the City could not complete its end of the bargain and the owners could not live up to their promises. All bargains, all promises were now certified as "kept." It was here, it was good and it would be here for a long, long time to come.

The players were perhaps the most disappointed. "We expected a sellout, and we knew the City was pretty excited to get a baseball team out here," pitcher Eric Johnson said. "It's pretty disappointing to get rained out, especially on a big day for the City and a big day for baseball."

The Yakima Bears players sat in the dugout watching Mayor Koho arrive in the helicopter. "It would have been exciting to play with all these people here opening night," Yakima catcher Jason Brown said. " Everybody was ready to go. We had nothing else to do but sit in the dugout and watch. It was very entertaining. It's not every day that a helicopter flies in and the mayor of the City gets out. That was definitely exciting."

C.J. Ankrum saw it from a different perspective. The Volcanoes' first baseman said," It takes a long time to get ready for a ballgame, and then to finally get ready and to have to shut down is tough. If it wasn't a brand new field and the fans and the City weren't so excited for the game, they probably would have called it a long time ago. They did everything they could. This City hasn't had baseball for a long time, and if it makes them happy then it makes us happy."

The game was played the very next day. Ryan Jensen delivered the first pitch ever at Volcanoes Stadium. It was a ball. On the third pitch, Rich Saitta belted it over the left field fence for the first hit and the first home run at the new ballpark. In the Volcanoes' half of the first inning, Mike Byas beat out a slow roller to short. He promptly stole second and third, establishing himself as having gotten the first hit and first steals at the new ballpark. He would later score the first Volcanoes run when Travis Young was safe at first on an error by shortstop Ricky Bell.

C.J. Ankrun slammed the first Volcanoes home run in the third inning. He would add another later in the game on his way to a four RBI night. There were many firsts that night before the crowd of 3,375. After Ankrum's second homer, catcher Tim Flaherty belted another, his third of the season. Back-to-back homers, even, in the opener. The Volcanoes went on to win by the score of 8 to 2.

And so it was done. The first game was over and the season went on its way. After starting the year with a 0-5 record, the team won nine consecutive games. The Volcanoes were a contending team for the rest of the year but were unable to overcome their tendency to be swept in series. They hit and ran and pitched well but not well enough. The team was very exciting all season long and the fans loved them and supported the team. Everyone was optimistic right up to the season end and the "Wait till next year" attitude could be sensed on the last day. All promises had been fulfilled and the fans had demonstrated the judgment of those that championed the stadium idea was correct. Its time had really come and it was here, and it was a success.

Jerry Walker and son Mickey, rode in the parade

Brother Ed Tucker visited (see Lafferty on mike)

Loyal fan Jan Suggs (she's the chick on the right)

315

Bill's relatives visited from New York - (l to r): Mary Anne O'Hara, Ed Tucker, Bill, Sean O'Hara, Barbara Galgano, Megan Rok; and handsome Danny O'Hara in front

They took the tour of Mount St. Helens

The Volcanoes line up for playoff game in Boise

The field at Boise after winning the championship

Several players celebrate in clubhouse - (l to r): Erik Mattern, Steve Hill, Jeremy Luster; and Sammy Serrano

Ryan Vogelsong and Doug Clark celebrate

Arturo "Scoop" McDowell and Carlos "Kool Aid" Frazier, whoop it up

"We're gonna size you up!"  Bill and Jerry remind team in clubhouse
of the rings they will receive

Steve Hill, "Kool Aid" Frazier and "Scoop" McDowell took the party outside

The Crater on a regular summer night

Crater

# CHAPTER SEVENTEEN: CHAMPIONS

You could not have been able to tell by the way the 1998 season began that this team was going to bring the first League Championship to Salem-Keizer. The team started off in mediocre or average fashion, winning one, losing one, winning one then losing two and then repeating that formula over and over. The team dawdled under .500 for the first part of the season as it struggled to find itself. For Manager Keith Comstock, it was a seemingly endless struggle as he tried to distill the available talent into a strong playing force, weeding out the lesser contributors from those more likely to succeed. There were some very talented players on the team, and, sooner or later, they were bound to hurt somebody with their bats and pitching.

As always, the season's approach brought considerable anticipation. The first season in the new ballpark in 1997 had been a roaring success from many points of view. The fans convincingly supported the team by coming out in droves, regularly, and cheering loudly. They were into the game, all the games, all the time and turned the "home field advantage" into a real advantage. In baseball circles, the Salem-Keizer experience became well known as a very enjoyable one for fans and players alike.

Don Porter, for example, virtually lived at the stadium during the season and with the players too. He made trips to the away games at Eugene, Portland and Medford and, occasionally, Spokane. His back wall at Porter's Pub was dedicated to the Volcanoes and, little by little, memorabilia of the team began to be accumulated there. Speaking of having the team in Keizer, he said, "They're an important part of the community. We were so lucky to get them. I think that's the finest thing in the world."

Not everyone felt that way it seemed. According to the Statesman Journal , some folks had not forgotten the experience of the team getting fast track approval to come and obtaining the City's help in constructing the ballpark. Sam Goesch, then Keizer Chamber Of Commerce President, mentioned some segments of the citizenry still rankled over the way the team was brought to Keizer and the rush and push to get the many approvals required. "I think it's still controversial" Goesch said, "and I think the people of Keizer would have liked to vote on it."

But that was distinctly a minority opinion. The team was immensely popular and well before the season opener in 1998 all the box seats were sold out and all but 70 of the season tickets had been taken. A good percentage of those seats were snapped up by Keizer residents.

The team had actually brought in Don Larsen, the Yankee pitcher who in 1956 accomplished the greatest single feat in baseball history by throwing a perfect game against the Brooklyn Dodgers in the World Series. His presence was intended to stimulate ticket sales at the ballpark before the season started but by the time he got there in late May, the tickets were sold. He became a glittering preview of the many quality personages that would be brought to the ballpark in the times ahead. People who would never be likely to get to Salem or Keizer unless the ballpark was there.

Wally Mull, now City Manager of Keizer, said he couldn't believe Keizer's own Field of Dreams was a reality. "Usually those kinds of things end up in Salem," he said.

Al Miller, the former Keizer City Councilman and a loyal and stalwart supporter of the stadium proposal, felt much the same way. He had been signed as a lefty pitcher by the Phillies out of high school. He was sent to Walla Walla for a year before deciding the law presented more chance of success for him. But he couldn't get baseball out of his blood. "If I could live in a ballpark, I would," he said. "I only missed one game all last year (1997), and that was for a City Council meeting. After the season, my wife and I went through Volcano withdrawal. "

Mike Witenberger, the OK Barbershop proprietor in Salem, echoed those feelings. He was officially the first fan into the new stadium when it opened and the love affair continued. "I go to the baseball games, and everything else comes after that," he said. There really is no truth to the myth, though, that he once left one of his haircut patrons sitting in the barber's chair half trimmed as Mike rushed out to get to the game.

The true acid test though was reflected in the opinion of Keizer Mayor, Dennis Koho. He had staked his reputation and political career on the stadium issue and it represented his legacy to the City. There can be no doubt the stadium would not have been built when and where it was had it not been for his loyal and steadfast support.

Koho was the first person to tell us it could be done and to tell the Volcanoes that he wanted season tickets. "I've never had baseball in my backyard," he said. "It's wonderful to take advantage of it. The concourse of the Volcanoes Stadium becomes Main Street, Keizer for the summer. You see a whole bunch of your friends and business folks from around town."

The team's arrival for the 1998 season was much more auspicious than in 1997. This time, there were no conflicting priorities such as getting the ballpark finished, finding host families and sorting out ticket snafus. The team would open at home this year, with a clean slate, contrary to the five game disaster in Spokane the year before. In 1997, when they limped home for the Grand Opening of the ballpark, they were 0 and 5. Then, they had no time to get acclimated to their new surroundings and arrived early in the morning of the scheduled opener after a long bus ride from Spokane. Tired and confused about their roots and where they would stay, they approached the season with trepidation. Not this year.

This time they had a chance to bask in their new surroundings. The stadium had already sort of established for itself a reputation of high quality in organized baseball. So the players worked out and got used to the ballpark, and themselves, leisurely. They schmoozed with the fans and signed autographs. It was a love affair at first sight and it would last far beyond the baseball season which had not even started yet.

Manager Keith Comstock was getting his baptism of fire, too. A rookie manager, he was impressed with the players on hand stating, "With the talent I've seen, we will be exciting to watch." He shepherded his new flock through the preseason and pre-game activities with a warmth and gentleness that were to become his trademarks. "This is what the lower levels are all about." he said. "The electricity you can feel already. Now if I can just find a place to live. No host family wants to take in a manager for some reason." They may not have taken him in, but they did take him to their hearts. Comstock was, and remains, an extremely well-liked and popular figure in town.

As Comstock unpacked his gear and organized his office, one could see a sealed plastic bag that had been carefully hung on the wall of his office. It contained a cigar. A special cigar. "I soaked it in 12-year-old scotch," he said. "I've saved it for my first managerial win." It would not soak in that scotch much longer.

It was a formidable task that lay ahead of Comstock and his only coach, Bert Hunter. There was no pitching coach, so Comstock, himself a former major league pitcher, would have to serve in that capacity as well. San Francisco had been outstandingly successful in the draft and signed 17 of its top 22 draft picks, and 20 overall. They were all coming to Salem-Keizer as their first stop.

The number one pick was a third baseman signed out of a California high school, named Tony Torcato, and he had not yet arrived. He stayed home to graduate from high school.. As the team stood that day before the season started, it had 37 players on the roster, including four on rehabilitation assignment after off season surgeries. Two more, both pitchers, Chris Jones and Jacob Estevez would join the team later, as would Torcato.

Dick Tidrow, the famous New York Yankee pitcher (he also played for Cleveland), nicknamed "Dirt", was the San Francisco Director of Development, and his assistant, Bobby Evans, came in. They were on hand to help evaluate the talent and help in setting up the lineups and pitching rotation. Their presence also demonstrated to the new professional players that San Francisco truly had a big interest in them, as well as an investment, and wanted them to succeed. It was an indication everything possible would be done to make that occur.

However, there was no question the backbone of the cadre of "experts" looking at the assembled talent was Keith Comstock. He would have the opportunity to see these players every day, in all sorts of situations. He would be their manager, helper, coach, sympathetic ear, confidante, and, when the occasion called for it, a quasi-parent. He would have to solve all sorts of problems as the season wound its way to a conclusion, and he was good at it. There was a mutual bond of respect and admiration between him and the players that would last a lifetime.

This year, the team even had the space and time to play a simulated game, the Saturday before the opener. It was a good way to get used to the stadium and themselves playing together. The year before, the 1997 team had no such opportunity. They were thrown together on the road, had a few workouts, and started the season in the unfriendly confines of Spokane Stadium. There can be little question that played some role in their woeful showing up there. Coming home five games down with no wins, even for a Grand Opener, had to be a downer. They worked courageously through it and in the end could be proud of the showing they made. This team would be different.

The Volcanoes' front office meanwhile continued to pursue finding a naming sponsor for the stadium. That was a big ticket item. Selling the naming rights to corporate sponsors had become the thing to do with all new stadiums in particular, and all stadiums in general. However, it was difficult to accomplish in Salem-Keizer where sponsors who could reap a sufficient public relations benefit to justify the expenditure, were rare. In the absence of such a sponsor, the fans were in effect naming the stadium, calling it Volcanoes Stadium or, even more affectionately, the Crater, and it stuck.

Many new items had been added since the first season. Mindful of the rainout of the Grand Opener, the Volcanoes purchased an infield tarp for the field. While it would be difficult to handle, as all baseball tarps are especially since they are only used on inclement and windy nights, it could prove to be saviour of games and avoid washouts. It would take 15 people to handle it on a normal rainy day and 20 if it was windy. It would take practice to get it laid out and retrieved, practice not gained under stressful conditions. The ground crew clearly had to get the practice in. "Now that we have it," Rick Nelson said, "it will probably never rain." That would be an unexpected benefit.

In addition, a computerized sound system had been purchased from the subsidiary of the Portland Trail Blazers. It would supply a limitless array of sound effects and made the storage of appropriate music and its recall very easy and practical. It was an expensive addition but increased the aura of professionalism for the fans. Jim Walker planned to play the organ for ballpark music the first two nights, but he would also record that music into the system for use when he was not in town.

Also added, was an inflatable and colorful pitching contraption. For a small fee, you could wind up and pitch three balls into the gadget. It would measure your pitch speed and give a numeric readout for all to see. It was a terrific new attraction and was located in the main concourse, very near the portable souvenir stand that became immediately popular. The investing by the owners, the "giving back", was continuing.

And the fans' appreciation showed. Phil Galloway really wanted to be the first fan into the ballpark on opening night so he camped out at the gate, literally for hours. Three year old Arny Ripp was being brought to his first game ever. "He's so excited" his mother said. " He thinks he's playing. He's not getting the whole picture yet."

Don Olheiser also couldn't wait for the season to start. Don and his friends pulled their vehicle into the Volcanoes' parking lot about 5PM on game day and proceeded to set up a portable grill. Not long after, the smell of cooking hamburgers and shish kabob wafted across the parking lot. Adding fruit, pasta, chips and dips, with cookies for desert, and soda and beer from a cooler, they sat on lawn chairs to enjoy the feast, the evening, the socializing, and eventually, the game. Tailgating was a tradition with Olheiser, something he started at University of Oregon football games during the absence of baseball from the local scene."There's nothing better than coming out here on a summer night and having some hot dogs and drinking a couple of beers and having a good time. I'm not a big sports fan, but for local stuff, I am a sports fan," he said.

Jim and Sandy Schulte epitomized the attitude of the fans. They were almost as new to Keizer as the team, and badly wanted to be part of the Volcanoes' fan club. They had received their tickets as a gift and looked forward to the game. "It's a new experience," Sandy Schulte said.

Even the weather cooperated. Opening day was a bright, sunny day with high, blue skies. It was a good omen that things were going to go the Volcanoes' way, that night at least.

Another helicopter ride was in order following the very brief pre-game ceremonies. This time, the elite passenger was Shawn Kintner, the McNary High School star athlete who had been a big factor in bringing the Oregon State High School Football Championship to Keizer. In the fall, he would enter Oregon State on a football scholarship and maybe help that team over his four-year career to a national championship. For now, he was being honored by being asked to throw out the season's ceremonial first pitch. And he did well.

The game began in the fading light of day as the sun went down over the Willamette Valley and across the mountains that still lay to the west. Nate Bump took the ball for the home team and pitched very well. He was to keep the Eugene Emeralds scoreless for the first three innings, allowing only three hits during his stint.

In the meantime, Jeremy Luster, in his first at bat as a Volcano, was really nervous. "The first couple pitches I was real nervous." he said. "I had hit right-handed like 15 times all year. ." He had worked the count full with uncommon patience for a young player. The next pitch was high and inside and the switch hitting Luster deposited it far over the left centerfield wall for a home run. " I just swung and guess I got lucky," he said. "I was feeling numb running around the bases. I couldn't ask for anything better than that." He was to complete the game by adding a single and a bases loaded walk for a pretty good day at the plate.

Comstock was to use three other pitchers that night; Randy Goodrich, Benji Miller and Todd Ozias following Bump to the mound. Goodrich got the win, with the only negative mark being a ninth inning home run to Al Castro off Ozias. "Goody was fabulous" Comstock almost sang. "He really created a great tempo. He threw strikes and kept the ball down." That location forced the Eugene hitters to beat the ball into the ground and the defense did the rest. So did the hitters. The team got eight walks, including three with the bases loaded. RBI singles by Brett Casper and Jeff Allen completed the scoring in the 6-1 game.

There was no question Luster's lusty hitting led the way. Jeremy had not been used to playing in front of crowds like the 4,182 fans who packed the Crater for the Opening Game. "These people were great," Luster said. "I enjoyed this so much out here. It's just amazing. I couldn't ask for anything more than this. Especially at this level. I never thought it would be like this."

Jerry Walker did. "I think that we 're trying to keep the honeymoon going," he said a few days earlier. "The goal is for each season to be special. We want to continue to create the atmosphere that was created last year with the energy and excitement."

Statesman Journal columnist Greg Jayne was to warn:

"Of course, the promoter in (Jerry)Walker wouldn't allow him to say anything else. He's P.T. Barnum without the top hat, and he's got a pretty good product to sell. The selling gets tougher in the second year. Last season was a grace period, a time when fans would have come to the park even if Attila the Hun were the owner."

Getting in the last word and speaking of Luster's home run, a very relaxed Keith Comstock said, "It got us on the board early. It generated energy for the team. They all felt that." So did Comstock. He got to smoke that special cigar.

But the bubble had to burst. The next night, still at home, the score was almost reversed. The Emeralds, who were to be the divisional doormats at the end of the season, rapped out a 5-1 victory. The team then followed Eugene the 64 or so miles south to the Emerald's ballpark. It is an old wooden stadium which everyone tends to describe as having a lot of character. It probably does because it attracts a good number of fans each season. Bob Richmond tells people it is his favorite place to watch a ballgame. It is different.

The Emeralds were not good hosts. It was their home opener and there were many fans root, root, rooting for the home

332

team against a few stalwart Volcanoes fans who had made the one hour trip south to Eugene. They treated us like relatives and almost gave us everything we wanted--the game-- but held out that carrot. They finally won the contest 6-5 and sent us on our way.

Off to Southern Oregon we went, where the team, recently renamed the Timberjacks, treated the Volcanoes unkindly. That team, located in Medford, and having already announced its intention to move the franchise to another location, (they were hoping for Vancouver, Washington) was to be the main competitor of the Volcanoes for the division title. The Timberjacks swept the Volcanoes three straight games, including a shutout. The team limped back into Keizer in the middle of the night, sporting a 1 and 5 record, with all losses coming in a row. As bad as last year after 6 games.

Yakima came in for a 5 game series, and they promptly shut down the Volcano offense and extended the losing streak to 6 games. Searching all the while for the winning formula, Manager Comstock finally found the key. Starting pitcher Masashi Kiyono held the Bears to three hits over his 5 inning stint and was then picked up by reliever Kevin Joseph who finished it off.

The home town crowd probably had something to do with it. Comstock said, "If you get the crowd into it, this game can be a lot of fun for us. The crowd responds to hitting and running, and all the fundamental things of baseball. When we get them behind us, it makes a big difference. "

The team needed to come out of that funk. They were hitting a puny team average of .171, last in the entire league. Only Jeff Allen stood above the .300 mark and Doug Clark, who had so much promise, was at an awful .055!

The next night, the team clawed its way to a 5-4 twelve inning win. Squandering an early lead, the Volcanoes also squandered several excellent scoring opportunities before Chris Magruder got a wild pitch thrown to him with the bases loaded in the bottom of the twelfth. It wasn't beautiful, but it was a win. The next night, they weren't so lucky. Ryan Vogelsong threw six solid innings, braving the rain through it all, but it wasn't enough. You have to hit to win, at least a little bit, and the team's hitters were collectively slumping. To add to the indignity of inclement conditions that kept the crowd down, the Bears shut out the home team, 5-0.

The next night, the Bears should have been hoping for rain. The Volcanoes literally erupted, pounding out 16 hits in a 19-8 rout. Jeremy Luster hit two homers and drove in 6 runs himself. Tony Torcato , who entered the game with a .064 average, went 4 for 5. Doug Clark also homered with a man on and scored four runs, a team record. The 19 runs was also a club record. (It was a new club.)

Luster tied individual club records for home runs and RBI's in a game. "We've been kind of waiting for our team to explode," he said. "You know we've got all the talent in the world. We finally got what we were looking for. We have to enjoy it now and put it behind us." In the game, right-hander Jake Estevez made his first and last start as a Volcano. He was called up to Bakersfield right after the game.

The team was in good spirits as the players boarded the bus for Spokane. They were headed for a 5 game series with the Indians who were touted as having the strongest team in the league this year. The rout of Yakima in the final game of that series was good for their morale and lifted the team record to 4 and 7. They could handle those Indians, they thought.

Perhaps it was the long bus ride or perhaps the apparent revolving door of players, but the confrontation with Spokane was a horror show. The Indians scored 8 runs in the bottom of the first and the Volcanoes could not catch up all night, falling to Spokane 13-6. At that point, four of the Volcanoes' pitchers had been called up to the next step on the ladder. Other players, late arrivals and late signers, kept coming in. "Pretty soon we're going to have a rotation full of teenagers," Comstock said. Shortstop Cody Ransom said it best. "It's the same game, just different people. Everybody wants to move up. If they don't, I don't know why they're here."

Owner Jerry Walker put a little different spin on it. "Fans are having a hard time finding an identity with this team, because so many players are shuffling in and out," he said. Bill Tucker, the other owner, thought it would all sort out. The talent was coming or was here. He said, "San Francisco has signed 20 of its top 22 picks from the 1998 draft, and all of them are on the Volcanoes' roster, or have been. It's maybe the strongest team we ever had and they just have to sort out who's who."

Meanwhile, the hitting drought continued. The Spokane Indians squeezed out a 3-2 victory on June 29 and a 5-4 victory the following night, to put an end to the month of June. The Volcanoes' record had fallen to 4 wins against 11 losses and the only hope on the horizon was the well known but yet unfulfilled promise of the talented players in uniform.

July started out better. After 4 straight losses in Spokane, and still looking for their first road victory, the Volcanoes got it together again. After lefty reliever Tom Nielsen had given up a 2-out, two-run double in the bottom of the eighth, Eric Mattern blasted a triple with the bases loaded to give the Volcanoes a 6-4 lead and the game. It ended their 4 game losing streak and gave the team its first win on the road and a winning record in early July. They still had a ways to go, since the team only had 5 wins now and was 6 games below the respectable .500 level. It also was the first Volcanoes win ever in Spokane, after having been swept up there all 1997 and June of 1998.

From there, the team limped home to face those Southern Oregon toughies from Medford. And toughies they were. That team sported Jason Hart, the league leader in home runs and he lived up to his reputation. In the sixth inning he struck a 3 run homer and a grand slam in the seventh to almost single-handedly beat the home team. Hart did open the door, turning a 6-5 Volcanoes' lead around which then continued to a 13-7 victory for the Timberjacks. The Volcanoes didn't help themselves that night either. The moundsmen gave away 11 walks in a game that had 24 hits, including 10 for extra bases. The game was only 2 minutes shy of 4 hours long.

The next night was the opposite story. The teams were going hard at each other before 2,745 fans and had battled to a 5-5 tie by the fifth inning. Manager Keith Comstock hit the right buttons though. With a Timberjack on first base with one out, he summoned Long Island lefty Tom Nielsen from the pen. Just hoping for a couple of ground balls to hold the visitors at bay, Nielsen struck out both batters remaining in the fifth, all three in the sixth and the first one in the seventh for 6 straight strikeouts. Nielsen was exultant and couldn't remember striking out 6 straight at any level.

In the bottom of the fifth, the Volcanoes erupted for 5 runs to take command. The big hit was a bases-loaded triple by John Summers. Chris Magruder followed with his first home run in the sixth to make the score 11-5 which is how it ended. Nielsen gave the bullpen a much-needed lift and rest and the team was feeling good, having come back to 6 and 12.

Before a sellout Fourth of July crowd of 5,269, and before a spectacular and dazzling fireworks display sponsored by Roth's was unleashed at game's end, the Volcanoes won again, 8-1. They then followed Southern Oregon to the Medford ballpark for a 3 game series. The Volcanoes swept all three to raise their record to 10-12 with a 5 game winning streak. Was all the patience and frustration beginning to pay off? The Volcanoes roster now included 2 first round picks, Tony Torcato and Arturo "Scoop" McDowell, and 2 "sandwich" picks in Chris Jones and Jeff Urban. The Giants had now signed their first 22 picks in the 1998 draft. The team was loaded with talent, but were they just 'paper' tigers?

Coming home to Keizer to face the Spokane Indians in a 5 game series, the Volcanoes now exuded confidence. They were closing in on that coveted .500 mark and still had a lot of season left to make it meaningful. The series would be a matchup between the two hottest teams in the Northwest League. Both had winning streaks on the line so one had to end. Unfortunately, the Salem-Keizer streak ended at 5 while Spokane extended its streak to 5.

It wasn't a blowout though. With any luck but bad luck, the Volcanoes could have won. The score was 2-1 and the Indians got their runs with the help of the Salem-Keizer pitchers. Leading 1-0, the Volcanoes pitcher issued a leadoff walk in the third, bounced a pickoff throw past first base, and then threw back-to-back wild pitches to score the runner. In the sixth inning, the Volcanoes reliever fielded a bunt and threw wild over first base to get that runner to second. He advanced on a single and finally scored what proved to be the winning run on a sacrifice fly.

Three games under. No room for mistakes, not against this team. Had they won, the Volcanoes would have moved to within a game of then Southern Division leader, Portland. By winning, the Indians moved into a tie for first with Northern Division leader, Boise. Salem-Keizer then lost the next game in a heartbreaker, 7-6. The team trailed all night but continued to battle back and almost made it. "I don't think we're ever too down to come back," Steve Hill said. " I've never played with a group that fights as much as these guys. It makes it fun to play with them."

Manager Keith Comstock was equally proud. "These kids battle," he said. "We never just roll over and die. They've got so much character, it's a lot of fun coaching them. That character will shine through at some point in the season." But when? The team was now at 10 and 14 with the season approaching midpoint.

The answer started to come right away. The team took the next three games from Spokane, 12-4, 11-5 and 6-5. The Friday night victory may have been a tribute to Manager Comstock banning roving hitting instructor, Carlos Lezcano from sitting in the dugout. Lezcano had visited several times earlier in the season and had never seen a victory. He was banished as a bad luck charm.

The players switched to red shirts and red hats. "It's not so much superstitious as it is out of respect for baseball lore," Comstock said. "I watched The Natural last night . One guy wore a lightning bolt on his sleeve, then they all wore lightning bolts, and they all started hitting. Don't put it past me to put lightning bolts on our sleeves." Nothing was sacred to produce a win, and win they did and kept winning. When they finished with Spokane that series, the team was one game under that coveted .500 mark at 13 and 14. Everybody contributed but Chris Jones and Jeff Allen were standouts. Let's go get those Yakima Bears.

It wasn't to be that easy. Even though Chris Magruder was playing his first professional game in his home town of Yakima, and he performed well, the team was lackadaisical, probably from the long bus trip. They held tight until the home seventh when two errors and three wild pitches let the Bears score five times to ice the game at 7-4. The Volcanoes were hitting now, though, Every starting batter had at least one hit and Tony Torcato went 3 for 4. Cody Ransom, Scoop McDowell and Chris Magruder each had 2 hits. However, the

Volcanoes' batters struck out 13 times. The team now was at 13-15 and couldn't seem to quite reach that elusive .500 mark. They also now trailed division-leading Portland by 4 full games.

The next night, July 15, the game started out as more of the same from the night before. Yakima came out with their hitting shoes on and Randy Goodrich was tagged for two homers in the first inning and a 3-0 Yakima lead. The Bears made it a 4-1 lead in the second but were shut down after that as the Volcanoes began to claw their way back. Led by Jeremy Luster and Chris Magruder, who each had clutch triples, the visiting Volcanoes struck for nine runs and held on to win at 9-5. Todd Ozias sparkled in relief and the team pulled to within 1 win of the .500 mark.

July 16 was a major turning point in the season. The Volcanoes outslugged and outlasted Yakima for a 11-10 win. More importantly, the team which had began so far under water, was now at .500 for the first time since winning the season opener. It was a flagship event.

Player confidence was now soaring. Despite all the hitting that went on, it was a sacrifice fly by Mike Dean in the ninth inning that produced the winning run. The game was topsy-turvy with the Volcanoes trailing first at 4-1 and then 9-7 after 5. That team of scrappers continued to battle back for this all important win and Benji Miller, who came in to relieve in the seventh, shut the Bears' bats down for the rest of the game. There had been 4 lead changes and the game produced a total of 21 runs on 27 hits with no errors. If there was a hitting star for Salem-Keizer, it was Tony Torcato, now hitting everything in sight, who had 4 hits and 4 RBI, including a two-run homer in the fifth inning.

Chris Jones was giving the loyal Volcanoes fans a big scare. He was going so good, they were concerned he would be promoted to long season A ball before the season ended and we would be forced to go on without him. He added to his luster again this night in Yakima. Jones threw 7 innings of shutout baseball, extending his scoreless inning streak to 21 and 2/3. He had allowed only 1 earned run in 27 innings all season. This night he struck out 6 and walked only 1 in getting his record to 4-0. Mike Huller relieved and yielded Yakima's only run in a 4-1 Salem-Keizer victory. The team was now over the break-even mark, having won 6 of their last 7 games and 11 of their last 14. Pretty good.

July 18, 1998, was the date of the first professional start of Mark Hills, a Keizer native. He had pitched before for the team, but not as a starter. Being off his home turf for the event probably helped. He turned in a stellar performance throwing 4 innings of 1 hit baseball. When he was replaced on the mound, the team led 5-0 and pulled away eventually to an 8-0 lead. There the good times ended.

The finish would be a nightmare, the kind of game that gives managers and pitching coaches gray hair and sleepless nights. Jeff Urban, Mark Hutchings and Todd Ozias replaced Hills and couldn't hold the Bears at bay. Yakima tied the game with an 8 run rally in their half of the eighth inning and won it on a Mike Balbuena homer leading off the ninth. It was a downer after being so far ahead in a game that could have given them some space above the .500 mark. This was minor league baseball "at it's best."

Despite the last game debacle in Yakima, the team was still in high spirits as the bus zoomed home over hill and dale back to the friendly confines of the Crater. The Portland Rockies were to be their guests for a three game series that could prove critical. Also, the season midpoint was approaching and tradition held that the team in first place on that date usually won the division title. Lots of reasons to push and pull out all the stops.

And push they did. In the Sunday game on July 19, the team scored the last two runs on Portland wild pitches and won 5-3. With some hitting and good running, plus excellent middle relief pitching, they eked out a victory. Kudos had to go to Keith Connolly and Tom Nielsen who got the outs they needed from the fifth through the eighth inning before handing the ball over to Benji Miller who was establishing himself as the all-star he was to become.

It was good to win right after such a devastating loss in Yakima. "I told the kids they could either go north or go south after a game like that," Manager Keith Comstock said. "Good teams go north. The best thing about tonight is we let that game go. One game doesn't take away all the good work they've done in two weeks. They got back in the pennant race. It's important for us to show we can compete with them, and it's important for us to show ourselves that we belong in this race."

They did belong. The win put the team back over .500 by a game. More importantly, it put Salem-Keizer in a tie for first place with the Rockies. That was a lofty position for a team that had had such a mediocre start, and was clear evidence the team was finding itself. Now the task was to keep it up.

The next night, the team pounded out 10 hits, including 3 doubles and 2 triples, winning again, this time 7-3. Everybody was hitting and several stars were beginning to shine. Jeff Allen, for instance, was enjoying a power surge and 15 of his 28 season hits were for extra bases. At this point he had 6 homers, 4 triples and 5 doubles and a league-leading slugging percentage of .656. Jeremy Luster was also making his name a household word, with 20 RBI's on 24 hits. Perfect production. The team was now 2 games over break-even and all alone atop the Southern Division.

The next night was more of the same. Josh Santos had what was probably his best start of the season and was the beneficiary of some timely hitting. Jeremy Luster homered again to help the team to 7 runs. The Benji Miller saga also continued. Entering the game in the seventh inning with the bases loaded and one out, Benji struck out the next two batters and continued to shut the Rockies' hitters down to preserve the 7-3 win and a sweep of Portland..

Next on the menu was the Everett Aquasox. The Volcanoes were rolling, fresh from their sweep of the Rockies at home. The team had now won 14 of its last 18 games with a 2-game cushion (Comstock referred to it as only a "pad") atop the Southern Division. The Aquasox were tough despite a record of 4 games under .500, good enough only for third place in the Northern Division.

The first game matched up two of the top pitchers in the league, Chris Mears of Everett and Chris Jones of the Volcanoes. It was to be a downer night for Jones, who saw his scoreless inning streak stopped at 23. He surrendered 10 hits in all and his earned run average puffed up to a still very respectable 1.72. The game got away though and the Volcanoes couldn't solve Mears until the sixth inning when they closed the gap to 7-6. The game continued in that vein and ended with Everett the winner 10-8.

That game marked the halfway point of the season. The Volcanoes were where they badly wanted to be at the midpoint--on top of the division. The standings at that time stood as follows:

| Northern Division | | | Southern Division | | |
|---|---|---|---|---|---|
| Team | wins | losses | Team | wins | losses |
| Boise | 24 | 11 | Salem-Keizer | 19 | 16 |
| Spokane | 21 | 14 | Portland | 17 | 18 |
| Everett | 15 | 20 | Medford | 17 | 18 |
| Yakima | 13 | 22 | Eugene | 14 | 21 |

It was a real horse race in the south, with only 2 games separating the first 3 teams. In the north, Boise was ahead by 3 but everyone thought Spokane might be a true dark horse and overtake Boise before long. At this point, among the stars establishing themselves was Doug Clark who had a 17 game hitting streak and was batting .321, and in the hunt for the league batting title.

The Volcanoes, in their second full season in their new ballpark, even though hampered by some tough weather early on, had drawn 64,110 fans for an average of 3,562 per home game. Both figures were above the inaugural season highs at the same point which were 63,342 for an average per game attendance of 3,519. The team had clearly caught on with the fans. Not many were questioning the wisdom of building the stadium anymore.

Despite the lofty position the team enjoyed, Manager Comstock had to guard against complacency. "These kids realize that it took hard work to get here," he said. 'It's certainly going to take hard work to stay here."

The players knew it too. "It's great to be in first," Jeremy Luster said. "But it's a long second half of the season. We can't get too happy about it." Cody Ransom spoke about it too. "We all know we can get beat at any time," he said. "Nobody's getting too big a head. We know what it's like to be in last place and we don't want to go back there. We just hope we can keep it going."

The second game of the Aquasox series would make anyone believe it was not going to be a breeze. Mark Hills started and threw over 5 innings, leaving with a 5-3 lead. However, some wild pitches and an error let the Sox tie it at 5-5. That put a lot of pressure on the offense but the players were up to the task. With two outs in the eighth and Kevin Tommasini leading off second, Tony Torcato hit it hard up the middle for a single and what proved to be the winning run. Todd Ozias dominated the Aquasox in the ninth, striking out 2.

The next day, the defense took a rest and, despite five shutout innings  by Jeff Urban, the team lost 8-3.  The Everett team boasted Jake Weber, the league's leading hitter at .350 and he was everything advertised.  He hit his fourth homer, a grand slam,  off Tom Nielsen as part of a 6 run inning to put the game away.  Losses happen, even to Portland and Southern Oregon that night, so no ground was lost.

With the bullpen experiencing a general case of the blahs, and Ozias and Miller his seemingly only reliable relievers, Manager Comstock changed the program a little.  Other teams were beginning to realize the Salem-Keizer bullpen was no longer at its best for the time being. So Comstock relieved starter Randy Goodrich in the sixth with Ozias who then pitched through the eighth, a little longer  than customary. Benji Miller was then brought in to preserve the 5-3 win after Sammy Serrano had broken the 3-3 tie with a solo home run in the seventh inning. Steve Hill, showing his versatility as well as his hitting ability, had 4 hits that night.

July 27 was a rare off day and the team left late that evening for the endurance trip to  Boise. That would not be easy as the 5 game series was expected to be as difficult heat-wise as game wise.  Boise was almost always tough and they were leading the Northern Division.  If the Volcanoes won their division, they could expect to meet Boise in the playoffs. It was time to stand tall.

The first game was a slugfest. The Volcanoes put a 5 spot on the board in their half of the first, but Boise matched it in their half. The second inning was almost the same with Jeremy Luster tripling with 2 on to cap a 4 run inning and a 9-5 lead. The pitching couldn't get it together and the Hawks answered with 6 runs in their half for an 11-9 lead. The Volcanoes kept battling though and loaded the bases with two outs in the ninth but couldn't get a run across, and lost 13-12.

The next night was different though. Mark Hills threw 4 shutout innings and the rest of the staff combined with him to hold the Hawks to 7 hits. Jeff Allen hit his seventh home run and Mike Dean drove in 2 as the Volcanoes won 6-2. Tom Nielsen pitched 2 innings in relief and got his fifth win.

July 30 was an unexpected day off due to inclement weather. That meant a doubleheader would be scheduled for the 31st. It was never welcome to play 2 games in 1 day this late in the season. However, league rules called for the games to be made up as soon as possible. This was the last scheduled visit of Salem-Keizer to Boise so it was now or maybe never.

The lousy weather continued and threatened to rain out the doubleheader too. Nevertheless, they started to play and got the first game in without a hitch. Jeff Urban threw 5 and 2/3 scoreless innings for his first win of the year. Benji Miller again closed it out for his league-leading eighth save as the Volcanoes won 4-1.

The nightcap had a different script. The Hawks jumped off to a 6-0 lead after 4 innings. Just as the Volcanoes started to come back by scoring 2 in the top of the sixth, the rain started to fall heavily After a long delay, the game was called giving Boise a rain-shortened win.

The doubleheader thus ended as a standoff. It was a fitting and appropriate end to the month of July. The standings now looked like this:

| Northern Division | | | Southern Division | | |
|---|---|---|---|---|---|
| Team | wins | losses | Team | wins | losses |
| Boise | 28 | 14 | Salem-Keizer | 23 | 19 |
| Spokane | 26 | 17 | Medford | 20 | 23 |
| Everett | 19 | 24 | Portland | 20 | 23 |
| Yakima | 18 | 25 | Eugene | 17 | 26 |

The race was tightening up in the Southern Division. Both Southern Oregon and Portland were in a dead heat and trailed the Volcanoes by only 3 and 1/2 games. Anything could still happen. It was still anybody's race, especially in this league where streaks were always going to happen. In the North, Boise was not comfortably ahead either. Spokane, which was rumored to be the class of the league, was now coming on and that race threatened to go down to the wire too. It was a promoter's dream but a nail biter for the managers and the players.

The league was prepared just in case the season ended with two teams tied for first. In such cases the league applied a formula for deciding the winner. It would not be decided by a playoff between the teams. The winner so declared would be the divisional winner for that season. The first level of the tie breaker was based on how the two teams fared against one another in head-to-head play. If it couldn't be decided by games won and lost, the next tie-break level would be on runs scored against one another. That was followed by other levels to break the tie if necessary. There was a similar formula arrangement to decide a 3 way tie. It had never been necessary for the Northwest League to apply any tiebreaker criteria.

Boise won the final game of the series by a score of 9-6. It had been a seesaw game which was decided by some lax pitching and a fielding error. It was important to right the ship immediately because Southern Oregon was coming to Keizer for a three game series. The team had lost the Boise series 2-3 but were in every game and could have won more if circumstances were changed only a little. There was no reason to fear Boise if that team proved to be the opponent in a playoff series. Spokane was a different matter. But we had to hold off the Timberjacks and the Rockies to win it, and that had to happen in head-to-head competition.

August 2 was Mike Dean's birthday. He celebrated by going a perfect 4 for 4 and driving in 4 runs. He led a 16 hit attack that shocked the Southern Oregon Timberjacks. The Volcanoes won 13-5 despite some less than stellar pitching by the usually reliable Benji Miller, who nevertheless rang up another save. "I think this is a crucial series for us and for them." Comstock said. "It's the last time we face these guys. Anytime it's the last time you face a division foe, you want to get as much out of it as you can."

Mike Dean also enjoyed the day. "I wish I could have hit forever," he glowed. "The way I was feeling at the plate, I thought I could get a hit every time. It's a great feeling. 4 for 4 nights don't come around so often. I'm going to sleep well tonight."

The next night was payback time in a wild and wooly contest. In a game that took 3 hours and 44 minutes to complete, there was plenty of everything for everybody. It featured 22 hits, 20 walks-14 by Volcano pitchers, 4 home runs and 7 errors. After Mike Dean hit a home run in the bottom of the sixth, the Volcanoes led 9-5 and seemed to be in command. However the Timberjacks scored 5 times in the eighth, capped by Omar Rosario's 3 run homer, to give Southern Oregon an 11-9 lead. In the bottom of the inning, that same Rosario made an error that led to a Volcanoes run and the score was tied at 11 when Sammy Serrano drew a bases loaded walk. In the top of the ninth, though, Jason Hart struck his 14th homer, his 5th in the Crater, for the winning run.

The next day, the teams played what would become the most important game between them in the entire season, even though only a few appreciated its significance then. The Volcanoes had won 6 of the 11 head to head games played thus far. If the Volcanoes won this game and these 2 teams finished the season tied, the division championship would be awarded to Salem-Keizer for having won the season series. If Southern Oregon won the game, the season series would be tied and the other elements of the formula, some of which were still undecided, would come into play.

Baseball is the popular game it is because any one day is independent of every other day. Each game starts with the score even, no matter what happened the day before. So, the Volcanoes who had such a disastrous game the day before, were able to start anew. This game was entirely different.

Where they had issued 14 walks the day before, Volcanoes' pitchers issued only three this night and held the Timberjacks to seven hits and only 4 runs. The Volcanoes capitalized on their hitting and opponent mistakes and pounded out 12 hits in a 10-4 victory. John Summers, Tony Torcato, Steve Hills and Doug Clark, still in the hunt for the league batting title, each had 2 hits.

They now had the important edge in case of a tie. "The reality of it is, we're four games ahead of Southern Oregon," Comstock mused. "When we see that number, we know there's an extra game on it in case we do tie." Prophetic.

Portland was up next for 3 games. In the first of the set, 6 errors and sloppy play cost the game for the Volcanoes. Losing 10-3 was no joy and brought out the bulldog in Manager Keith Comstock. He held his first "team meeting." The next night, he was ejected from the game for arguing too vigorously on a call by the umpire. The team rallied to close to a 3-3 tie, then pulling ahead to win 8-5. Now they were 3 games ahead again, and really counting.

The stimulus didn't last long. The next night, they lost the rubber game of the series to Portland, falling 8-7 in 11 innings. "These kids don't handle pressure very well, and it's not going to go away," Comstock said. "They've got to learn to deal with it and quit trying so hard. When you try too hard, inevitably you're going to overdo it. They're trying to be the hero. It just looks to me that their engine is revved up too dang high." Portland and Southern Oregon were now tied, only 2 games back.

Before that last game with Portland, the Volcanoes and San Francisco Giants said "I do" to each other again. The two signed a two year PDC agreement to stay together through the year 2000. The Giants wanted to remain with Salem-Keizer because of the state-of-the-art facility and the strong fan base. The Volcanoes had a different motive. "Why would we leave the Giants?," part owner Bill Tucker asked. "They have one of the richest traditions in baseball." Jerry Walker chimed in, "We never considered going anyplace else. We think the community can associate with a West Coast team. As long as we keep this wonderful relationship that we have, the Giants will be our No.1 choice."

It was off to Eugene for 3 games now. Eugene had not fared well throughout the season as the honeymoon between the Emeralds and the Braves frayed. The team was dead last in the Southern Division and had no hope with only 3/4 of the season gone. They still had a role to play as the division teams went at each other as the season rushed to a close.

The Volcanoes took the first 2 games in the series, 7-4 and 12-2. A sweep was avoided by Eugene as it's hitters broke out for a

9-3 victory. That loss prevented the Volcanoes from moving 6 games above .500 for the first time in team history. It was on to Portland for a tough 3 games now, followed by 5 games in Everett to wind up the long, 11 game road trip. It was a freak of the schedule that did not favor the Volcanoes.

Southern Oregon had been climbing steadily. The Volcanoes, probably feeling the heat, blew a 5 run lead to Portland and suffered a 9-8 defeat which they could not afford. Even Benji Miller couldn't stem the tide and gave up a grand slam to the first batter he faced, Salvador Duverge and the winning run in the bottom of the ninth. Salem- Keizer and Southern Oregon were now deadlocked at the division top.

The Volcanoes were shut out, 2-0 in the next game and fell to second place. By the skin of their teeth and a 3 run homer from Chris Magurder, the Volcanoes won the final game of the series by a score of 4-3. Magruder had just rejoined the team from San Jose in time to help, really help. The team ended a 3 game losing streak which came at the wrong time, and stayed 3 games above .500.

In Everett, the team stayed 1 game off the pace by winning 5-2. Southern Oregon rallied to beat Yakima to preserve their lead. The next day, the race remained in status quo as Everett smashed the Volcanoes 17-5 and Yakima squeaked by the Timberjacks, 8-6. The Volcanoes reversed the fortunes on that Sunday, pounding the Aquasox 11-2. They eased back into a tie with Southern Oregon for first place as the Yakima Bears beat them 7-4. However, they slipped back to second place the next day as they lost by 12-8 and the Timberjacks won. The see saw action continued as the Volcanoes won again 7-1 on August 18 while Southern Oregon fell to Yakima, 5-2.

It was a tired bunch of puppies that bussed home from Everett that night. They were happy to be at least still tied for the lead, and coming home for 7 games, even though 5 of them were against the Boise Hawks. The race had actually narrowed down to two teams in each division. Boise led a tough Spokane team by one slim game and Salem-Keizer and Southern Oregon were in a dead heat again. The Southern Division lead swayed back and forth but mainly it was the Volcanoes that would slip out of the first place tie, and then crawl back.

August 19 was another day off in an unusual schedule. The Volcanoes looked forward to playing on their home turf again.. Things seemed to go much better for them there although the Crater did not have the reputation of being a hitters park. The days were narrowing down to a precious few and there were only 14 games left on the schedule. Not many innings, not many outs.

The Volcanoes won the first three games of the series against Boise. They won the first game by 11-4. Carlos Valderrama, activated that day from the disabled list, led the charge. Sammy Serrano, Cody Ransom and Jeff Allen hit home runs for Salem-Keizer and Bill Mott hit 2 for the visitors. That put them ahead of Southern Oregon for the time being. They won the third game 4-3.

Sammy Serrano had come alive as a hitter, with 5 homers in his last 10 at bats. Chris Magruder was back, voluntarily accepting a "demotion" from Bakersfield to help out the team

354

he started the season with. We thought it was love. John Summers snapped out of his slump in the second game with the winning hit. He had seen his average plummet from the lofty .340's to almost .300 flat during his hitting drought.

The next two games were losses though. They were tough, too, losing 12-8 and 8-4. Now, with 9 games left, the Volcanoes were ready to take on the Eugene Emeralds for the next 6. The schedule appeared to favor the Volcanoes since the Emeralds were the doormats of the division. It looked easy for a change. Over confidence seemed to be the chief concern of Manager Comstock. Southern Oregon, meanwhile was playing the very tough Portland Rockies.

But Salem-Keizer lost the first two games of the series. The Emeralds were not expected to beat the best team in the league at this critical stage. The first game was one of frustration and the team fell 7-3. Southern Oregon took advantage of the opportunity and climbed back into sole possession of first place, beating Portland 6-5.

The second game was also a heartbreaker, with the Volcanoes falling 5-4 in the bottom of the ninth on a bad hop grounder that turned into a run without much hitting. The Emeralds were clearly relishing their role as spoiler, the only challenge left open to them.

In the third game of the series, the Volcanoes turned it around and put together some solid hitting and clutch pitching. They hit and held on for a 10-6 win. The next game was probably the most memorable of the season thus far, a season with many memorable games. Trailing by 2 runs in the bottom of the ninth, Jeremy Luster (yes--him again) struck a 2 run double to tie the score. In the bottom of the tenth, Eric Mattern hit a solo home run for a real big win.

"Every night it's a different hero," Luster said. "That's what it's going to take." Erik Mattern was gracious, saying," Jeremy's hit was bigger than mine. If it wasn't for him, I would never have been put in that situation." Tony Torcato had been hit square in the mouth by a thrown ball the night before, and the team learned today that he was out for the season, hot bat and all. Bad break. Now they would really test destiny.

The final game of the series showed the true mettle of this team. They had to win and they did, winning it in rare fashion. Jeff Allen hit a 3 run home run, his tenth of the season, and Jeremy Luster, Mr. Reliable, lashed a two run single to bring home an 8-5 win. The game was the last scheduled home game of the season for Keizer and the team gave the fans something to remember them by. In the second inning, a walk and a fielder's choice put runners on first and second for Eugene with no outs. It had the makings of a big inning with the Emeralds tallying several runs to put the Volcanoes into a real crater. However, luck was on the Volcanoes side.

Bry Ewan hit a sharp grounder right at third baseman, Steve Hill. Alert as always, Hill clutched the ball and stepped on third. One out. He then whipped the ball to Erik Mattern who was standing on second base. Two outs. Erik then threw to Jeremy luster at first for the third out in a triple play. It was a rare treat. "My first one ever," Steve Hill said. "I've never been that pumped about a defensive play. It was the most exciting thing-except last night's win- that's happened to me this summer." There would be more.

Teams that get triple plays usually win the game. For some strange reason, that seems to be the rule. That win, coupled with the Timberjacks 3-1 loss to Portland that day, created another dead heat in the standings between Southern Oregon and Salem-Keizer. So, it would come down to the last 27 innings of the season, probably all of them, before the issue was decided.

"Eugene played us tough," Comstock said after the game. " I think Eugene will go down there and play them the same way. I think you can bet on those guys (Eugene) winning one of those games, possibly two. But we can't count on that. We either win it or lose it in Portland." There was no doubt though that the cards were clearly stacked in favor of the Timberjacks. They were playing the division doormats in their home park while the Volcanoes were playing tough Portland in the Rockies' ballpark. In the Northern Division, things were just as tight as Spokane had caught and passed Boise and was threatening to pull further ahead on a late season surge.

The game that ended the month of August was another white knuckle game for the Volcanoes. Mike Dean, Jeremy Luster and John Summers each drove in 2 runs with lusty hitting and the Volcanoes led 6-1 going into the ninth inning. A couple of hits off Randy Goodrich and an error by the usually very reliable Steve Hill gave the Rockies a 3 run burst. Comstock called on a tired Benji Miller to quell the rebellion, and he was up to the task. The Volcanoes won 6-4.

"I was starting to get scared," Mike Dean admitted later. "Any time a team  strings together a couple hits, and you get an error on top of that, in the back of your head you kind of get to worrying."

Manager Comstock was more in character. "We just tried to make too much happen with the ground ball.  The bottom line is , we won, and Benji got the save.  Everything worked out. We did a lot of good things.  I didn't want it to go unrewarded." The Timberjacks kept pace, easily manhandling the Emeralds, 8-1.

It had already been a rewarding season and San Francisco was counting its prospects..  Doug Clark had raised his season's average one point to .343 in that game, going 2 for 5.  That ranked him third in the league and still in the hunt for the batting title.  Jeremy Luster was on a 14 for 28 streak in his last 7 games.  He raised his batting average to .310, making him the fourth Volcanoes player batting over the magical .300 number.

Lefty Josh Santos had given 7 strong innings in that game, throwing only 90 pitches and allowed only 1 run on 4 hits.  He struck out 7 and walked 2.  It was a fine clutch outing.  His record now was 4-1.

It was 1 down and 2 to go.  Destiny was now in the team's hands for sure.  If they won the last 2 games, they would win the division no matter what those Southern Oregon guys did. They would both be tied if they both won both their games and the tiebreak rule would award the championship and playoff berth to the Volcanoes.  There was no margin for error.

The next, and second last of the season, game was an even tighter squeaker. The Volcanoes won 8-7 but the ninth inning was a nailbiter. Portland, which never quit and proudly never gave in, rallied again in their half of the ninth. Benji Miller had to be called on again. He was tired and lucky. He threw 1 pitch for a grounder to short for the game-ending out. He said he didn't think he had much more fuel left in his tank. Southern Oregon again kept the pressure on and beat Eugene again.

Now it was down to the final 9 innings, 27 outs, of the regular season. It was win and the playoffs, or lose and possibly go home. It was all on the table. Mark Hills, the Keizer native, knew it would come down to his start for the finale. He was able to figure out the rotation and knew it would be him on the hill for all the marbles if it came to that, and it did. He was somewhat happy to be out of town in Portland rather than at home. Less pressure-he thought. It was clearly the most important game of the Volcanoes' season, and possibly the biggest of Hills' career, certainly thus far.

So this was it. All or nothing. Needing a win and expecting no help from the Eugene Emeralds in their game with the Timberjacks, the Volcanoes went out and took care of business right away. They came out with their hitting shoes on and put up runs to enjoy a 10-3 lead at the end of the fifth inning. Everyone seemed to pitch in at the plate. Steve Hill, Sammy Serrano and Chris Magruder had triples, making it a team total of 49 triples for the year. That eclipsed a league record that had stood since 1972 when Lewiston (Idaho) hit 47. Chris

Magruder went 5 for 5 plus a walk, breaking his own franchise record set a month earlier. "It's been a long time since I had a game like this," he said.

Magruder had been promoted to San Jose earlier in the year and had been sent back to help the team close on the pennant. He was of immense help and ignited many rallies and drove in some very important runs and scored others. That was unusual. "We don't want to be perceived by other baseball organizations as being primarily focused on winning", said Bobby Evans, Assistant Director of Player Development for San Francisco. "That is not our primary focus. But other than to help Salem-Keizer, there was no reason to send those guys back down."

As always, though, the Rockies kept pecking away at that lead. They finally closed to 11-8 and tired and worn Benji Miller had to be summoned again to save the Volcanoes' chestnuts. He responded again in grand style.

As the last out was recorded, the dugout exploded and the field players circled en masse around the pitcher's mound. Soon, Bill Tucker and Jerry Walker and the entire Walker family were in the melee. It was a joyous group and they didn't seem to want to leave the field. The lights of the stadium had to be dimmed before they all headed for the dressing room.. They had done it. They had swept Portland, they had achieved the impossible dream. When asked if he knew the final score in Southern Oregon, "Kool-Aid" Frazier, a player who saw precious little playing time during the year but kept quiet as a team player should, said, "Who cares?" Southern Oregon had won so the win in Portland was a necessity.

The locker room was one huge noise center. Bill Tucker and Jerry Walker strode into that pack to congratulate them. Cigars seemed to pop up everywhere. Over the din, Bill Tucker held up the Balfour ring sizer box. He reminded them about needing to win against the Northern Division champions to get the rings. No one seemed concerned about that. They were in a joyous state. The ride back to Keizer was equally happy. When they arrived to a large local celebration by the fans, they finally found out the playoff opponent would be Boise.

It was somewhat unfortunate, but better than nothing, that the playoff games would begin the very next day, in Keizer. No day off, no rest, no time to bask in the glory of the achievement. Even worse, there was no time to advertise to alert those members of the public who did not closely follow the team's fortunes. There would be radio and newspaper announcements but only for the one day, the very day the playoffs started.

It was an off day from school so it should have helped swell the attendance. However, it was also coming into the big Labor Day weekend so people already had plans made which could not be broken. There were many factors both ways, but the main difficulty was the inability to advertise properly and no time to get special souvenirs to sell at the games. The first 2 games of the playoffs would be in Keizer. The rest would be in Boise.

Rick Banning told the Statesman Journal that he couldn't think of a better place to take his kids on a weekday night, to see the first playoff game ever for the Salem-Keizer Volcanoes. "I think it's great we have something like this. The kids can stay out late, and we get autographs after the game." It was the first time since 1982 that a Salem minor league baseball team would be in the post season hunt. There was never before a Keizer minor league team so this was the first there also.

"It's only their second year and they have done real well," said Carol Pacholl of Keizer who walked to the ballpark from her home. "But I'm surprised at the low attendance (for the first playoff game). They did so well this season. They made us like baseball again." She was speaking of the attendance that night, which would only reach 2,601, well below the season average of 3,526 or the ballpark's capacity of 4,296. "With less than 24 hours to plan, the attendance was actually very good," noted League President Bob Richmond.

But the occasion was festive. It even drew out-of-towners Lana Doyle of Toronto and Russ Scharn of Newberg who said, "This is the first time I have ever been to a game. It's great." Even the umpiring was different. There were 4 umpires instead of the usual 2. "We try to get the 4 best," league President, Bob Richmond said. He picked them and they would work the entire playoff series. Honored selectees were John Woods, Bill Van Raaphorst, Tony Prater and Paul Chandler. They would have a major influence on this first game.

Before the game, Jerry Walker and Bill Tucker distributed souvenir championship t-shirts to all the players. "This is just to wet your appetite" Bill said. Jerry said, "This is just a warm-up to the rings."

Jerry's reference was to the rings the league champions can receive. Not all teams buy them for the players but these two owners would, and the Giants would help do it right. In fact, at various times throughout the season, Bill Tucker would visit the team locker room, make a little inspirational speech and tell the players about the big ring they would get if they won the championship. He would hold up his '92 ring and show it to them as an example of what it would be like. "This one will be bigger." he said. He believed in motivation.

Bill had even obtained from Notre Dame, a copy of their locker room motto "play like a champion today" and had it hung on the locker room wall. They also had Bob Feller, Hall of Fame pitching legend, make an inspirational speech to them when he visited the stadium. Incentive.

Pre-game ceremonies were kept to a minimum but were nevertheless observant of ancient baseball traditions. The teams and dignitaries were introduced but no windy speeches and not a lot of fanfare. The fans had come for the game and they would see one to remember.

Neither team looked particularly sharp or fresh in the game. So it was kind of sloppy. The Volcanoes jumped right off in the bottom of the first and hung a 3 spot on the board. The Hawks, probably still suffering jet lag from that long trip overnight from Boise, never fully recovered from that rally. That trip took 71/2 hours. Bill Perreira double bused them down to give more room to each player and allow for better rest. However, it appeared not to be enough after an emotion draining pennnant race and waiting for hours to find out who they were going to play before embarking on the trip.

The game was filled with excitement but less than good plays and umpiring calls. For instance, Mike Dean attempted to score from second on a single to right by Scoop McDowell. Dean, the ball and catcher Jason Hill arrived sort of together. Dean, a catcher himself, flattened Hill in a clean play. After hitting the ground hard from that hefty block, Hill nevertheless hung on to the ball. The umpire called Dean safe in a clear break for the Volcanoes.

The ninth inning saw the most bizarre play. With runners on base in the top of the ninth with two outs, the Boise batter hit a popup just behind Volcanoes third baseman Steve Hill. He had to catch it. For some reason he didn't and the ball dropped to the field. However, the baserunner had swung close by Hill as he was going for the ball and may have had a hand in his missing that routine popup. There was no call from the umpiring crew. Everyone seemed lost in space. Finally, Manager Keith Comstock ran out to plead his cause for an interference call. After a conference among the umpires, they called the batter out for baserunner interference, and the game was over.

It did not sit easily with Boise Manager Tom Kotchman. "You just can't stand there and let the game end like that," he said. "It was a helluva way to end a playoff game. But it's the right call, so next game." Hill was more accurate. " I can't say that was the reason I missed the ball," he said, "but the guy bumped me." Steve had immediately called interference to the umpire. It was the delay in call that was probably the worse thing.

But the game packed in a lot of excitement. Most of the fans stayed to the very end and got their money's worth. "I'm getting hoarse and it's only the second inning" said Bob Hawley. "It's better than going to the movies. You can get up and walk around and visit people. There's everyone from newborns to 80-year-olds here tonight."

The team had to say goodbye to Chris Magruder though, who left to go up in the chain again. He had done his part to bring the pennant home. It would be tough without either Torcato or Magruder. Could this really be a team of destiny?

The second game of the playoffs was a laugher, as they say, for Salem-Keizer. The crowd had swelled to 3,369 and they roared like lions as the Volcanoes got 4 in the fifth and 3 in the sixth to break the game open. Boise had opportunities throughout the night but could only score 5 and lost the game 14-5. Now there was only one game to be won for the championship flag to fly over the Crater. It was not in the bag by any means. Just last year, in 1997, the same Boise Hawks had been ahead 2 games to none and had lost to a tough Portland team that swept the remaining games. It could happen again.

"I feel like with our team because we've got focus, it's going to be tough for us to lose 3 games in a row," Steve Hill said. The main worry might have been overconfidence. "I'm pretty sure we'll take it as a 0-0 series" said pitcher Josh Santos who benefited from the scoring attack and got the win. It was a confident, happy and joyous group that departed that night for Boise. They had a 71/2 hour bus ride facing them. Many of their loyal fans would drive cars and take planes to Boise for what could be a 3 day stay.

The team was now clearly in the driver's seat. This team which had to have been established as underdogs simply because of the way their year went, now had command of the league flag and their own destiny. They would have to put together nine consecutive innings of winning baseball at any time over the next three days to bring home the championship. Salem had celebrated only one professional baseball championship since 1940. Keizer never had any. Would this be the one?

For the final game it would be aces up. Ryan Vogelsong, with an aching arm, would take the ball for the Volcanoes against Hawks' ace, Doug Bridges. Unfortunately, Ryan didn't have much this night, he would have to rely on courage and guile. Boise tagged him for a run in the first and it looked like it could be a long night for Volcanoes fans and a short night for Vogelsong. He hung in there and got the side out, limiting the damage.

Destiny's tots struck back in the second as Jeremy Luster hit another home run to tie the score. Ryan was not up to controlling the home team Hawks, though. Boise struck three times in the third to jump to to a 4-1 lead, which looked pretty safe the way Bridges was throwing Sticking with his ace, the guy who really helped get them there, Keith Comstock, serving as both manager and pitching coach, nursed Vogelsong into the sixth inning.

It was a gutty performance by both Vogelsong and Comstock. "I kept him in there because he was throwing with his heart," Comstock would say later. "I'll take heart over arm any day of the week." Vogelsong, who was to get the win, was exuberant in his compliments. "A lot of it was the guys on the bench," he said. " They kept telling me to just keep plugging away. When you have guys believing in you, it gives you confidence."

Randy Goodrich relieved Vogelsong with one out in the sixth. The turning point may have been Doug Clark's fourth inning homer which cut the deficit to 4-2. It was a  bomb and the entire stadium knew it was gone when it left the bat. It seemed to surprise the Hawks that this team would continue scratching and clawing its way back into the game. As Clark rounded the bases and touched home plate, he looked up at the collected fans of the Volcanoes who had followed the team to Boise. He sort of grinned as if to say "We got 'em now."

Maybe it was so. From that time on, the Hawks looked like dead men just going through the motions. They fielded and hit, but not much in the hitting category. Goodrich shut them down holding their offense while the Volcanoes threw their offense into high gear. Sammy Serrano tied the game with a two-out, two-run single in the fifth.

The Volcanoes took the lead in the top of the sixth, and added another in the seventh on 3 walks and an error. The team led by 6-4 going into the bottom of the ninth. Three more outs needed.

Comstock followed the pattern he had all year. He summoned Benji Miller from the bullpen to put the game away. Miller, clearly the ace of the bullpen and of the entire league bullpen, an all-star, and a reliable arm on all occasions, answered the call. The Hawks continued to play like dead men and Miller overpowered them. The first batter struck out, the next tapped the ball back to Miller for an easy out and the third batter grounded to Cody Ransom, our slick fielding shortstop who threw a bullet to first for the out, the game, the championship.

The dugout erupted and surrounded Benji on the mound. There was a release of tension and the players jumped on and hugged each other with abandon. They had won. They were champions. This team that had to fight so hard to find itself in the beginning of the season and had to struggle so often and find hits and runs and pitching to come from behind so often, was now the champions. They ruled the league. The impossible dream had happened to come true.

That last game was like a sample of the entire season. Everyone contributed. The Volcanoes got 7 hits from 7 players, including home runs from Luster and Clark. Steve Hill and Mike Dean had bunted for base hits and each of the team's runs were scored by a different player. Everybody counted. It was a true team effort. "I wasn't surprised to have only one guy on the All Star Team," Manager Keith Comstock said. "Teams like this win championships."

Amid the melee on the field were Jerry Walker and Bill Tucker. Bob Richmond was carrying the league championship trophy and wanted to deliver it then and there. It is not even a good looking trophy, old and tarnished as it is,and it gets passed on to the winner from year to year. Neither Bill nor Jerry wanted to take it. They would make up their own again. However, they did have to honor league standards so Bill took the trophy.

In the stands, the faithful Volcanoes fans were celebrating too. One could see Don Porter and Al Miller on top of the dugout taking photos and yelling and screaming. After a while, the players made their way into the dressing room for more raucous congratulations and celebration. They celebrated like World Series winners. They were learning to act like winners too.

Bill and Jerry followed them in. Trying to get their attention and doing his best to shout over the din, Jerry held up the ring sizing box for all to see. "We did it," he shouted. "We're going to size you up for those rings we've been promising all year. You'll be proud to wear it. " Bill Tucker shouted. The celebration would continue.

Back at the hotel, there was some mixup as to where the impromptu party would be held. Don Porter had come prepared for a party in his room but the players had other ideas. They had a site for their celebration. Jerry and his entourage left to join them and Al Miller tried. Unfortunately there were two places with similar names and Al had some difficulty locating the correct one. The partying went on into the night and neither the players nor their fans came back to earth and reality until the wee hours.

It was a tired group of Salem-Keizer enthusiasts who made their way back home the next day. Tired but happy, they smiled all the way home. Meanwhile, Jerry and Bill were trying to put together a welcoming party and a parade in honor of the champions. It had been a memorable year, and no one seemed to want it to end. It would end the right way.

It had been a great season.  A truly great season.

The Victory Parade gathers in front of Keizer City Hall

The team rode in Pepsi delivery trucks

371

The Keizer Fire Department got into the act

An Irish donkey wagon carried Jennifer Knudson

Sometimes children say it best

Fans greeted the parade at the ballpark

373

For the parade - Bill sits on fender of Roth Antique Fire Engine

The Roth Engine was painted green - naturally

Keith Comstock showed off the League "Trophy"

At the end of the parade, the team assembled at the ballpark

The team responded to the fans cheers

376

The ring ceremony in Scottsdale

A group of future big leaguers show off their rings - (l to r): Tony Torcato, Jeremy Luster, Chris Jones, Jeff Allen, Chris Magruder, Benji Miller; and Doug Clark

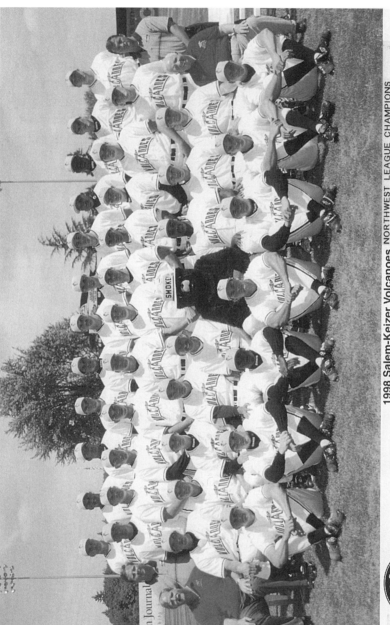

## 1998 Salem-Keizer Volcanoes NORTHWEST LEAGUE CHAMPIONS

**BOTTOM Row (L-R):** Kevin Joseph, Mark Hills, Carlos Frazier, Erik Matern, Guillermo Rodriguez, Tom Nielsen, Chris Jackson
**SECOND ROW (L-R):** Jerry Walker, Eric Johnson, Steve Hill, Chris Jones, Masashi Kiyono, Keith Comstock, Smokey the Bear, Bert Hunter, Cody Ransom, Doug Clark, Bill Tucker

**THIRD ROW (L-R):** Billy Carpine, Jeff Pohl, Randy Goodrich, Mark Hutchings, Jeremy Luster, Brett Casper, Nate Bump, Ryan Vogelsong, Shawn Lindsey, Joe Ojeda, Joe Farley, David Kenna, Eric Reisinger

**TOP ROW (L-R):** Ben Bertrand, Mike Dean, Erasmo Ramirez, John Summers, Carlos Valderama, Tony Torcato, Todd Ozias, Jeff Allen, Pedro Mota, Luis Mercedes, Benji Miller, Mike Huller

251

# EPILOGUE

The parade might have been the biggest sports parade ever in the entire county. Certainly it was the biggest such event in Keizer. The newspapers and radio got the message about the parade out to the people. It was on short notice so nobody was willing to predict how big it would be or how many people would come out for it.

Jerry had contacted John Preston to try to enlist him to line up the details. Then he got Mayor Dennis Koho involved to get all the necessary bureaucratic work done. Preston and Koho would collect regular and antique cars, floats and convertibles for the parade. Orville Roth's vintage fire engine, naturally painted green, would lead the parade with bell clanging. Of course everything would be preceded by police cars with their lights flashing and police would direct traffic around the City.

The parade participants collected in front of City Hall on Chemawa Drive. Bill, who had seen some outstanding New York City parades in his day, was really impressed. It wasn't that so many had shown up on such short notice that got him. It was the variety of vehicles and the enthusiasm of the participants.

Walking down the parade line, Bill met Dale and Betty Emery, loyal fans and outstanding people, already in place in the parade line. Preston had arranged for Pepsi trucks to participate, with their cargo doors up. The players rode in those cargo stacks which were open on both sides of each truck. It was a good idea. There was a vehicle with a fake calliope on it spouting music from inside. Janet Walker rode in that vehicle, making gestures as if playing that instrument.

There were pony drawn wagons, bicycles, motorcycles, and many others, humorous and regular, all driven by enthusiastic people. There was even an Irish donkey wagon carrying Jerry's sister, Jennifer Knudson. The parade was indeed a big event. Bill and Jerry rode atop the back seat of Jerry's BMW convertible, driven by Lisa. Jerry held one-year-old Mickey and repeatedly held him up for all to see. It was near his birthday so Mickey probably thought his dad had done all that for him.

The last car was an antique vehicle with a rumble seat. Keith Comstock rode in that rumble seat, clutching and hugging the trophy. He deserved the spot of honor. He had just been honored as Manager of The Year in the league. He deserved that too.

The parade wound its way out to River Road, then along Lockhaven Drive to Radiant Drive where it entered the ballpark parking lot. Along the way there was at least a thousand people lining the way, yelling and shouting and holding up hastily constructed signs of congratulations. The Statesman Journal had published a special placard and distributed them widely, proclaiming the Volcanoes as champions.

When we got into the parking lot, it was jammed with people who crowded in on the vehicles and cheered and shouted. The team front office had announced that soda(contributed by Pepsi) and hot dogs would be available at the Stadium concession stand for free. Everyone made their way into the stadium for the formal shindig.

The team was brought out onto the field amid loud cheers. Dennis Koho read a proclamation declaring the ENTIRE month of September as Volcanoes Baseball month in Keizer. The Mayor of Salem, Mike Swaim, also had a proclamation from that City. Then Bill Tucker and Jerry Walker spoke. They had been asked by Keith Comstock to hold the proceedings brief so they said little beyond congratulations and thanks to the fans. Comstock was different.

Swept up by the moment, Keith was euphoric. All the celebration of the victory and the victory itself had gotten to him. He was overwhelmed by the support the team had received all year and by the outpouring of affection he had seen just minutes before along the parade route and during the on-field ceremony. When he took the mike, he was effervescent.

Keith made a nice little speech of his own from his heart. He then began introducing each player separately, of course to loud cheers and applause. He had something to say about each of them and they in turn each had an opportunity to express their own feelings. It took time but it was a memorable event. One could appreciate Comstock's memory and concentration. He had noted so many things during the year about each of the players and remembered them. It was an uncanny performance and a very good demonstration of his talent, both as a human being and as a leader. Having seen that performance, you could never look at Keith Comstock the same way again.

Then all the tumult and the shouting was over. It was getting dark now and the people filtered out of the ballpark slowly, like water escaping down a clogged drain. They really didn't want to go. The ballpark had been the scene of such big moments and so many triumphs that season. It was a time to remember, a snapshot in all our lives that would endure for a long time.

The players, Keith too, would be gone from this field shortly, possibly forever, drifting into that vast abyss of life, possibly never to surface again in such an outstanding way. Certainly several of them would march on through the minor league system to the big leagues, either in San Francisco or elsewhere and would be the subject of conversation among the Salem-Keizer fans whenever the limelight struck them again. Others would be just names in a parade of players who came upon the scene, banded together, and had one memorable season in the sun as ballplayers on a championship team. They were winners, indelibly marked forever as champions, at least once in their lives.

Many fans who came there that day, or during that season, even if only once, would remember them all. Many more players would follow, taking their places on the team, perhaps even for more championships. But this one would always be special. These players were special. This team was special, and would always be special. It was the first championship team of what would hopefully be many in seasons to come. These cities, this franchise, these fans deserved it.

Bill and Jerry thought about the team often and worked at designing and arranging for an appropriate ring to celebrate and remember that grand season. The Giants, like the great organization it is, wanted to do it right for the players too. They contributed to the cost and thereby allowed us to order a magnificent ring for each of the players as they deserved.

It did not seem long before Spring came creeping round the bend. Spring brings out many thoughts, of love, and certainly baseball. Bill and Jerry ventured to Scottsdale, Arizona that March to see Spring Training and view the progress our former players had made and possibly get a look at those who would be coming to us for the 1999 season. Among the items on the agenda, though, was the presentation of the championship rings.

On March 27th, the Volcanoes and the Giants threw a lavish party in a hotel in Scottsdale. All the players except one had made it back and were present at the ceremony. In addition, besides Bill Tucker and Jerry Walker, Northwest League President Bob Richmond, and Giants organization's Jack Hiatt and Bobby Evans were also present. Keith Comstock and Bert Hunter were there of course. Pat Lafferty, the Voice of the Volcanoes, was there in good form and acted as master of ceremonies. Several of the Volcanoes' fans also came to Scottsdale for the ceremony.

Lafferty perfomed admirably and each of the players there were called up, handed their ring and applauded. When they sat down you could see them trying them on and chuckling over how well they looked wearing that ring.

The ring is truly impressive both as to size and detail and is now worn proudly by anyone associated with that team. It was a night for everyone to remember. As Pat Lafferty was to write in his personal summary of the season, "As an epilogue to a championship season, this was an evening--and a team-- to remember. And remember them we will. For this is the team against which future editions of the Volcanoes will always be measured. And with each ring come the memories of a lifetime and a championship they will never lose."

Over the 1998/1999 winter, the Giants switched managers between Salem-Keizer and Bakersfield. Comstock went there and Frank Reberger came to guide us. However, the 1999 team did not fare as well. It got off slowly and required some time to distill it into a good baseball machine. We suffered some move ups and injuries. Our big hitter Seam McGowan got hurt and went down for ten days. That is near disaster in a short season league. But we had no excuses. The games were good and we were in most of them. In fact there were a large number that we had big leads in only to lose to late rallies--the sign of an incomplete team. Reberger did what he could, but we were just not good enough.

Eventually, however, the team jelled and we started to win. Unfortunately we had dug ourselves into a big hole, too high to scale with late season lightning. We finished in a flourish, made it close and even scared the leaders and the second place team in Medford a little bit. Reberger had them really clicking at the wire. By then, we were definitely the best team in the league. We landed in third place, two games under that magic .500 level but we had made it exciting and the fans were pleased. The team finished just two games out of first place.

Fan support continued to be tremendous and life at the Crater was a joy all year long.

Bill and Jerry do not consider the championship in 1998 as any vidication of the decision to come to Salem-Keizer or to build the ballpark in Keizer. Neither is it vindication of the supportive position many people took on behalf of the team and the stadium during those difficult days the issue was still open. However they are all vindicated by the record which stands as immutable testimony to the propriety of the decision to proceed.

In the three years the stadium has been there, close to half a million people have come to baseball games there. They are not all citizens of Keizer, or of Salem. They are not all adults or not all children. It is a mix of all types of people from both cities and others. And those numbers are swelled even more by the many who attended other events that have been brought to the stadium. Included are a concert by singer Patty Loveless, several recreational vehicle shows, Halloween and Christmas parties, and other countless events.

Chief among them, though, was the Oregon Ducks Spring football game and the Nike World Masters Baseball Series, international in scope. In 1999, the Volcanoes played (and beat) the USA Olympic Team at the Crater. These are events and entertainment that would never have reached Keizer, or the general area, without the stadium being there. The quality of life of the people in the area has been visibly improved by the team and the stadium, without any doubt. This serves to enhance the reputation and identity of the City.

Those items are clearly the vindication of the position of those who supported the stadium idea with their lives, their careers and their reputations. Bill and Jerry are eternally grateful to them for their help and support.

But what about the economics of the decision by the City of Keizer to go out on the limb to enlarge the Urban Renewal District to include the stadium site so that bonds could be issued to generate funds to foster the project. The enlargement of the District boundary was a timely idea by then Councilman Al Miller. It made the entire dream feasible. Dennis Koho, then Mayor and Dotty Tryk, then City Manager, all helped immensely and got the stadium built. It stands as their legacy, their contribution from public service careers for the City. Miller, Koho and Tryk are all gone now from City government, but never forgotten.

Dotty Tryk's budget is on record. The facts are there for all to see. The City of Keizer has unquestionably profited from the project. One would find it difficult if not impossible, to measure the quantum of profit the City may enjoy. Properties that were miniscule on the tax rolls now generate much more in tax revenue, parking income and event monies. The economics are difficult to measure simply because of the added property the City condemned and still holds. What will that eventually be worth? Future development may provide some more details to an ever elusive equation but it will never be capable of accurate ascertainment.

There are so many intangibles here. Property values, tax revenues, quality of life, entertainment, future development, attraction of new growth and population increases, all of which may come to Keizer now that its identity has been staked out. What is that worth? What will all that be worth?

If profit is to be measured in terms of the youth of the area and the new level of entertainment they have enjoyed, the issue is beyond question. All one has to do is to visit the Crater during a game and count the many happy young faces in the crowd or those waiting for the players to exit after a game, clamoring for autographs. Those things cannot be replaced or evaluated. They are priceless.

The quality of life of middle aged people or seniors, or even parents of the present youth of the City have gained immensely from the team's presence. It has given the City a common bond and people from different walks of life, and different age groups, have been blended together by summers filled with the exploits of young men vying for a place in the major league sun. They cannot wait for the new seasons to come, and expectantly look forward to new faces on the diamond for them to see, and know , and root for.

The bond issue did not raise anyone's taxes one single dollar although it did stretch out the payment of the existing bond issue a little further. The ultimate yearly cost, if one wishes to express it that way, was miniscule to each citizen, and probably not even noticed. The fact is, that by the time the stretch out period arrives, the same people who were taxpayers at the inception, may have rolled over many times, and it may be applicable only to people entirely unfamiliar with the entire issue.

The results of that economic computation are clear. Yet, economics is not the only way the project is to be judged. Its success shows through in many of the intangibles itemized above for sure. However, it is also serving as a catalyst for development out at the interchange, as expected. Now talk of such development including plans for same, have been identified and being spoken of more realistically. It is only a matter of time.
Success?

# Keizer Stadium Dedication - June 22, 1997

### By - Al Miller

It is truly an honor and a privilege for me to deliver the dedication remarks here today. When I was first asked to give these remarks I told my wife that, for me personally, other than our wedding vows, this is the most important thing I have been asked to say in my entire life. As I prepared my remarks, and as I stand before you today, the words of Lou Gehrig keep coming to mind when he said, under much different circumstances, "Today, I feel like I am the luckiest man on the face of the earth".

Where do I begin? I begin with baseball, our national pastime. A game whose legends and heroes, with their great feats, have provided us with excitement and lasting memories, who have inspired us all in one way or another, and who have caused Bill Tucker and Jerry Walker to love the game almost as much as life itself. I begin with Mickey Mantle and Whitey Ford, who sponsored a camp in Florida, where, by fate, Bill, a New York lawyer, and Jerry, a Washington realtor, met for the first time. That chance meeting has led to the construction of this fine stadium and all of us being here today.

But more than that, this stadium is the realization of a dream, a product of the vision and perseverance of Jerry Walker. When Jerry first came to our area he told others of his dream, but time was short and to make it happen everything had to be done in less than a year. It seemed impossible. The City of Salem could not do it. Then he contacted Keizer Mayor Dennis Koho. Dennis contacted other city councilors who wanted to hear

*Keizer City Councilor Al Miller delivers stadium dedication address*

more. Meetings were held where Jerry communicated his dream. It still seemed impossible. How could it happen, especially in a small town like Keizer? But Jerry kept talking and making believers out of us one by one. Maybe it could happen.

Negotiations began, public hearing were held, and issues were discussed and debated. The many meetings seemed to be endless, often going into the wee hours of the morning. Many times specific issues were decided by a 4 to 3 vote of the Keizer City Council. During this process City Manager Dotty Tryk, City Engineer Bill Peterson, Public Works Director Wally Mull and Community Development Director John Morgan worked long and hard to budget and plan the city's proposed participation in this project. When Measure 47 passed, the city's financial participation in the project appeared to be impossible, but Dotty Tryk immediately went to work and found a way

for urban renewal bonds to be issued prior to the deadline.

Many times the project seemed doomed, but Jerry Walker kept talking and Mayor Koho kept looking, as he put it, "for a way to get to yes". On a fateful night in December of last year, the final city council vote was taken. The City of Keizer had indeed agreed to form a partnership with Jerry Walker and Bill Tucker.

But could the land be acquired and construction completed in time? The groundbreaking occurred in January and construction began in February, continuing at a feverish pace until just a few days ago. During the process issues and problems arose, but everyone involved, the contractors, Jerry Walker and the city staff worked together with a common purpose, the building of this stadium, on time and under budget.

This stadium is a tribute to the extraordinary efforts of all those who helped make it a reality. It is truly our field of dreams. It represents what our community stands for: dedication, hard work, strong family values, a commitment to our youth, and the ability to work together to accomplish a common goal, even in the face of seemingly impossible odds.

When you come to events here, be proud of this facility and take pride in what has been accomplished. Invite others to come and share the experience. Use it, but don't abuse it, for it is representative of all of what we stand for and is an extension of each one of us.

It is with great pride that I hereby dedicate this stadium. May it long serve as an inspiration to others and as a symbol of who we are and what we are.

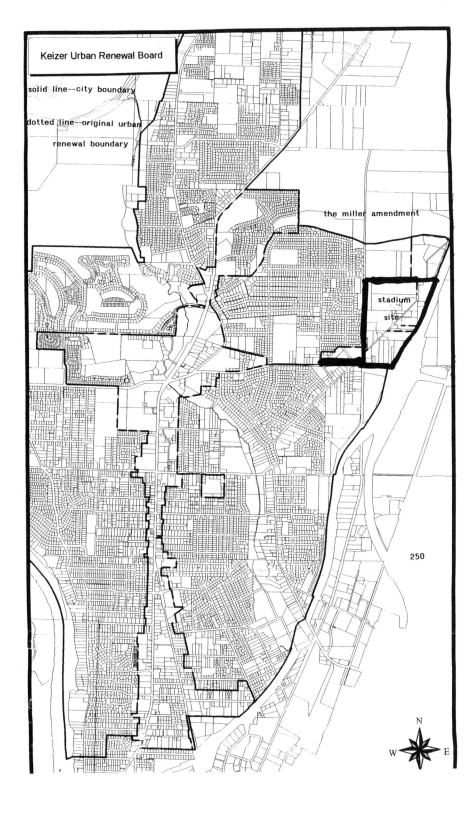

Keizer Urban Renewal Board

solid line--city boundary

dotted line--original urban
renewal boundary

the miller amendment

stadium site

250